Starstruck
Cosmic Visions in Science, Religion, and Folklore

STARSTRUCK

Cosmic Visions in Science, Religion, and Folklore

Albert A. Harrison
University of California, Davis

Berghahn Books
NEW YORK • OXFORD

Published in 2007 by
Berghahn Books
www.berghahnbooks.com

© 2007 Albert A. Harrison

Library of Congress Cataloging-in-Publication Data
Harrison, Albert A.
  Starstruck : cosmic visions in science, religion, and folklore / Albert A. Harrison.
    p. cm.
  Includes bibliographical references and index.
  ISBN-13: 978-1-84545-286-5 (hardcover : alk. paper)
  ISBN-10: 1-84545-286-0 (hardcover : alk. paper)
  1. Stars--Folklore. 2. Stars--Mythology. 3. Outer space--Folklore. 4. Cosmology-
-Folklore. I. Title.

  GR625.H34 2006
  398'.362--dc22

                                                          2006101304

British Library Cataloguing in Publication Data
A catalogue record for this book is available from
the British Library.

Printed in the United States on acid-free paper.

ISBN 978-1-84545-286-5 hardback

For my family:
Mary Ann, Kathy, Rich, Ally, Ricky, and Sherman

CONTENTS

PREFACE

Reverend John Young's path to the Union Theological Seminary began as a child when his parents took him on Thursday nights to a secret concrete bunker located at the end of a long, unpaved, and unmarked road in the desert foothills near Austin, Texas. When they arrived, his father, a former Pentagon intelligence officer, would don a white plastic jumpsuit and a pair of emerald-colored goggles. While John played in the dirt, his father and a group from "Project Starlight" operated radios, cameras, and sensors, while a noted psychic stood on the top of a white platform and attempted to establish mental contact with orbiting UFOs. "We have no weapons," the psychic indicated with energetic hand signals, and then motioning to a nearby field: "Land over there!" (Young 1998).

Young's father was working with a group known as the Association for the Understanding of Man. The U.S. Air Force had given money to Project Starlight to help with their semisecret search for extraterrestrial life. "Had I stopped to reflect upon it," Young continues, "I would have assumed that everyone's dad spent their time looking for UFOs using sensitive government electronics ... The world of psychic phenomena, extraterrestrial life, and reincarnation was perfectly normal to me."

Not everyone's childhood is quite like Reverend Young's, but many if not all of us have encountered the amazing barrage of claims and counterclaims about our place in the universe. Originating in science, religion, and folklore, these claims reflect different combinations of fact and imagination, of reality and belief. This book traces often disparate, sometimes parallel, and occasionally intersecting efforts of people who maintain profoundly different worldviews to locate contemporary humanity in the greatest of all possible contexts. These efforts challenge, stimulate, inform, amuse, and sometimes infuriate. Our comprehensive tour includes the outer limits of science, the search for life beyond Earth, UFOs, religion and spirituality, mysterious visitors from afar, deception and dirty tricks, apocalypse and resurrection, perpetuating human legacy, and preparing Earth for entry into galactic society. Throughout, we see how people seek meaning and purpose in an age largely dominated but not entirely controlled by science. To appreciate the breadth of thinking about cosmic issues, we must consider the work of people who eye one another with suspicion, and sometimes with hostility and contempt.

We begin with a brief review of scientific discoveries that challenge former understandings of our place in the universe. Different world-views, based on varying mixtures of science, religion, and folklore, help people understand and interpret these discoveries. Worldviews are lenses that alter the images that register on individual conscious-ness, bringing some aspects of reality into focus, distorting others, and blocking still others from view. Contrasting worldviews fuel controver-sies that are especially sharp when information is sparse or ambiguous, as is currently the case.

Science, as a method and as a social institution, is flush with success in our materialistic culture. The accumulation of reliable knowledge is slow, and as they attempt to speed scientific progress, people speculate freely and anticipate discoveries that may never come. Frontier science is a vast gray zone between widely accepted facts and unfettered imagi-nation. It is easy to enter the fray emboldened by imperfect visions of science, and vague expectations that twenty-first century physics makes anything possible. We consider the skeptic's roles of cop, scientist, and philosopher, and see why some people are skeptical of the skeptics.

A series of scientific discoveries has increased the plausibility of extra-terrestrial life. We review the basic rationale for NASA's astrobiology, which studies the origin and distribution of life in the universe, and for SETI, the scientific search for extraterrestrial intelligence. Recent devel-opments include searches for extraterrestrial lasers, and new techniques for detecting chemical indicators of biological and industrial processes on distant planets. People seek to inform future generations about their lives, times, and accomplishments. Space-age efforts include launching probes that bear greetings from Earth, and powerful interstellar broadcasts. Entrepreneurs have made it possible, for a small fee, for anyone to send unedited messages to the stars. Are these efforts harmless, or could they attract the attention of an aggressive or berserk civilization that chooses to exploit Earth or eliminate humanity as a threat?

UFOs annoy, amuse, and inspire. According to the extraterrestrial hypothesis, at least some UFOs are alien spacecraft. Many reports of UFOs come from competent, credible witnesses, but anecdotal evidence is not good enough. We compare event-dependent explanations of UFOs, which focus on the sighted object, and observer-dependent explanations, which focus on people who report UFOs. Over sixty years of vigorous UFO research has failed to uncover unequivocal physical evidence in support of the extraterrestrial hypothesis. Despite the weak evidentiary basis, belief in UFOs remains high, and whether or not these beliefs invite derision they have a powerful impact on society, culture, and individual lives.

Religion thrives in an age of science, and remains important bedrock for people's cosmological views. Many ideas from religion have entered into discussions of our place in the universe. These include multiple paths to knowledge, hidden realities, and superior forms of intelligence beyond Earth. We explore superficial parallels between God, UFO passengers, and putatively wise and benevolent aliens that may be beaming microwave transmissions to Earth. Scientists, who claim that the discovery of extraterrestrial intelligence would represent the final triumph of evolution over creationism, confront theologians, who counter that the discovery would provide further testimony to God's greatness. We review lowbrow flying saucer religions, and introduce highbrow theologies that are formulated to accommodate a universe brimming with life.

Throughout recorded history, people have reported mysterious visitors from afar and today's little gray aliens are a contemporary manifestation of this. We compare the claims of the self-styled realists, who contend that alien abductions actually occur; the positivists, who deem that abductions are important in a psychological sense; and skeptics, who contend that no matter how real they seem to the reporter, abduction stories are not true. A substantial and growing research base strengthens the view that abduction reports rest on cultural and psychological factors.

Fraud and illusion play profound roles in our attempts to make sense of the universe and "UFOlogy" in particular is marred by misrepresentations, hoaxes, and dirty tricks. Chapter 7, "Tricksters," reviews the history of fraud, deceit and misunderstanding in UFOlogy and examines claims of government cover-up. To some extent, the latter can be understood in terms of declining trust in government, the mismanagement of official UFO investigations, and the immigration of ideas from right-wing conspiracy groups. Conspiracy theories at once terrorize, because they imply great evil in this world, and reassure, because they imply that the world is ordered rather than random (Barkun 2003). While it is all but impossible to disprove a cover-up, we can point to convincing alternative explanations of conspiracy claims.

Millennial thinking is rampant in discussions of our place in the universe and, indeed, there are many ways that the world could come to an end, either slowly (global warming, resource depletion) or abruptly (nuclear war, pandemic, major asteroid or comet impact). We find similar messages in the Book of Revelation, rare Earth theorists' predictions of our planet's demise, and abductees' visions of civilization's end. Themes of salvation, resurrection, and immortality permeate both mainstream and UFO religions. New scientific discoveries raise new hopes for secular paths to eternal life. According to some futurists a series of breakthroughs in biotechnology will extend life indefinitely. Others foresee a confluence of computer science, nanotechnology, robotics, and neuroscience that would allow us to survive forever within the reverberating circuits of computers. Prophets who foresee these paths to immortality are exuberantly optimistic about the future of technology, while brushing aside crucial philosophical issues.

The first microwave search was underway in time to influence the Brookings Report before it was presented to the U.S. Congress many years ago (Committee on Science and Astronautics 1961). Commissioned by NASA, and prepared by a large team of experts and consultants led by psychologist Donald Michael, this report presented a wide range of ideas on how peaceful space exploration might affect human affairs. Most of these ideas had to do with technological innovations such as communications satellites. Encountering extraterrestrial intelligence was one small part of this report, and the committee stressed that contact could occur at any time. Whereas the committee felt that the consequences were largely unpredictable, they urged ongoing studies to prepare us for the great discovery.

From the start, SETI scientists acknowledged that their search could have profound implications for society, and they involved social scientists and humanists in their planning efforts. The SETI Permanent Study Group of the International Academy of Astronautics is responsible for the most serious and sustained planning on the cultural implications of SETI. These exercises revolve around the standard SETI detection scenario, which consists of intercepting radio or laser transmissions that are the functional equivalent of a telephone dial tone. Other planning has evolved around a broad spectrum of scenarios and proposes multiple strategies for managing relations with nonhuman intelligence. One such effort was based on three critical uncertainties (familiarity of the intelligence, the speed with which contact unfolds, and the favorableness of the anticipated net effects), five societal sectors (government, business, religion, science, and the media), and four response strategies (cooperation, adaptation, containment, and fight). Each strategy includes shaping public perceptions of the situation, maintaining social cohesion and international stability, and assembling and positioning the resources necessary to mount an effective response. As long as SETI remains little more than an exercise, governments can afford to treat search activity with benign neglect. As soon as detection is confirmed, expect vigorous intervention on the part of governmental authorities. As we plan for the discovery of life beyond Earth we must be wary of creating fantasy documents; that is, optimistic plans that rest on little evidence but generate great confidence and reassure the public.

In the final chapter I suggest that the overall success of our efforts to rethink our place in the universe may be less dependent on any one perspective than on the collective thinking that Howard Bloom has described as the Global Brain. In a sense, people with very different worldviews are brainstorming our place in the universe. Successful brainstorming requires imagination, to ensure that many ideas are presented, and quality control, so that only the best ideas earn closer scrutiny. Imagination fails us when we are unwilling to consider new possibilities, and when we become so enamored of an idea that we cling to it despite growing evidence to the contrary. Quality control is extremely difficult in an era of mass communication, the Internet, and widespread gullibility and cynicism. Presently, we can generate new ideas at a far faster pace than we can evaluate them. Over time, as new evidence rolls in, many of the ideas that circulate today will be shown to lack viability. As the less viable ideas are withdrawn, we will achieve greater if imperfect consensus on our place in the cosmos. In the meantime, thinking broadly rather than narrowly may ease our transition from citizens of Earth to citizens of the universe.

Many people have contributed to this project. This work would not have been possible without benefit of membership, over the years, in a number of committees, panels, and study groups focusing on astrobiology, SETI, space travel, paranormal phenomena, and "planetary defense," that is, the protection of Earth from asteroids and comets.

I am particularly indebted to the "Contact: Cultures of the Imagination" conferences held annually at Moffett Field, California where science and science fiction meet, and to Robert T. Bigelow, the Science Advisory Board, and the former staff of his National Institute of Discovery Science in Las Vegas, Nevada who introduced me to many new ideas. Special thanks to Eric W. Davis, Richard Haines, Mary Ann Harrison, Joel T. Johnson, H. Paul Schuch, Allen Tough, and Douglas A. Vakoch, who offered helpful comments on preliminary versions of this manuscript. Their advice was invariably good, but not always followed—as author, I assume full responsibility for the views expressed in this book. I am particularly indebted to Marion Berghahn for her confidence in my manuscript, to the copyeditor Meredith Massey, and to Vivian Berghahn, Melissa Spinelli, and the production staff at Berghahn Books for transforming a computer printout into an attractive monograph. Most of all, heartfelt thanks to my beloved wife, Mary Ann Harrison, who gave unstinting support, encouragement, and advice over the excruciatingly long time that it took to bring this project to fruition.

A. A. H.
Davis, California
December 2006

One

THINKING BIG

One of the greatest science fiction films of all time, *Close Encounters of the Third Kind*, tells of an unambiguous encounter of human and extraterrestrial civilizations, and of the struggles and triumphs of people who are caught up in this event. The name of this 1977 Steven Spielberg blockbuster derives from a system for classifying unidentified flying object or UFO sightings. A close encounter places the observer within 500 feet of the UFO and that of the third kind requires sighting the spacecraft's occupants. The movie consists of a complex series of interlocking plots unfolding around the world.

In Muncie, Indiana, electric power company technician Roy Neary is sent to explore a progressive power failure that is darkening the town. As he drives to a critical substation at Crystal Lake, the earth trembles and mailboxes shake on their stands. His flashlight, radio, and truck ignition malfunction, and a deep roar accompanies flashing lights as a UFO passes over his pickup truck, from back to front. Police pursue blobs of light that race through tollgates, leaving the collectors dumbfounded. Airline crews and flight controllers witness UFOs, but fearing condemnation or ridicule from their superiors, decline to file reports. Jillian Guiler and her young son Barry are perplexed when electric appliances and battery-operated toys run amok. In the middle of the night Barry wakes up and wanders outside towards a diffuse light. Awakening only later, Jillian is horrified by her son's disappearance.

Roy never does solve the problem at Crystal Lake. Despite his best efforts to regain his composure, Roy is so preoccupied by the experience that he is fired by his boss and abandoned by his wife. Increasingly, he is obsessed with a distinctive silhouette that he models in successively larger scales using shaving cream, mashed potatoes, and finally mounds of dirt. Eventually, the shape's significance is revealed on television.

During an evening newscast it stands in the background as military police evacuate an area that they claim is contaminated with nerve gas. Roy realizes that he has been sculpting Devil's Tower, a distinctive peak within Wyoming's Grand Teton mountain range.

He immediately sets forth to Wyoming, as do Jillian and other people who have an inexplicable, newfound interest in Devil's Tower. Soon working as a team, Roy and Jillian overcome great difficulties to reach the Tower where they nestle on a ledge overlooking a landing field. There, they watch government scientists communicate secretly with small UFOs before a huge mother ship materializes. Accompanied by awesome light displays and throaty, pulsating sounds, the ship descends, lowers a landing ramp, and disgorges several generations of missing persons, including Barry. Transformed by their experiences, Jillian and Barry return home, while Roy joins a team of intrepid explorers who swagger on board to accompany the giant spacecraft skyward.

Most obviously, *Close Encounters* is good science fiction with action-packed adventure sequences and stunning special effects. It offers audiences high suspense and a great plot. It is a space-age version of the hero's journey. Seized by a vision, Roy ignores the entreaties of his family and the recriminations of his friends and sets forth to find his destiny beyond Earth. Like renaissance sailors sailing for the Indies or immigrants driving Conestoga wagons to the American West, Roy is drawn to an ill-defined but promising new world. And, to the delight of everyone whose unconventional beliefs have been met with a chilly reception, he is vindicated. His boss, wife, and chuckling neighbors were the ones who got it wrong.

Close Encounters resonates with science, religion, and folklore. For this reason it offers something for everyone. In this book, we explore the complex roles of science, religion, and folklore in ongoing attempts to understand the universe and our place within it. We will travel through a vast and shifting gray zone bordered by encrusted knowledge on the one side and unfettered imagination on the other. This gray zone attracts a diverse set of enthusiasts including astrophysicists, mathematicians, military officers, entrepreneurs, cowboys, journalists, veterinarians, clinical social workers, CIA operatives, artists, pathologists, theologians, engineers, and astronauts, with a few anthropologists, sociologists, and psychologists sprinkled in. I propose that we live in a period of time when almost anything seems possible, but that as additional findings roll in, science will apply brakes to imagination.

The success of *Close Encounters* both reflects and promotes a dawning realization that we are both citizens of planet Earth and citizens of the universe. This recentering or expansion of perspective rests in part on an explosion of scientific knowledge, some of which is frightening in its implications. Although bound together by our fascination with the realms beyond Earth, we vary in terms of the knowledge, skills, and degree of imagination that we bring to bear. In the course of refining our views about the universe and our place within it, we either reaffirm old answers or seek new ones to great existential questions: Who are we, how did we get here, and what will become of us?

Michael Michaud was one of the first to describe how a convergence of forces is fostering a new sense of affinity with the cosmos (1995). Steven J. Dick's *The Biological Universe* traces twentieth-century scholarly thought on this, especially the prospects for extraterrestrial life (1996). Later, he proposed the idea of cosmic humanity, a transformation of humankind shaped by a new understanding of the evolving universe, the likely discovery of extraterrestrial intelligence, and the lure of interstellar travel (2000a). For some people the transition to cosmic humanity is accompanied by spiritual overtones, and confers a sense of purpose, meaning, and hope for the future. Science provides the discoveries, but myth and popular culture shape people's interpretations of science's findings.

For approximately three hundred years science has probed the mysteries of the skies, displacing Earth from the universe's center, discovering that the universe is far vaster than previously supposed, and generating evidence-based accounts of its origin and evolution. In the last half century, science strengthened the rationale for extraterrestrial life, a rationale that has gained widespread acceptance. So far the evidence is circumstantial. We have long known that there is an abundance of galaxies and stars and, by the last years of the twentieth century, astronomers discovered that in addition to our Sun, many other stars have planets that are potentially life bearing. Although there is modest agreement that simple forms of life—such as single-celled organisms and grasses—may be fairly commonplace "out there," there is less agreement that these will evolve into intelligent beings capable of making their presence known to us. Still, a small group of influential scientists moved SETI, the scientific search for extraterrestrial intelligence, from the outskirts of science to its center. Science provides a rationale of sorts for *Close Encounters*, and the movie contains scientific trappings galore, even if the storyline is unmistakably fiction.

For many people the idea of intelligence beyond Earth is not a scientific hypothesis but a confirmed belief. In Paleolithic times people personified the sky and developed myths about a sky god that created Earth out of nothing (Armstrong 2005). The vast, towering, mysterious, and eternal sky, she notes, has reminded people of the sacred ever since, but this early form of monotheism gave way to polytheistic religions that included numerous special purpose gods, many of whom resided in the heavens above. Ancients believed that Atlas held the world aloft, and that Apollo carried the Sun in his chariot as he rode across the sky. For thousands of years, fixed celestial events have regulated ritual and agricultural cycles. Beyond this, spectacular, transient events including comets, meteor showers, supernovas, and solar eclipses have impacted cultural traditions throughout the world (Masse 1995). For instance, the arrival of the volcano goddess, Pele, in Hawaii, has been traced to a cluster of spectacular celestial events between 900 and 934, and transient celestial events influenced the names of Hawaiian royalty.

Prophets from the sky have played defining roles for Judaism, Christianity, and Islam, and many new religious movements as well. There is extensive religious, even Christian symbolism in *Close Encounters*. Neary sees the light and then, as an act of faith, overcomes successive obstacles to reach Devil's Tower. There, amidst miraculous special effects, infinitely wise and compassionate beings descend to Earth. As the door to their mother ship opens there is an act of resurrection: they restore to our midst alive and healthy people who had long been written off as dead. Neary accepted the challenge and passed the test. His reward—or perhaps we should say salvation—is spiritual fellowship with those aboard the awesome spaceship that streaks towards the unknown.

Science presents itself as objective and value-free, divorced from issues of purpose and meaning. Religion is laden with values and subjectivity, and is specifically devised to address existential questions. Most scientists would prefer to preserve this distinction, but in recent years the lines between science and religion have blurred somewhat. Scholars are looking for points of complementarity, correspondence, and integration, as well as indifference and conflict (Peters 1998; Barbour 2000, 2002). Whereas they do not necessarily accept the biblical story of creation, intelligent design theorists contend that evolution alone is hard pressed to account for the complexity of human life (Behe 1996). Nonscientists look to science for confirmation of religious beliefs.

Today, generously financed philanthropic organizations, such as the John Templeton Foundation, sponsor scientific research that bears upon religious, spiritual, and ethical issues. Books published as science (and often cross-listed by publishers under spirituality) have religious or quasireligious overtones, as revealed in their titles. These include *God and the New Physics* (Davies 1984); *Einstein and Buddha: The Parallel Sayings* (MacFarlane 2001); *Quantum Theology: Spiritual Implications of the New Physics* (O'Murchu 2004); and *The Physics of Immortality: Modern Cosmology, God, and the Resurrection of the Dead* (Tipler 1995).

Historian David Noble (1999) shows how ancient imaginings and religious myths have shaped science's offshoot, technology, for thousands of years, and continue to do so today. In his view, religion and modern technology have coevolved with the result that the technological enterprise remains suffused with religious beliefs. Much technological development, like religious thought, is aimed at perfecting humankind, creating paradise on Earth, and evading (or at least forestalling) death and extinction. Noble traces the interplay of religion and technology from ancient times through the Rosicrucians and the Freemasons to contemporary engineering.

Many of the great minds that formed science were interested in metaphysical issues and studied scripture, prophecy, and the occult (Noble 1999). Whereas they valued science they valued God more, and in some cases believed that their achievements were possible through God's grace. Even the inventor Thomas Edison, perhaps the ultimate utilitarian, had a spiritual side. He built a Congregational church, and joined a religiously inspired group for moral rearmament. Persistently interested in the nonquantifiable aspects of reality—that is, realms beyond—Edison remained fascinated with mysticism and tinkered with ways to communicate with the dead. Throughout his life his mind visited mystical realms, and on his deathbed he awoke from his final coma just long enough to report that he had glimpsed heaven, and that it met expectations.

Folklore refers to the stories that are widely accepted within a given culture, and whatever else they may or may not be, UFOs and alien abductions are a part of contemporary folklore. These stories are told through the visual arts (painting, tapestry, sculpture) and the performing arts (theater and dance) as well as through prose and poetry. Although folklore may seem incomprehensible or silly to outsiders, it is laden with symbolism and meaning for insiders. Folklore tells the members of a given culture what is important and helps them come to grips with issues that concern them. It provides a common frame of reference, shared understanding, and vehicles for interpretation.

Folklore may be based on real events—accurately or inaccurately interpreted. It also includes stories that are exaggerated, understated, twisted to prove a point, or totally fabricated. Because folklore is a mixture of fact and fiction, it is open to multiple interpretations. Whether or not a particular piece of folklore withstands rational analysis or scientific proof, it still affects people's thinking, perhaps more profoundly than unassailable facts. Some folklore is openly acknowledged as folklore (jokes, parables, and cautionary tales), but UFO folklore is presented as factual in many articles and books (Ziegler 1997).

Of the different interpretations of UFOs the best known is that they are signs of intelligence from outer space. Just a few of the touches that add folkloric authenticity to *Close Encounters* include luminous spheres, strange cloud formations, flashing lights, a huge mother ship, failing car ignitions, jeering skeptics, and sinister government agents who use intimidation and deceit to hide the truth from the public.

Myths are inseparable from religion and play a crucial role in folklore. Myths are stories that place our lives within a larger setting, and explain experiences that are otherwise incomprehensible. Myths address transcendental issues, such as the relationship between humans and unearthly beings, whether these are gods, UFO pilots, or Jedi. Myth is an "eternal mirror in which we see ourselves" (Bierlein 1994: xiii). Myth inspires hope and "pushes us beyond the safe certainties of the familiar world into the unknown" (Armstrong 2005: 35).

Today, ancient myths are reemerging with a scientific spin and cloaked in space-age garb (Colavito 2005). Thus, rather than subject to God's scrutiny, we are watched by naturally evolved entities whose level of intelligence is beyond our ken. Rather than being visited by angels in all their natural glory, we are visited by humanoids that drive advanced spacecraft and wear shiny spacesuits. Links and parallels between science and myth are a central theme of this book, but in seeking support for their views many people are too easily drawn to alternative histories and pseudoscience, not recognizing the flimsy nature of these substitutes for their laboriously established counterparts.

As a skeptic, Paul Kurtz is concerned by the power of myth to divert people from science (1991). In his view the "transcendental temptation" lures us to embrace ideas that make us feel good, rather than those that are scientifically valid. New discoveries about the universe may strengthen this temptation. He writes: "What lies beyond the dark reaches of outer space, punctuated by the flickering bright lights of distant galaxies? The transcendental temptation is just at the point of taking its greatest leap forward, soaring this time not on the wings of angels but on the gigantic wings of telescopes and the radar antennae of astronomers and the Promethean promise of the new technologies of space travel" (Kurtz 1991: 446). People do not always realize that they have made the jump from science to wish, stoutly maintaining that they have remained faithful to science, if not as it is right now, then as science may become someday.

Four converging forces prompt us to recalibrate our place in the universe and find new answers to old questions. These include cosmic evolution and new threats to planet Earth, as well as astronomy and spaceflight.

Cosmic Evolution

For astronomer and philosopher of science Eric Chaisson (2001), cosmic evolution—the history of our universe over time—has been a continuing shift in the direction of order, organization, and complexity. Following its inception at the moment of the "Big Bang," the universe moved from pure radiation or energy to particulate matter. About twelve billion years ago matter began clumping into galaxies, followed two billion years later by the debut of stars or suns. Our own Sun and planet date back maybe five billion years, but stars and planets continue to be born and die today. Earth had sufficient plant life to qualify as a biosphere about three billion years ago. Over a billion years ago, single-celled organisms gave rise to multicellular organisms including mammals (250 million years ago) and apes (fifty million years ago). The human body began to take shape about four million years ago, and about five hundred thousand years ago our brains began gaining immense power. A hundred thousand years ago new technologies allowed people to leave Africa and begin filling other ecological niches throughout the world.

Over time, the increasing complexity of our ancestors' nervous systems gave rise to the mind, that is, conscious thought. Our level of intelligence, including our ability to develop complex artifacts and use language, makes it possible to think about other times and other places, to take the perspective of other people, and to contemplate the self. Large, modern societies (which historians and sociologists date back approximately five hundred years) are of such recent advent that using Chaisson's notation system they have no age at all. Unless cosmic evolution reverses itself we can expect greater levels of complexity, more intricate cultures, and higher levels of consciousness.

Human evolution has been accompanied by the emergence of increasingly larger social groupings brought about by population growth, improving communication technologies, and new political forms. In business, we see evidence of this in seemingly endless rounds of mergers that produce larger and larger corporations. We also discern this in organized religion. This includes the merger of several small Protestant churches to form the United Church of Christ in 1957, ecumenical activities intended to build bridges between different faiths, megachurches with congregations numbered in the tens of thousands, and radio and television evangelists who minister to millions of people. More and more these social systems cut across international boundaries. Although not every nation belongs and they exert only spotty control over people's lives, the European Union and the United Nations are examples of this. A hundred years ago, when many people even in Western societies spent almost their whole lives within fifty miles or so of their hometown, ideas like "international government" and "global community" would have seemed like nonsense. Today, both notions are commonplace.

Historian David Christian proposes "Big History" as a new defining paradigm for his field (2004). Since there is no agreed-upon starting point for history, we should start at the very beginning. In addition, he objects to the standard practice of organizing history by time and nation-state (such as France in the Renaissance, German history since 1945) since this artificially segments the flow of events and encourages "we-they" feelings. Christian starts at the Big Bang, when the universe began, and interweaves cosmology, geology, and environmental studies to describe the origins of stars, planets, and life, including human life. He then proceeds from the Paleolithic era through the transition to agriculture and the industrial revolution, and even offers glimpses of the possible future such as the results of global warming. In this manner Christian weaves natural history and human history into a single narrative.

James Lovelock's conception of Gaia presents our entire planet Earth—rocks, water, atmosphere, vegetation, animals, people—as a living system with self-regulating and self-correcting properties (1986). To him, Earth is less akin to a machine than to a living organism, an organic whole. Whereas most analyses focus on how Earth's geology set the stage for life, Gaia (named for the Greek goddess of the Earth) stresses how living beings shape the environment—through the creation and absorption of oxygen and carbon dioxide, for instance. The key is the interdependence of everything in the natural world. Gaia, according to

Stephen Scharper, fuses scientific insight and religious imagination and has become well entrenched in popular culture (1994).

Who knows where the trend towards increased complexity, consciousness, and size will lead? Ronald Bracewell coined the term "galactic club" to describe a vast but sparse network of extraterrestrial civilizations (1975). If extraterrestrial civilizations that are much older than our own began searching for one another millions of years ago, a few of these civilizations may have entered into ongoing communication. They may be sharing ideas and perhaps even undertaking joint commercial ventures. Although from our perspective cost and efficiency would dictate that they communicate by means of radio, some of these civilizations—perhaps from within the same solar system—may have overcome the difficulties of interplanetary travel and regularly visit one another. At first, one or two civilizations might form an association. Then, with sufficient time and continually improving technology, many additional civilizations would join, both individually and in clusters.

Astronomy

Folklore is rife with myths regarding the Milky Way, a pathway to the heavens that "looks like a gossamer cummerbund on the black tuxedo of the night" (Krupp 1995: 411). To a large extent, air and light pollution have obscured our vision of this "frosty rainbow," which again becomes a source of wonder and awe during a dark night in the desert or after an earthquake or other disaster has extinguished city lights. Despite our decreasing opportunity to witness celestial spectacles first hand, modern astronomy draws our attention to the skies. We view the awesome wonders of the heavens in magazine pictures and television documentaries, if not with the naked eye. Rapid technological advances that have brought us closer to the stars have further sensitized people to cosmic issues.

The invention of the telescope by Galileo made it possible to obtain a clearer view of the heavens, to separate the planets from the stars, to see the rings of Saturn and moons of Jupiter. By the late 1800s increasingly powerful telescopes led some observers to identify canals on Mars, but a few years later, even better telescopes showed that these patterns were only in the eye of the beholder. In less than another hundred years astronomers were operating behemoths such the 200-inch reflector at Mount Wilson and opened the Keck Observatory, located high on a mountain in Hawaii, isolated from city lights and at an altitude where there is minimal interference from clouds and pollution. One of the crowning achievements of the space age was the deployment of the

Hubble space telescope. Because it is beyond Earth's atmosphere, it can outperform comparably sized devices on Earth. The pictures returned by the Hubble have informed science and, for many people, delighted the senses. Properly chosen and edited to best advantage, some of these pictures seem to communicate meaning and significance, and their artistic qualities serve the National Aeronautics and Space Administration [NASA] well.

In the 1930s, radio operators noted a static-like hiss emanating from far away. What they heard was a cooling of the universe, background radiation leftover from the Big Bang. Stars also emitted radiation within the microwave range; thus it became possible to use the new technology to map the stars, to identify new phenomena, and to analyze patterns in the images collected on the giant mirrors of optical telescopes. Operating day and night, these telescopes probe deep space and have led to some of the most startling and important discoveries of recent times. Now some telescopes are harnessed to seek electromagnetic radiation—radio waves—or laser flashes from extraterrestrial civilizations.

Space Flight

In the 1760s, humans achieved flight by means of hot air balloons. In 1903, at Kitty Hawk, NC, two bicycle mechanics, Wilbur and Orville Wright, harnessed an internal combustion engine to a glider and undertook the first heavier-than-air flight. Very few experts thought that heavier-than-air flight would be possible, and, indeed, the Wrights seem surprised when their airplane actually took off (Cornish 2004). The initial flight lasted only three minutes and took place at a relatively sedate twenty-five miles per hour—less than a third of the speed that could be attained by a superbly conditioned bicyclist on an all-out sprint on a carefully prepared track. Now, every day of the year, groups of 200 to 300 passengers climb aboard fleets of airlines that fly between continents at over five hundred miles per hour, while the fastest military planes can achieve better than three times that average.

The transformation of rockets into practical tools began in the 1920s, with the work of Robert Goddard in the United States and the amateur Rocket Clubs in Germany. The dawn of the space age was unmistakable by October of 1957 when the Russians put *Sputnik* into orbit, a feat that required accelerating the basketball-sized satellite to twenty-four thousand miles per hour. The chief German rocket scientist Wernher von Braun, who relocated to the United States, envisioned orbiting satellites as a millennial event that ushered in a new cosmic age (Noble

1999). Thus began the great space race of the 1960s. America and the Soviet Union were locked in a political and technological battle to be the first to reach the Moon. This required building bigger and better spacecraft and acquiring the means to keep small groups of people alive in space during the few days that it took to complete a lunar mission.

Both the Americans and the Soviets made great progress, but it was U.S. astronauts Neil Armstrong and Buzz Aldrin who planted a flag on the Moon in July 1969. The last astronauts returned from the Moon in late 1972, and subsequent spacefarers have been confined to low Earth orbit ever since, prompting critics to complain that the space program has stalled (Klerkx 2004). As it recedes in time, the race to the Moon has gained mythic qualities, causing a great yearning to return to that brief moment of triumph (Launius 2005). Space activists, hoping that we will become a multi-planet species, point to Apollo as a model of a resolute nation moving outward into the unknown. There is a growing nostalgia for the heroic astronauts of that bygone era and the steely-eyed rocket men with butch haircuts, horn-rimmed glasses, and pocket protectors who helped them get there (Launius 2005). But governments are unwilling to pay to move humanity outwards, and, in the private sector, suborbital pocketbooks prevent the realization of interplanetary visions.

Still, we have steadily improved the capabilities of our unmanned spacecraft. Armed with TV cameras and other sensors, and in some cases capable of performing laboratory analyses in situ, these compact spaceships give us a close-up look at distant conditions. What we can't achieve in outer space we can achieve in cyberspace, so celebration of space travel has been replaced by a celebration of electronic technology (Dean 1998). Our probes have sailed beyond Pluto's orbit and, over periods so long as to be meaningless to us, they will reach other solar systems. In 2004, President George W. Bush's Space Exploration Initiative injected new life into NASA. This calls for a return to the Moon in 2020, a flyby of Mars in 2030, and a landing there somewhere around 2035. Today's space program does not match the mythic proportions of the space program of the 1960s, but many people remain enthusiastic about space exploration and hope for a continuing human presence beyond Earth.

Threats to Planet Earth

In the last half of the twentieth century we became increasingly aware of threats to human survival. Until recently, advances in technology have offset major boosts in human population. Now there is evidence that our voracious needs are outstripping our planet's resources

(Diamond 2005). Environmental scientists warn us of growing ozone holes that allow vast amounts of radiation to seep through to the Earth's surface and contribute to global warming, poisons and pollutants that kill off plants and animals, deforestation, and the elimination of species. Global warming causes ice caps to melt and ocean levels to rise, in the process contaminating valuable farmland. Warming water kills off useful species, such as whales and fish, and establishes fertile breeding grounds for viruses and bacteria that are harmful to people. Five times in the past, major natural disasters have led to mass extinctions; now, we are in the midst of a "sixth extinction" caused by our mismanagement of our home planet (Williams 2000). Like the voraciously growing plants Scotch broom and kudzu, we are crowding other species out of their ecological niches. Over the long run, we risk descending into a new and fatal ice age. Several times glaciers have ground their way south from the Arctic and we may be living in a relatively narrow sliver of geological time (still measured in thousands of years) that separates two ice ages.

Only recently were we alerted fully to the threats posed by near-Earth objects: asteroids and comets that arrive in the vicinity of our home planet. Countless balls of metal, rock, and ice cross Earth's orbit and even enter our atmosphere. Most of these objects are so small that they burn up on entry and of those that survive very few do serious damage. But on occasion asteroids and comets wreak havoc. An impact of a 10 km-sized asteroid 65 million years ago led to the extinction of the dinosaurs, and there is reason to believe that other impacts in Quebec and in Australia led to mass extinctions 214 million and 250 million years ago (Raup 1991). Fairly regularly, astronomers spot objects that could hit Earth. In December 2004 they located a civilization buster that initial calculations suggested would reach us in 2029. Continued observation and recalculations showed that it will miss Earth, but this comet should be an awesome spectacle when it eventually heaves into view.

To protect ourselves from such threats we look upwards—for divine intervention from God or for sage advice from members of older and wiser civilizations. Or, we see it as within our own power to venture into space to solve our own problems, for example, to find the additional resources that we need to support burgeoning populations, to divert Earth-threatening asteroids or comets, or at least to preserve our species by dispersing beyond Earth.

Worldviews

As different people grapple with new discoveries they appeal to different evidence and draw different conclusions. How can we differ so dramatically, for example, in our interpretations of a microbe-like structure in a meteorite, a light in the sky, or a purported message from the great beyond? As Mark E. Koltko-Rivera explains, worldviews are sets of assumptions and beliefs that describe reality (2004). Worldviews define what does or does not exist (either in principle or actuality), what can be known and what can be done, and how it can be known or done. They are based on assumptions that may be unproven, and, indeed, not even subject to empirical testing. But they serve as foundations for people's understandings about human nature, meaning and purpose in life, the composition of the universe, and our place and future within it.

Worldviews may be viewed as frames of reference, that is, contexts that put a distinctive spin on reality. Or, we may think of them as lenses that alter the images that register on human consciousness, bringing some parts of the picture into focus, distorting others, and blocking still others from view.

Different worldviews prevail in different times and cultures. Few contemporary worldviews correspond to those that dominated medieval Europe. But there is substantial variation within a culture and historical period. Within contemporary society we find people who maintain radically different views on the origin of the universe, the best way to determine the truth, and the ultimate source of moral guidelines. Cultural norms and conformity pressures have not, and may never, eliminate contrasting perspectives on reality.

People are involved or absorbed to differing degrees in their worldviews (Koltko-Rivera 2004). Here we may draw an analogy between being absorbed in a worldview and engrossed in a book. A person who is highly absorbed tends to stick with it (for example, reading the entire book in one sitting) and is impervious to distractions. "Glued to the chair," he or she may not hear the phone ring or the TV droning in the background. In the case of low absorption, the mind wanders. The reader alternates attention between the book and the TV, runs to the refrigerator for snacks, or takes a snooze. Similarly, a person who is highly absorbed in his or her worldview is enthusiastic, involved, and not easily distracted. Information that confirms the worldview is eagerly sought, while evidence that is inconsistent with it is ignored or rejected. Highly absorbed people are drawn to other people, books, magazines and Web sites that confirm their worldview, and are prone to accept even flimsy supportive evidence. Highly absorbed people may see themselves as beacons of light and fearless champions of truth, while others see them as rigid and close-minded, or, in extreme cases, fanatics and nuts. For people who are heavily invested in a worldview, its failure is more than a disappointment and embarrassment. It is catastrophic, and because of this people have many lines of defense and hold on ever more tightly when their worldview is under attack.

Personal experience plays a tremendous role in people's views whether one is an astronomer, a personality theorist, an airplane pilot or a short-order cook. This is particularly important to remember when we hear claims that do not quite jibe with the scientific-pragmatic view of reality. An academic ridicules UFO believers and considers UFO studies a waste of time. Then her personal sighting of a glowing orange orb flying low near a freeway prompts a complete change of heart. After one or two hours of sleep, an overworked executive slams the snooze button to silence his alarm clock. During the brief period of grace, a rapturous being of light appears at the foot of the bed, and explains the mysteries of the universe. When the alarm sounds again, the apparition is remembered, but only a sketchy and vague approximation of what it said. Perhaps the executive sets forth on a new life quest.

Many times people are aware of prosaic explanations of such events. Perhaps the orange orb was exhaust from a jet, and the night visitor a hallucination, but somehow, the mundane explanation just doesn't fit. People who have had such experiences and who are sensitive to the impressions that they make on others realize it is prudent to avoid mentioning the experience, or, if it is too late for that, make light of it, attributing it to too much beer. Unusual experiences, coupled with concerns about other people's reactions (loss of a grant, a missed promotion, failure to be re-elected, becoming the target of neighbors' jokes) give rise to "closet believers" whose expressed opinions do not square with their private beliefs. They may embark on a search for evidence proving that the experience was real. Of course the search will be difficult, but who knows what they might find?

Imagination and the Possible

Imagination, through its influence on our sense of reality, helps determine what we accept and reject (O'Connor and Aardema 2005). For centuries, philosophers debated the role of imagination in people's sense of reality, but in 1900 the concept all but disappeared from view when the emerging field of psychology sought to establish its scientific nature by focusing on observable behavior rather than invisible mental life. There remains a strong temptation to separate perception, the process through which sensory information informs us about the real world out there, and imagination, purely internal processes involving mental images and stories. Although we may enjoy a good fantasy, we do not want to fall victim to runaway imagination. And, we fear, if our imagination does run wild it may diminish critical thinking, cause trouble with other people, and give rise to delusions, hallucinations, and other stigmata.

Certainly the material world, as known to us, influences our sense of reality. But our conception of the possible and impossible also derives from other people: family, friends, work associates, and the many different groups to which we belong (or aspire to belong). The media plays a powerful role: science textbooks, magazines, tabloid exposés, newscasts, television documentaries, movies, and Internet offerings shape definitions of truth. Because as a child Reverend John Young accompanied his father as the latter sought to communicate with UFOs telepathically, he considered extraterrestrials, psychic communication, and reincarnation as normal and real (Young 1998). A person with a different pattern of experiences would develop different ideas about the possible and the impossible. It is doubtful that someone raised by high school science teachers, who went on to earn an advanced degree in engineering and then joined NASA, would entertain such possibilities as telepathic communication and UFOs.

People with good backgrounds in science, strong religious upbringings, or heavy immersion in myth are likely to have very different definitions of truth. After a scientist, priest, UFO witness, or anyone else develops a sense of reality, they are not easily dissuaded by arguments and evidence to the contrary.

People who are strongly invested in a particular worldview have strength of conviction and consistency on their side, but other people may see them as closed-minded and inflexible. At the other end of the continuum are people who are somewhat capricious in their efforts to separate fact from illusion and myth. While they strike others as fickle or disorganized, they may not be aware of their own inconsistencies. People have remarkable abilities to compartmentalize ideas, favoring one set (such as evolution) in the classroom and another (such as creationism) at church. In different settings their minds are drawn to different principles and "facts."

Perception and imagination define our sense of the possible (O'Connor and Aardema 2005). Because of perception, the real world out there counts. For this reason, claims that reality is only a figment of the imagination or a social construction are off the mark. Because of imagination, though, there is a strong subjective element. Science offers a set of tests to help people decide whether an idea is consistent with the real-world-out-there. But everyone's worldview has an imaginative component, no matter how vigorously they insist that they are strictly adhering to the facts. In part because differences in imagination lead to different interpretations of history and science, controversy reigns.

From Imagination to Belief

In the 1980s, psychotherapists listened to clients describing the terrible abuse that they suffered as small children. In the course of satanic rites they were tortured and raped, and saw the perpetration of unspeakable acts. Many of the accused were childcare workers or teachers. Patients who recounted these disturbing events were extremely emotional, and gave a wealth of gruesome detail. As the psychotherapist listened, two things stood out: the person was earnest and sincere, and the report itself was vivid and compelling. The only hitch—the abuse never happened (Victor 1998). While hoards of patients were identified as victims of satanic ritual abuse, their accusations were never authenticated.

Narrative truth, as it is revealed in people's stories, is not the same as historical truth, what "really" happened in the past. And, even historical truth is open to dispute. Consider, for example, the changing tales of what happened in Dallas when President John F. Kennedy was assassinated there in 1963, or different accounts of the purported UFO crash at Roswell in 1947 (Harrison and Thomas 1997).

Such findings prompted Theodore Sarbin to develop the notion of "believed-in imaginings" (1998a, 1998b). He refers here to ideas that have made the transition from imagination to belief. Believed-in imaginings begin as an image or story, and, over time, gain the status of fact. People assign believed-in imaginings unconditional credibility, despite their subjective origin. The concept is not meant to be pejorative, and it rests on nonpathological processes that lead someone to believe things that other people (often from different times or cultures or confronted by different circumstances) regard as untrue, perhaps even ridiculous or bizarre.

In Sarbin's view, imagination manifests itself in narratives that organize personal experiences. These stories flow from fantasies and daydreams. People get highly involved in some of these narratives, and the resulting powerful emotions affect judgments of what is real. Merely thinking about something makes it seem more likely. In one experiment, investigators asked research participants to express their degree of confidence that certain childhood events had happened to them personally (Garry et al. 2001). They were then asked to imagine some of these events, and as a result of this contemplation became increasingly confident that these events—maybe tipping over a cake at a wedding reception, being lost in a mall, or being attacked by a dog—had actually occurred. In other studies, participants who imagined symptoms of real (and fictitious) ailments became more convinced that they would contract these diseases (DePalma et al. 1996). This is, in a sense, a form of "medical student disease," suspicions that one has the same ailments as a recently studied textbook case. In this experimental research, imagination affects both memory of the past and expectations about the future (Sherman et al. 1985).

The transition from imagination to belief starts when people say to themselves "suppose this were true," and, as they continue to think about it, qualifiers (such as "suppose") drop out (Sarbin 1998a). As a result of psychological, social, and cultural forces, ideas become beliefs and beliefs become facts. In some cases, believed-in imaginings take another step and become lived-in realities. This happened for the patients who falsely believed that they were victims of satanic ritual abuse, and may have happened to Desmond Leslie, who tried to write a fictional account of aliens that contacted Earth in the past and then became convinced that he was dealing not with fiction but with fact (Bennett 2001). And, as we shall see, this also offers a plausible partial explanation for some people's strong convictions that aliens had kidnapped them.

Cultural Narratives

We love stories, and, for many of us, a good story is worth reams of carefully assembled statistics. Stories that circulate widely within a given culture—cultural narratives—are major feeders of imagination. Both children and adults have a predisposition to accept stories as true (Gerrig and Pillow 1998). Simply comprehending a story is the first step towards believing it, and if that story arouses powerful emotions, we are even more inclined to accept it as factual. Powerful stories, delivered through the media, have profound effects on us. Human life, writes Karl Scheibe, "did not start off being a movie, but is fast becoming one ... we take our attitudes, gestures, ways of thinking, dressing, conversing, loving and hating, and fighting from the movies" (Scheibe 1998: 53). Quite a few of these movies have space themes: *ET: The Extraterrestrial, Alien, Contact,* and *Independence Day.* They give rise to "what if" thoughts that seem increasingly real even though one should know better. Of the Fox Television Network show, *The X-Files,* Lisa Nocks wrote: "*The X-Files* borrows from many sources—including ancient mythology, urban legends, UFOlogy, political conspiracy theory, and the daily news—to uncover 'The Truth' which the series' regular character, FBI agent Fox Mulder, believes is 'out there.' While the truth may be out there, it is usually nowhere between the pages of the series' weekly scripts. Yet avid viewers (myself included) come away from many episodes with the feeling that *The X-Files* truth is at least as plausible as anything anyone else has to offer" (Nocks 1998: 295).

In their book, *The Media Equation,* Byron Reeves and Clifford Nass report that people equate (or at least confuse) media portrayals with real life (1996). This is easily understood in the case of children, who are inexperienced, and adults who are distracted and later remember an event but do not recollect that they saw it on TV. But Reeves and Nass's research suggests that people often confuse media and reality in a fundamental way, and are not aware of their mistake. Asked directly, people will tell you that they can keep media presentations and reality straight, but in practice this requires a lot of effort, and is difficult to sustain. Symbolic representations and their real-life equivalents trigger the same neurological reactions, and, of course, the media deliberately plays on our emotions.

People long for single, overarching accounts of the unexplained, and when these are not available feel free to manufacture them. These grassroots explanations, suggests Donald P. Spence, begin as a jumble of chaotic facts, become believed-in imaginings, and then gain a life of their own as they are spread through the media (1998). Grassroots explanations are simplified, sensationalistic, and impervious to disconfirming facts. Spence suspects that people prefer exotic and glamorous grassroots to more accurate but prosaic explanations and for this reason can be blind to the uninspiring truth. Grassroots explanations belong to the people. They survive not because they are supported by data but because they offer a comprehensive mythic account of unexplained happenings. If more and more evidence shifts the balance in the direction of a scientific or mundane explanation, people lose interest and move on to a new mystery.

Over time, recollections become aligned more closely with cultural narratives (Victor 1998). This is reflected in changing recollections of "Our Lady of Fatima." Fatima is located in a rugged section of Portugal that was lightly populated in 1917. At that time, three children—Lucia dos Santos, and her cousins Francisco and Jacinta Martos—repeatedly saw an apparition of a lady in white. Later, Lucia, the only child who conversed with the apparition, entered a convent and her two companions died. Researchers discovered that many of the children's initial accounts did not fit well with prevailing notions about Marian apparitions (Fernandes and D'Armada 2005). They compared Lucia's early statements with those that she made later in life. Over the years, she became more certain that the mysterious apparition was indeed the Blessed Virgin. Her description became more vivid, and the apparition became more Mary-like. The Lady in White's incorrect prediction that World War I would end in 1917 disappeared from the record, replaced by the prediction that, if people prayed, peace would be obtained. New references were made to the grace of God, and to the seer's destiny. As she aged, Lucia recalled new facts about the sightings, even though she could no longer remember events that would stand out in most people's minds, such as the date of her father's death. As these researchers note: "Each person's truth carries with it the cultural charge of the individual, the influence of his or her environment, and the logic of the circumstances" (Fernandes and D'Armada 2005: 10).

Most successful science fiction writers know full well where their stories depart from reality and in their everyday lives are scientific materialists, believing that "all that exists is matter and that the laws of physics are the only ultimate truths" (Colavito 2005: 343). But the same factors that spur imagination—rapid advancements in science, and the interpenetration of science, religion, and folklore—relax reality constraints. Other people, who have more experience, more impressive credentials, and carry greater intellectual and institutional authority can serve as sounding boards to help people separate reality and fantasy and to evaluate ideas before they are promulgated widely. Perhaps our culture's tolerance of variations in religious and political beliefs now extends to the nondemocratic spheres of science and nature. Still, scientists would strongly dispute the claim that *The X-Files* truth is at least as plausible as anything anyone else has to offer. From science's perspective, validation by intuition or popular acclaim is not good enough.

Two

FRONTIER SCIENCE

In 1845, John James Waterston submitted a lengthy article to the Royal Society, Great Britain's most prestigious association of scientists. In this paper, he claimed that a gas consists of tiny colliding particles whose behavior determines the properties of the gas as a whole. The article, under consideration for publication in the Society's journal *Philosophical Transactions*, was sent to two experts for review. One, according to Waterston's biographer David Lindley, called the article "nothing but nonsense" while the other conceded some good points but concluded that the ideas were "very hypothetical" and "difficult to admit." (Lindley 2001: 1). Waterston was ahead of his time, and for another fifty years it was possible for credible scientists to proclaim that atoms do not exist.

It's easy to judge the work of a scientist who has already won a Nobel Prize. The achievements that led to the award are not only pivotal but also durable, since they must withstand many years of close scrutiny before establishing the winner's eligibility. It's also easy to dismiss work that is conspicuous for its shaky assumptions, flawed procedures, forceful contradiction by other data, and hopelessly naive and wishful interpretations. There is, however, a vast zone of frontier science where research is difficult to assess, as evidenced by the controversies that erupt when the work is mentioned. Much of the science that bears on space travel and life on other worlds falls into this zone, an area that becomes particularly murky when researchers move into completely uncharted waters or assault entrenched knowledge.

Suppose we could take a time machine back to the year 1000 and ask a group of bright and well-tutored Europeans to forecast our world of today. At that time, technological and cultural change were slow (the 1030s were not unlike the 1020s or 1010s or 910s for that matter) and while people understood that subsequent generations would come and go, they did not expect the future to be much different from their day. Who could guess how advances in agriculture would lead to hardier and more abundant crops? Who could guess how biology, ranging from the germ theory of disease to nuclear medicine, would give us so much control over health and survival? And who could foresee tremendous advances in weaponry, transportation, communication, and labor-saving devices? Could those of us who are alive today be equally limited in our views of the future?

The anticipation of even greater scientific discoveries is one way to cope with the rapid influx of knowledge about the universe and our place within it. Even as science has raised interesting questions, we hope it will find satisfying answers—and soon. We look for hints or portents that mysteries will soon be solved. Drawing on our own understanding (and in some cases, misunderstanding) of science, we hypothesize, speculate, guess, and fantasize about great discoveries that may be "just around the corner." Maybe the key discovery has already been made, but because of the closed minds and authoritarian views of senior scientists it has not yet entered into the literature. Or, maybe the discovery has not yet been de-classified and released to the public. Perhaps that huge, silent, flying black triangle is one of "ours." No matter that some of these guesses are based on arcane theories and isolated facts. They represent a vote of confidence in the potential of science, even though scientists are not always eager for such accolades. Novel interpretations of space-time continua, mysterious sources of energy, and rampant paranormal phenomena are all a part of our coming of age in the universe.

The Game of Science

Science is materialistic, meaning that it deals with the objective world of matter and energy (or particles and waves) that exists independent of any observer. Through empirical methods (relying on the evidence that confronts their senses) scientists can identify and verify nature's patterns—physical, biological, psychological, and cultural. Science is also deterministic, resting on the assumption that there are lawful relationships between cause and effect, but in recent years science also acknowledges a role for chance. Science is flexible and adaptive, and can be brought to bear on questions that are rooted in or even touch upon the material universe. The scientific method is analogous to a large and powerful spotlight that has the potential to illuminate anything and everything within its beam. Careful naturalistic observation and controlled experimentation yield scientific data or facts—the provisional body of knowledge that stuffs science journals and textbooks.

A primary goal of science is to create maximum consensus (Ziman 1978). This is sought through rationality and reason, as well as through careful research. Yet, this is not to say that science advances with the inexorable logic of a computer. There are many fits and starts—and about-faces. "Einstein," writes Paul Halpern, "was not the resolute thinker who created ironclad theories every time he put his thoughts to paper. His working career was full of many aborted attempts, astonishing sudden changes of heart, and curious episodes when he would say one thing and then do something entirely different" (2004: 6-7).

The organization, clarity, and logic that distinguish so many scientific papers mask the messy nature of the creative process that led to their writing. This theme appears in Harry Collins and Trevor Pinch's view that science is "neither a chivalrous knight nor a pitiless juggernaut" (1994: 1). Rather, it resembles the golem of Jewish folklore. The golem "is made by man from clay and water, and with incantations and spells. It is powerful. It grows a little more powerful every day. It will follow orders, do your work, and protect you from the ever-threatening enemy. But it is clumsy and dangerous. Without control, a golem may destroy its masters with its flailing vigor."

Scientific theories are explanations or accounts of things that occur in nature. They are sets of statements intended to logically and convincingly capture or express some aspect of reality. Theories impose order and meaningfulness on observations that might otherwise seem chaotic, and tell us what should be expected under conditions that have not yet occurred. Theories are enabling, in that they help instigate and guide research. They give rise to new hypotheses that can then be put to a test. Testability is crucial. For scientists to take a claim seriously, it must be subject to proof, and one of the main characteristics of science is the energy with which scientists challenge their own findings (Moldwin 2004). Theories must be consistent with the facts and if inconsistent facts pile up, the theory must be changed or abandoned. Sometimes, people overlook the important link between theories and facts and mistakenly dismiss an important and well-supported idea because "it is only a theory." The theory of evolution, which has overwhelming empirical support, is a good case in point when it is disregarded by people who accept the biblical story of creation (Morrison 2005). All else being equal, scientists prefer simple theories to convoluted theories, general theories to narrow theories, and useful theories to those that represent little more than mental games.

Theories also constrain, in the sense that once a theory is in place it may be difficult to acknowledge pieces that do not fit. Scientists are very suspicious of findings that conflict with widely accepted theories and may discard their own findings if these run counter to prevailing theory (Hawkins 1997). Scientific theories exclude or prohibit entire classes of events. As Erich Goode points out "Without an explanatory theory, some scientists go so far as to say 'I don't care what evidence you have. What you say is all but impossible,' a stance that strikes many people as close-minded" (2000: 26-27). Heavy investment in a particular theory may create expectations so strong that they bias studies and make it easy to overlook inconvenient facts. For instance, a researcher might discard "deviant" observations on the grounds that they could not possibly be correct, and then rejoice that the remaining observations support the theory. This does not mean that researchers tend to cheat or "fudge" results (although both happen from time to time), only that subtle biases in observational procedures and data analysis can nudge results in a particular direction.

Science is also a social institution. Science exists within a culture that encourages some pursuits but discourages others. As an institution, science has its own hierarchy (power structure and pecking order), its own beliefs and conventions, and its own methods of quality control, which sometimes includes ignoring discrepant findings and silencing dissenters. Academies, in Paul Kurtz's estimation, may push people away from really big ideas, so that truly basic and significant questions remain unanswered (1991). Biases, rivalries, and politics accompany the steady accretion of reliable knowledge. Prevailing theories, vested interests, and professional politics help dictate those parts of the material universe that will be illuminated and those that will remain cloaked in darkness.

Science includes opinion leaders, who tell other people what to think, and who favor the scientific elite at the exclusion of upstarts and outsiders. Through selecting, training, and rewarding junior scientists, senior scientists shape successive generations of scientists in their own image. Gatekeepers control membership in professional organizations, and dictate which information will be disseminated within science and to the general public. Joel Achenbach writes that Carl Sagan "was the gatekeeper of any serious discussion of extraterrestrial life. He became the go-to guy for anyone with a new idea.... Only he could decide ... if a creative idea should be allowed into the lecture hall or instead left outside, panting on the sidewalk" (Achenbach 1999: 55). None of these control mechanisms are unique to science. They are a reality of social life that applies to governments, churches, industries, professions, academic disciplines, and UFO study groups. Assemble people in a group and they will establish a hierarchy, develop standards and conventions, and find ways to bring dissenters into line.

Leonard Hayflick devoted his long career to studying cellular aging and death (2003). At the time he was a graduate student, in the early 1960s, biologists believed that in the absence of external forces normal cells would reproduce ceaselessly, that is, live forever. (The experiments that purportedly showed this were improperly conducted and the results depended on an infusion of fresh living cells.) Hayflick and a fellow graduate student found that under carefully controlled conditions that prevented the infusion of fresh living cells, normal cells would die. Aware that their challenge to a widely accepted belief would end their professional careers before they started, they asked six senior scientists to verify the findings in their own laboratories, so that critics could not claim that the original results were due to improper handling of the materials, flawed storage, or other error. Every one of these scientists, operating on their own turf, verified the original result. Nonetheless, the editor of the first journal that received their report speedily rejected it on the basis that it contradicted a well-known fact. The second journal accepted the paper, and it went on to become one of the most frequently cited research papers in science. This suggests that scientists with nonconforming results have a fighting chance if they can somehow persuade other scientists to replicate their results.

Resource availability also determines which ideas pull ahead. Donald MacKenzie points out that for years, airplanes used mechanical devices to navigate to their destinations (1996). In the mid 1970s an alternative arose, called the laser gyroscope. Compared to its mechanical counterparts, the laser guidance system would be lightweight and relatively inexpensive. An influential aviation writer pushed the idea of the laser system and, with only so many millions of dollars to spend, companies chose to invest in this new technology. For some time after its introduction, the laser system was heavier and bulkier than mechanical systems of comparable accuracy. The mechanical system remained in use in certain situations that required very high accuracy, and it took a while before the price of the laser system became competitive. MacKenzie concludes that it is difficult to attribute the laser gyroscope's success to any inherent technological superiority. Proponents of the mechanical system argued that with less money they could have produced a superior system but the funding decision insured the outcome of the competition.

Zones of Science

Science includes a core of ideas that are widely accepted and controversial ideas that fall outside of the core. Mainstream science fits comfortably within the core. Frontier science refers to research that focuses on sometimes sensationalistic and as-yet unproven ideas. At the outer reaches we find "fringe" science, which is even less firmly anchored in prevailing theory and fact. According to Michael Friedlander, "Mainstream science must have its fringe component if it is not to atrophy. In this fringe there are discoveries that will later graduate into the ranks of the accepted, and others that will never receive confirmation. How scientists will view this novelty will depend on its immediate degree of plausibility" (1995: 173).

Beyond fringe science is pseudoscience, which is not science at all. Pseudoscience may appear convincing, particularly if it panders to our desires, or if we do not bother to take the time to uncover its weaknesses or listen to the arguments of people who have done so. Pseudoscience is nothing more than simple assertions backed by belief rather than by rational argument and fact. Oftentimes it rests upon its own invented terminology, has no significant mathematical support, is presented in popular venues rather than in peer-reviewed professional journals, and panders to the uninformed. While science generates hypotheses and then tests them, pseudoscience assumes conclusions and then seeks evidence to back them up (Kaminar 1999).

Whether comfortably nestled at the core or dancing at the fringe, scientific research remains scientific if it follows the assumptions and rules of science (Bauer 2001). Both scientists who operate in the mainstream and those who push the envelope would agree that since science is progressive, it is tentative and inconclusive. At any point in time our understanding of the universe is provisional. Where they are likely to differ is in their relative emphasis on what science has accomplished so far, as compared to intriguing possibilities that may or may not become established fact. If we think of present-day scientific knowledge as a half-filled glass, mainstream scientists point with pride to the filled portion while the empty half fascinates their less-conventional colleagues. Perhaps, in a sense, mainstream scientists are more interested in facts while frontier scientists are more interested in possibilities. From the perspective of frontier science, mainstream science is not necessarily wrong, but it is limited and incomplete.

Attempts to understand the universe and our place within it often brush up against the paranormal. Erich Goode defines as paranormal events that scientists perceive as contrary to the laws of nature. Accounts of the paranormal, he adds, "invoke or make use of forces, factors, dynamics, or causes that scientists regard as inconsistent with a satisfying, naturalistic, or materialistic cause-and-effect relationship" (2000: 18). Paul Kurtz includes anomalies and the supernatural in his definition of the paranormal (1992). Anomalies are strange, unusual, or exceptional phenomena that are inconsistent with mainstream science's beliefs about how everything works. These phenomena emanate from another realm of being, or a hidden dimension of reality, exactly as do myth-based stories (Armstrong 2005). Paranormal experiences, according to Kurtz, conflict with past experience and common sense, do not tie in well with things that we already know, have no ready scientific explanation, and often have a mental or spiritual dimension. Scientists who do study the paranormal, however, do not see their research as discontinuous with other forms of science. According to Dean Radin all paranormal means is that it is something beyond the range of current scientifically known phenomena—there are no unnatural or supernatural phenomena, only large gaps in our knowledge and understanding (1997). These gaps are likely to be particularly large when we consider strange and infrequent events.

In George P. Hansen's view, scientists disdain the paranormal because it represents science contaminated by religion (2001). He places paranormal events somewhere between the material and spiritual worlds. Hansen reports that interest in the paranormal increases during times of culture change. Interest in parapsychology and UFOs was particularly high in China during the 1967 Cultural Revolution, in the United States during the turmoil of the 1960s and 1970s, and during the collapse of the USSR in the 1990s. Russia has yet to restabilize and interest in the paranormal there remains high. One possibility is that surging interest in the paranormal represents an attempt on the part of a troubled society to develop a more satisfying culture. Pursuit of this goal is reflected in enthusiasm for psychic powers, UFOs, past life regressions, and other New Age phenomena.

Working at the Edge

Relatively few scientists work at the frontier because they are reluctant to address a research topic unless it is both tractable and profitable. To pass the tractability test, a problem should be amenable to current theory and methodology. It must be solvable in principle, and there must be a fighting chance of getting the resources required to make a credible attempt. Scientists are likely to have a particularly rough journey if there is little in the way of accumulated knowledge to build upon. To undertake the profitability test, scientists have to assess what they would gain and what they would lose by pursuing the issue after they have decided that it is tractable.

Mainstream science is overflowing with important, interesting research topics. Adventurous scientists have to ask themselves if wandering down an unbeaten path would be more interesting and rewarding than continuing their current lines of research. Are they willing to risk loss of funding, denial of access to premiere peer-reviewed journals, and the ridicule of their former colleagues? For many established scientists, who thoroughly enjoy their present lines of research, this is not a difficult decision. It is very tempting to do what one does well and not move off in new directions.

As we applaud scientists who march off into the wilderness, let's keep in mind that it is easy to get lost there. Scientists outside the mainstream have to settle for unconventional funding sources that, rather than being impartial, may have a particular axe to grind. And because within any discipline those who work at the frontier are relatively few in number, they must depend on a small, scattered group of peers who are tied together by the Internet. An all-new finding may meet with a chilly reception because other scientists have no idea what to do with it. It's not easy to beat a path where few have gone before, and the formidable prospects of failure may offset some of the attractions of breaking new ground.

Fact and Fiction

Interesting, attractive artwork has always been among the tools that NASA has used to build public interest in the space program (McCurdy 1997). Some of this artwork, although plausible and convincing, depicts our expectations for the future, our vision of the universe as it might be. There are no false claims: because the captions allude to the future, everyone understands that the illustration is prophecy, not history. Still, since the pictures drawn by NASA artists and other science illustrators are based on educated guesses and used to illustrate scientific texts, they seem to have a certain level of authority. Intended to engage, enthuse, and build support for space exploration, they seem more "real" than imaginative renditions in other outlets, such as comic books. For some people the huge, immaculate spaceships of the future seem as real as the cramped, cluttered spacecraft of today.

Some analysts suggest that there is little interplay between science and science fiction, that science leads rather than follows science fiction (Cornish 2004). Yet there are at least five ways that science fiction influences science. Science fiction prompts creative thinking and innovative research. Science fiction interests and enthuses people, and may help recruit the next generation of scientists. Science fiction generates hypotheses for later verification. And, science fiction builds self-confidence, convincing us that we can extend the realm of the possible.

Jason Colavito describes how science fiction stories written by H. P. Lovecraft in the early part of the twentieth century shape present-day folklore about alien influences on Earth (Colavito 2005). Drawing on myths, legends, spiritualism, and misunderstood or misrepresented archaeological finds, Lovecraft and his colleagues suggested that an alien form of intelligence arrived on Earth in the dim past and has been influencing biological and cultural evolution ever since. These writers developed, across stories, a fictitious mythology with alien beings, ruined cities, and documents containing forbidden knowledge. Eventually, many people came to believe that one these fictitious works, the *Necronomicon*, was real and in use for worshipping the devil, a claim denied by the Church of Satan (Colavito 2005).

The idea of an ancient, mysterious presence on Earth began to take form in the early 1920s and persevered after Lovecraft's death in 1937. The thesis appeared, disappeared, and reappeared at different times and in different locations, surging forward with fury after the Swiss hotelier Erich von Däniken published *Chariots of the Gods* (von Däniken 1973). This was followed by a host of other books by von Däniken and others, and then a welter of speculative TV shows. The themes were varied: aliens bred with monkeys to produce the first humans; ancient Mesopotamian sculptures of half-men and half-beasts are actually faithful artistic renditions of extraterrestrial visitors; ancient cave drawings depict men wearing spacesuits; visitors from afar entrusted remote African tribes with advanced scientific knowledge long before it was rediscovered by terrestrial scientists; interstellar interlopers built the pyramids; and aliens maintain a presence in Antarctica, under the New Mexican desert, and on the ocean floor.

Oftentimes, these claims are presented rhetorically. Could we be the descendants of extraterrestrial entrepreneurs that arrived here to mine precious metals? Could this mysterious Persian artifact be a toy helicopter? Some of the books that make such claims are patently fabricated, while others represent varying levels of research and scholarship. While it has not been possible to investigate all of these claims, those that have been scrutinized tend to wither away. At an earlier time, when archaeology and ancient history were in their infancy, the evidence was spotty, so sensationalistic claims were hard to disprove. Today, with more of the pieces of the puzzle in place, archaeologists and historians find claims about extraterrestrials' intervention in human history impossible to believe. Colavito believes that by mixing science and myth, science fiction writers in Lovecraft's tradition enable us to understand present-day science in terms of a romantic and comforting past.

Some of the most prominent scientists who conduct research on life in the universe, notes Steven J. Dick, were drawn to the field in part by their interest in science fiction, and, indeed, some scientists such as Sir Arthur C. Clarke, David Criswell, and David Brin became science fiction writers (Dick 1996). The last half of the twentieth century saw an increasingly intimate relationship between science and science fiction, and the adaptation of these themes to spectacular movies and TV programs. All of this, Dick concludes, added authenticity to the idea of extraterrestrial intelligence.

Smithsonian Air and Space Museum curator Roger Launius makes a similar point about manned space exploration (Launius 1998). Over the years science fiction has become more closely tied to the realities of space exploration. Some things that were once imaginary are now real, and science fiction influences serious discussions of spaceflight in respected magazines and journals.

In 2001 the European Space Agency teamed up with the *Maison d'Ailleurs* (a French museum dedicated to science fiction, utopia, and extraordinary journeys) and the OURS Foundation (a private foundation that introduces, nurtures, and expands the cultural aspects of our efforts in space). They joined together to sponsor a project intended to cull science fiction for ideas to be used to advance our progress in space. This was known as the ITSF project, for Innovative Technologies from Science Fiction (for space application). The goal was to find technologies that would assist unmanned and manned spacecraft, space stations, and lunar and planetary bases.

Participating scientists, engineers, science fiction writers, and fans were instructed to prepare fact sheets on their most highly prized science fiction books and movies. These fact sheets included descriptions of concepts and technologies contained in their favorite works. Experts reviewed the fact sheets and eliminated technologies that had already reached fruition or were known not to work. The sponsors intended to extend the borders of science and technology, develop the most viable futuristic options, and launch new trends in science fiction.

Author Ben Bova reports that some of his science fiction has been mimicked by history (1998). His first novel, begun in 1949, described how Russia beat the United States into space, thereby triggering a crash program to put Americans on the Moon. It was rejected as too unbelievable. Not all of his predictions have come true, but in 1962 he anticipated the discovery of organic chemicals in outer space, and in 1976 he predicted the Strategic Defense Initiative (Star Wars), President Ronald Reagan's plan to develop a technological shield to protect the United States from enemy missile attacks.

As evidenced in a March 2002 eulogy for science fiction writer Poul Anderson, science fiction may have played more than a minor role in the Strategic Defense Initiative. Science fiction authors Jerry Pournelle, Larry Niven, and Vernor Vigne described how they collaborated with Anderson and others to develop the Star Wars scenario that was presented to the newly elected President Reagan. They wrote a one-page précis, a lengthier executive summary, and the report itself in the hopes that Reagan would at least read the précis. Reagan was enthralled, read the entire document, and commissioned the Star Wars effort. This hugely expensive endeavor could not be matched by the Soviets, and was one of the reasons that detente became more attractive to them than continued conflict.

Black Projects

Speculation is fed by recognition that much scientific research occurs behind locked doors. In medieval times, craftsmen were secretive about their tools and practices in order to protect the value of their skills. Trades were handed down from father to son, and secrecy prevented the growth of competition. In industry today, clandestine work, usually described as "propriety," is protected by nondisclosure agreements that allow the company to sue employees who leak company information to outsiders. Secret research projects conducted by the government and its contractors are sometimes referred to as "black projects" because they take place in the dark; that is, out of public view. Code names as well as the contents are kept from prying eyes, and only the most intrepid and skillful investigator can find the source and amount of funding in obscure government documents. A huge community of government-sponsored researchers work on advanced aircraft, communications systems, code breaking, nuclear energy, weapons and warhead design, and all sorts of enigmatic and esoteric ideas.

Projects are never fully cloaked in secrecy, so usually bits and pieces leak out. In some cases, there is deliberate disinformation: misleading clues made plausible by a small element of truth. Additionally, despite the threat of huge legal penalties people step forward from time to time and reveal those parts of the picture that are known to them. All of this fuels speculation about discoveries and inventions that do not appear in the science texts. Do aliens work alongside humans in Nevada's mysterious Area 51? Does the government have an antigravity device? Did speculation in the 1950s about aircraft powered by antigravity disappear in the 1960s because the concept proved worthless, or because it went underground when it proved feasible for powering secret aircraft? As the imagination roams, small tidbits of information assume tremendous significance. There are endless possibilities that are unlikely to be discarded because none of them can be disproved. Accurate claims that the so-called clues are fabricated or meaningless are taken as further evidence of their significance while anything of real scientific interest remains in the dark.

Ironic Science

At the frontiers of science, writes Erich Goode, there are "always controversies, unsettled issues and imaginative speculation. To the scientist trained a half-century ago, contemporary writings on black holes, quarks, mesons, antimatter, cosmic strings, virtual particles, ten-dimensional space and the nature of chaos must resemble science fiction" (2000: 72). Moreover, "speculation, improvable assumptions, and investigations into unobservable phenomena" (69) may be the rule rather than the exception in contemporary science.

Perhaps nowhere is the intermingling of science and imagination as evident as in discussions about our place in the universe. The "new physics," that of Einstein and Bohm, is a constant source of inspiration. It has a heavy theoretical slant, and includes—in addition to the ideas mentioned by Goode—space-time curvature, tunneling effects, multiple universes, hidden dimensions, implicate order, nonlocal action, and many other ideas that excite the imagination. The world that confronts our senses is just the tip of the iceberg; much of reality is embedded in hidden dimensions. "Modern science" writes Brian Greene "has spearheaded one assault after another on evidence gained from our rudimentary perceptions, showing that they often yield a clouded conception of the world that we inhabit … Assessing existence while failing to embrace the insights of modern physics would be like wrestling in the dark with an unknown opponent. By deepening our understanding of the true nature of physical reality, we profoundly reconfigure our sense of ourselves and our experience of the universe" (2004: 5). The exotic ideas of modern physics seem compatible with myth, and encourage us to revel in endless possibilities.

Science writer John Horgan describes this brave new era as "ironic science," a form of science that is based on ideas that are fascinating, even enthralling, but that cannot be tested by empirical means (1997). Ironic science is a postempirical, speculative form of science that generates interesting but unanswerable questions. Its chief function is to remind us of what we do not know, and its theories may claim to transcend the Big Bang, quantum mechanics, or natural selection. Commenting on a science symposium that he attended, Horgan wrote: "many of the presentations addressed issues hopelessly divorced from reality, from any possible empirical test. What was the universe like when it was the size of a basketball, or a pea, or a proton, or a superstring? What is the effect on our universe of all of the other universes linked to it by wormholes? There was something both grand and ludicrous about ... bickering over such issues" (1997: 93).

Different speakers, he continues, arrived at private understandings of quantum mechanics, couched in idiosyncratic language. No one seemed to understand, let alone agree with anyone else. The bickering brought to mind what Niels Bohr reportedly said of quantum mechanics: "If you think you understand it, that only shows that you don't know the first thing about it" (Bohr, quoted in Horgan, 1997: 91). If eminent scientists have trouble grasping enigmatic ideas, why should they seem to come so naturally to members of a bowling club speculating on the fastest way to get to the other side of the galaxy, or spiritual people seeking a new theory of consciousness? Perhaps because they promise satisfying answers to questions that are otherwise unanswerable right now.

Paradigm Shifts

Science changes by small increments, and sometimes by leaps and bounds. According to Thomas Kuhn, at any point in time, normal science has a prevailing way of viewing the world (Kuhn 1970). This worldview is called a scientific paradigm. Scientific paradigms encompass dominant theories of how things work, define ways that research should be conducted, and generate expectations about likely results. Although science claims to be open to new ideas and evidence, it is worth reiterating that scientists tend to resist those that run counter to the prevailing paradigm. If the new ideas cannot be accommodated within the prevailing paradigm, the discrepant observations may be discarded as the result of methodological or procedural errors, or perhaps simply ignored.

Still, rational and open-minded scientists can ignore accumulating facts for only so long, and as more and more data are collected it becomes increasingly evident that a paradigm is flawed. Pre-Copernican ideas about a geocentric universe could not account for new data that followed upon rapid advances in math and the invention of the telescope. At some point the balance swings and yields a paradigm shift. Thus, there have been shifts from a geocentric to a heliocentric view of our Sun and planets, and from Newton to Einstein. Progress is slow, and for long periods of time normal science prevails. Paradigm shifts occur only when it is no longer possible to ignore a mounting body of discrepant findings. According to some researchers in the paranormal, scientists can ignore mounting bodies of good evidence for extended periods of time (Radin 2006).

The most important implication of paradigm shifts is that at any point in time (including right now) there will be many observations or "facts" that are either misinterpreted or ignored but might at some future time contribute to acceptance of a radically new view. Perhaps in just a few years the pronouncements of some of today's top scientists will seem as out of date as Robert Millikan's 1928 proclamation that "There is no likelihood that man can ever tap the power of the atom. The glib supposition of utilizing atomic energy when our coal has been run out is a completely unscientific Utopian dream" (Cheney 2001: 262). Unfortunately for present-day speculators these discoveries and their significance can be understood only after they have induced the new paradigm. While we can see this in retrospect we cannot see this in prospect; thus, we have to be wary of arguments that a particular anomaly will lead to a major change in science.

The history of science is littered with episodes when a popular theory was supported by study after study (Polkinghorne 1998). Later generations of scientists discovered that the theory, the results, or both were wrong. But these episodes reveal strengths as well as the weaknesses of science. False theories and erroneous findings can hold sway for only so long. Science is cumulative and self-correcting. The emphasis on observation and verification means that, over successive generations of research, we come closer and closer to the truth.

Science and the Public

Filtering processes introduce simplifications and distortions as scientists communicate their ideas to colleagues, students, and to the general public. As already mentioned, scientific papers may overstate the level of organization, logic, and rigor that characterized a research project. Review articles written for scientific colleagues and textbook accounts prepared for students are necessarily simplified. Some studies are featured and others are mentioned in passing or neglected as the author attempts to weave many disparate threads together into a consistent narrative. As late as the 1950s, French physics textbooks presented science as a "fully realized achievement, encased in certainty" (MacKenzie 1996: 70). These textbooks ignored Albert Einstein and the principles of relativity, since this would undermine the predictability, elegance, and harmony that could be preserved by focusing on Newtonian physics.

Today textbook publishers thirst for new editions to minimize the economically catastrophic effects of the used textbook market. One path to renewal is focusing on very recent studies and findings. Unfortunately, in many fields, the most recent discoveries are among those that are the most likely to be retracted. The primary function of a textbook is to convey reliable knowledge. Books that include findings that have yet to be replicated or properly interpreted put glitz before substance and undercut science education by feeding students dubious facts (Bauer 2001).

The elite or highbrow media—*The New York Times*, the *Washington Post*, National Public Radio, and the Public Broadcasting System—are strong allies of science and report stories in ways that withstand the scrutiny of skeptics and educate the public (Goode 2000). Most newspapers and magazines do not run UFO articles, not because of an orchestrated government conspiracy, but because such stories are hard to verify and too often fail to lead anywhere (Huyghe 2001). One UFOlogist who quit the field (and who shall remain anonymous) mentioned to me "There is always something new and exciting but at the end of the day we are still at the same place." Such cautiousness and conservatism is not true of the tabloids that we find at the supermarket checkout stand.

The mass media capitalizes on the fact that bizarre, unusual, and weird stories attract the public's interest. A person who sights a spacecraft from the Pleiades makes news; someone who mistakes a C-5A cargo plane for a flying saucer does not. Airwaves and cables are overloaded with programs about UFOs, ancient astronauts, communicating with dead people, and similar phenomena. Each year a new set of programs about the paranormal debuts (accompanied by a geometric progression of reruns). These shows are not necessarily limited to entertainment networks but appear also on channels featuring geography, history, and science.

Broadcasting is a commercial venture that depends upon revenue from advertisers, which in turn hinges on audience size. Thus, even documentaries on "life in the universe" may have a sensationalistic tinge. Interviewees who express complex ideas, offer reservations and qualifications, or make comments that run counter to the show's premise find that their material ends up on the cutting room floor.

Colin Bennett states that entertainment replaced news in about 1980, when Ronald Reagan was elected president (Bennett 2001). It is not always easy for today's television viewers to separate news, entertainment, and commercials. In these days of consummate special effects and the ability to modify pictures pixel-by-pixel if necessary, seeing should not lead to believing. Brief previews featuring pictures of flying saucers or aliens are accompanied by wild claims ("If you didn't believe before, you will believe now"). Supremely confident self-styled experts (sometimes on both sides of an issue) rely on their credentials rather than an in-depth knowledge of the topic to back their assertions. Popular television and movie stars who serve as hosts lend an air of credibility, even though they lack qualifications in areas that really count, such as science or education. Mixing interviews of reputable scholars with dubious film clips and people who make flimsy claims add to the confusion. Douglas Raybeck notes that those media moguls who demand a large audience must accommodate limited intelligence and a short attention span (Raybeck 2000). This means "dumbing down" the content to reach the largest possible audience. In order to remain competitive over the years, major news magazines have cut the length of their articles and increased the size and number of pictures. Some of the material is set off in "side bars" or "boxes" to keep the article brief enough that people will read it. The sentences are short and the vocabulary is basic. Most broadcast news accounts are superficial, based largely on visuals, and replace in-depth discussion with sound bites.

As for making the world simple and palatable, it is hard to outdo Internet offerings. Through the Internet, any idea can be presented to large audiences. Fact is presented as fiction, and fiction is presented as fact. On many sites there are few words and lots of pictures. Read what you like, live with superficial, fragmentary explanations, and skip anything that seems difficult or unpalatable. By carefully choosing congenial Web sites and subscribing to electronic magazines that cater to like-minded people, one can, in effect, design one's own universe. Through the Internet it is possible to find other people who support your views. Once ensconced it is possible to survive indefinitely without having pet ideas challenged.

Simplified materials enable producers to reach large groups of people, but at the same time they help create uncritical audiences. The readers or viewers do not have to apply critical thinking or stretch their intellects in order to grasp the concepts. This makes them lazy, which in turn encourages producers to develop even simpler materials, thereby creating a vicious downward spiral. Raybeck fears that this will lead to a loss not only of literacy but also a diminution of other cognitive skills, such as abstract reasoning. All of this would mean "a more gullible electorate, more pliable consumers, more vacuous entertainment, and an increasing bifurcation of the social order," (Raybeck 2000: 48) with even greater power concentrated in the hands of people who are truly literate. As everything else becomes more complicated, people's views become simpler.

Skeptical Inquiry

Science and skepticism are intricately linked, and one of the skeptics' goals is to prepare a scientifically illiterate public. Skepticism, notes Paul Kurtz, founder of the periodical *Skeptical Inquirer*, comes in many forms (1992). One can, for example, doubt everything and accept nothing. But skeptical inquiry as a foundation for his work is an outgrowth of John Dewey's pragmatism and is closely allied with science. Organizations of skeptics are intent on educating the public.

Skeptical inquirers use rational thought and empirical data in an effort to acquire reliable knowledge. They think like scientists and practical, reality-oriented folk. When they evaluate ideas skeptics ask: "Is the person who makes this claim credible? "Is this claim consistent with what we already know?" "How good is the evidence?" "Can we find a simpler, better explanation?" Through logical analysis and the careful assembly of evidence they cast significant doubt upon claims of the paranormal, which many other people find appealing. Kurtz's mantra is that when we hear an unusual claim we must evaluate it in light of reliable knowledge (1992). Skeptics realize that we live in a complicated world that is hard to understand and urge us to look to experts within a field for leadership and guidance, hoping that we will not call too often on experts whose credentials are tangential, old, fading, or overstated.

Skeptics operate at three levels: cop, scientist, and philosopher, and their work at each level should be differentiated. As cops, skeptics see themselves as correcting errors, clearing up misconceptions and sending liars packing. Within the pages of the *Skeptical Inquirer* we learn how under the unflinching gaze of skeptics, self-proclaimed psychics suddenly find themselves unable to perform. We read how a few simple tricks that are well known to stage magicians explain the illusory successes of fortune-tellers and seers who claim to converse with the dead. We discover how charlatans create impressions of magical cures—for example, by offering free wheelchair rides to ambulatory patients who are quite able to walk away from the altar after the faith healing has been performed. As cops, skeptics do their best to protect us from scoundrels who bilk us by offering false cures that lure us away from effective medical help, give us poor advice after pretending to predict our future, or falsely claim to put us in touch with lost loved ones. We should rejoice at these policing efforts.

Because they see contemporary science as practical and successful, skeptics almost always speak out against (or at least find prosaic explanations for) the paranormal. Professional skeptics consistently reject paranormal explanations of mystical and near-death experiences, UFOs, and alien abductions and interpret weird phenomena in terms of observational error, neurology, psychology, and myth. At the level of scientists skeptics enter into debates over the most appropriate research procedures and data analysis techniques and what constitutes convincing results. Here their work should not be evaluated as a public service but as the work of scientists. At this level we cannot presume that they occupy a moral high ground over the people whose work they criticize; their arguments and data have to stand on their own merits.

The third hat that is worn by some (not all) skeptics is that of the philosopher. As philosophers, skeptics adopt the same metaphysics and epistemology as scientists, but also accommodate humanistic ethical values. At the level of philosopher, for those who choose to engage, atheism reigns and religion is a favorite target. The pragmatic-scientific viewpoint has no need for God, transcendence, mysticism, and spirituality. It's not that we should be bad people—far from it; we can refer to practical principles for treating one another decently and getting the most out of life. As philosophers, discussing weighty issues with fellow philosophers, skeptics have no special advantage or disadvantage.

Dean Radin, a leading parapsychologist who is known for his devotion to the scientific method, reports having read (in the proportion of two to one) books written by authors who are interested in the paranormal and by skeptics who refute their research (2006: 10). He writes:

"Both sides of the controversy seemed sensible enough; both argued their sides convincingly. But after reading all of these books I noticed that the debate followed a predictable pattern. One side presented experimental evidence that something interesting was going on; the other argued that the evidence wasn't good enough to be taken seriously. Some skeptics pushed doubt to extremes and insisted that positive evidence was always due to mistakes or intentional fraud." One side, he concluded, consisted of explorers willing to take risks to advance knowledge; the other side was more interested in defending dogma, sometimes "through passionate and vicious denial" (11).

But there is another kind of skepticism, one that originates at the grassroots level (Dean 1998). This form of skepticism involves asking awkward questions about scientific institutions and challenging the opinions of scientists. Grassroots skeptics do not accept the worldview of scientists as proven. A sense that their experiences, interests, and views are ignored or rejected by the scientific elite makes people distrustful and moves us further and further from consensus. For these people science and skepticism are not seen as voices in the wilderness or candles in the dark; rather, they are seen as a relentless juggernaut mindlessly squashing anything that gets into their paths.

For many people, the term "skeptic" has a negative connotation: naysayer, refuter, spoilsport, and debunker (Borgo 2005). Attempts to find a more neutral appellation—such as by calling themselves "brights"—have not gotten very far (Shermer 2006). But despite their characteristic hard-line stance, skeptics insist that knowledge is provisional and it is important to remain open to new ideas. Almost without exception they express interests in UFOs and other paranormal phenomena, even though they approach these with a strong sense of doubt. Susan Blackmore spent twenty-five years searching in vain for evidence of telepathy, clairvoyance, psychokinesis, and life after death before going on to other interests. She concluded that such phenomena do not exist, but, as a scientist, adds that she has been proven wrong and is not afraid to be proven wrong again (Blackmore 2001). Carl Sagan and Ann Druyan identified three claims within parapsychology that, while not proven, might deserve further study: psychokinesis, telepathy, and reincarnation (1997: 302). James Alcock stresses that although conventional psychologists and parapsychologists may look at reality in different ways, they share a common desire to use science to put their ideas to the test. He writes that "While we [skeptics] may 'tut-tut' the parapsychologists for their unending quest to put belief in the paranormal on a scientific basis, we need to recognize that we and they have much in common—a shared belief that the scientific method, with its insistence on the careful testing of theory against experience, is the best path toward the true understanding of the world around us" (Alcock 2001: 38).

Michael Shermer points out that science is always a matter of probabilities and whereas we can make reasoned guesses we cannot tell for sure what science will find next (Shermer 2006). Elsewhere he admonishes that by being intolerant we may squelch the truth or part of the truth. At least, by failing to attend to someone else's ideas we may fail to benefit from their mistakes. Besides, "being tolerant when you are in the majority means you have a greater chance of being tolerated when you are in the minority" (Shermer 1997: 186). Paul Kurtz states repeatedly that everyone—including scientists and skeptics—has to be open to the possibility that they will be proven wrong in the light of new evidence. This includes being skeptical about the skeptics. He is not interested in wasting a lot of time on silly arguments but he is willing to admit the possibility of error. "Only with open dialogue may we draw upon alternate conceptions and perhaps better approximate the truth. In an open market of ideas, no group can demand immunity from criticism" (Kurtz 1991: 325). When it comes to UFOs, the ultimate challenge according to Randall Fitzgerald is to avoid falling for a "continuous dribble of faked UFO photos, bogus alien bodies … fabricated alien artifacts and banal channeled messages" without adopting a rigid mindset that leads to "cynicism and a sniveling disbelief instead of doubt" (1998: 2). But it is hard to beat General Charles Cabell, Director of Central Intelligence in 1951. Addressing a group of subordinates who were assessing UFOs he demanded, "I want an open mind; in fact, I *order* an open mind! Anyone that doesn't keep an open mind can get out now" (Swords 2000: 103).

Three

EYES ON THE UNIVERSE

Early in the twentieth century Yugoslavian-born physicist Nikola Tesla applied scientific thinking, engineering skills, and theatrics to problems ranging from the brilliant to the foolish, triggering cheers and jeers from diverse audiences (Cheney 2001). Tesla radically improved the electric motor and helped George Westinghouse electrify the United States with alternating current (AC), thereby defeating Thomas Edison's efforts to promote direct current (DC). Supported by wealthy industrialists and financiers of that time, along with Hertz, Marconi, and DeForrest, Tesla developed radio. In 1902, near Fort Collins, Colorado, he detected rhythmic patterns that he was convinced had been beamed to Earth from Mars. Few people paid attention until a celebrity scientist, Lord Kelvin, proposed to a *New York Times* reporter that Martians could see the bright lights of New York, and were signaling Earth. About thirty years later, scientists understood that despite their regularity the rhythmic patterns that Tesla heard from outer space resulted from impersonal natural forces, not extraterrestrial intelligence.

If there is any single area of science where rapidly expanding knowledge captures the public's imagination, it is the search for life and intelligence beyond Earth. There is a strong circumstantial case (but no conclusive proof) that such life exists. Scientists are finding more stars and more planets, and identifying more conditions that stack chemical reactions in life's favor. The parade of discoveries is stunning: water on Mars, planets orbiting distant stars, life in terrestrial environments that just a few short years ago were considered lethal, chemical constituents of life in deep space, and much more (Darling 2001). Rather than a rare and unusual occurrence, life may be a cosmic imperative, although it is less clear that once initiated, life will evolve in the direction of human-level intelligence.

These findings encourage people who make very different assumptions and apply very different search strategies to anticipate the discovery of extraterrestrial life. Despite their profound differences, people who comb the Bible in search of ancient astronauts, look speculatively at an unfamiliar object in the sky, and listen for chatter between distant civilizations share a profound interest in what may be found beyond Earth. This chapter focuses on scientific searches for extraterrestrial life, efforts that fall under the rubrics of astrobiology and SETI. These constitute the gold standards against which other searches should be gauged.

Astrobiology

Astrobiology offers a biological perspective to many areas of NASA research and is defined as the study of life in the universe (Darling 2001; Harrison et al. 2002). The field is organized around three central questions. First, how does life begin and develop? This requires studying how life arose on Earth; looking for general principles that govern the organization of matter into living systems; exploring evolution at the molecular, organism, and ecosystem levels; and trying to understand the coevolution of our planet and its biosphere. Second, does life exist elsewhere in the universe? To answer this, scientists specify the environmental limits for life and locate promising sites for life as well as seeking indicators of past and present life. Third, what is life's future on Earth and beyond? Astrobiologists consider how Earth's ecosystem might fail and explore human-directed processes that might allow us to migrate from one world to another.

Astrobiologists look for extrasolar planets (planets orbiting distant suns), try to understand conditions that make some of these planets habitable (suitable for life), explore the conditions that give rise to life, and trace the course of evolution. They seek biosignatures, the direct consequences of biological activity, and geosignatures, alterations of the environment due to industrial processes. Astrobiology is, in part, the latest incarnation of a field first known as exobiology and later known as bioastronomy. Perhaps because it specifically includes life on Earth, astrobiology has generated levels of excitement and enthusiasm among scientists that its predecessors never attained (Staley 2003). Astrobiology is geared for finding life "as we know it": carbon based, and dependent upon on metabolic processes similar to ours.

The universe, as understood by most scientists, began in a huge explosion known as the Big Bang. It has been expanding outwards for the past twelve to fourteen billion years and may continue to do so indefinitely. The universe consists of plenty of space, enough matter to comprise trillions of galaxies, and some mysterious dark energy and matter that we do not know very much about. Each galaxy consists of billions of stars—there are 10^{11} stars in our galaxy alone. Stars are classified in several ways, primarily by letter designations O, B, A, F, G, K, and M that designate spectral types or effective temperature (Ulmschneider 2003). Our Sun is a G star, which means that it has an effective temperature of approximately 5,800 Kelvin (degrees above absolute zero), as compared to cool M stars (3,200 K) and really hot O stars (41,000 K). Not all stars are promising hosts for life-bearing planets. Stars so big and hot that they roast the planets that orbit them, run out of fuel in a paltry few million years, or spew forth huge amounts of lethal radiation do not give life much of a chance. Still, this leaves a substantial pool of K, F, and M stars that, along with G stars, are relatively hospitable.

It requires ingenuity to explore conditions at great distances; for example, to find extrasolar planets. Ultimately, searching for reflected starlight or infrared energy emitted from the planet itself may be the best way to find them, but at present this is largely unworkable because from great interstellar distances suns and planets appear so close together that the sun's blinding glare makes it impossible to detect the small orbiting planets (Sparks and Ford 2001). The Sun emits *two billion* times as much light as is reflected from Earth, and in the infrared range the Sun is still ten million times more prominent than Earth (Ulmschneider 2003). For such reasons, today's scientists rely on indirect methods to find planets.

As a planet moves it exerts a slight pull on its sun and causes it to wobble. Beams of starlight from its sun are run through a prism known as a spectroscope that splits the light into its constituent colors. When a planet tugs its star towards the telescope, known absorption lines shift towards the red end of the spectrum, but when it pulls away there is movement to the red end of the spectrum. By analyzing these shifts scientists measure planets' gravitational signatures and estimate their size and distance from their suns. Another procedure, based on transit dimming, involves looking for a slight dimming of a star (a decrease of 2 percent of its illumination) brought about as one of its planets "transits" or passes across its face (Ulmschneider 2003). As of October 2006 scientists have discovered about 210 extrasolar planets, but most of these are giants and not promising sites for life.

Planets that can support life fall within their star's habitable zone—not so close to their stars that water will boil, nor so far away that it freezes. In the 1950s, the habitable zone was considered rather narrow, but with the discovery of extremophiles that live in frozen areas or in boiling water that bubbles up from thermal vents or contains radioactive waste scientists now suspect that a planet's habitable zone could be rather large (Darling 2001). Guesses of the number of habitable planets in our galaxy have varied widely over the past forty years. Using modern techniques Ulmschneider reckons that there are 4×10^6 habitable planets (2003). If he's correct, this means that only one in forty thousand stars has an Earth-like planet. Keep in mind, though, that right now we are considering habitable planets as sites for life. A civilization with immense wealth and advanced technology might engineer otherwise hostile planets to make them habitable, or use some combination of genetic engineering, artificial intelligence, and robotics to adapt to planets that are otherwise lethal. Or perhaps extraterrestrial life occupies artificial satellites, spacecraft, and other fabricated worlds.

Life's chemical building blocks—such as hydrogen, carbon, nitrogen, and oxygen—are widely distributed throughout the universe. Nature constrains chance, meaning that it is not necessary to run through endless combinations before scoring a hit. Physical, chemical, and environmental boundaries limit the role of chance and stack the odds in life's favor. Whether or not life will evolve in the direction of human-level intelligence is a more complex and controversial issue. Some species of animals have thrived for millions of years without having to reason, solve problems, or engage in elaborate communication. They have no need to compose fugues for pipe organs, engineer nuclear weapons, paint intricate murals inside chapels, chat over the Internet, or restore antique automobiles. Eric Chaisson proposes that we do not differ in kind from other organisms: we differ in degree. Our complexity is revealed in our consciousness, in our culture, and in our metropolises. And, he adds: "no evidence whatsoever implies that humankind is the end-point of cosmic evolution, nor are we likely the only sentient beings in the universe" (Chaisson 2001: 196).

Advocates of the rare-Earth hypothesis suspect that extraterrestrial life is unusual and, where it does take hold, it is unlikely to evolve in the direction of human-like intelligence (Ward and Brownlee 2000). These scientists do not deny the possibility that scattered throughout the universe there are many life-bearing planets. What they do question is that many extraterrestrial organisms have attained human-level intelligence. Countless planets may house single-celled organisms, grasses, simple sea creatures such as jellyfish, and perhaps even small land animals. But, according to the rare-Earth hypothesis, only a negligible fraction of extrasolar planets will host civilizations.

The hypothesis posits that human-level complexity depends on an amazing combination of events, a confluence so remarkable that it is unlikely to have occurred anywhere else. Our existence as a species required—among other things—the presence of huge planets such as Jupiter, a Moon that is neither too big nor too small, and a particular geological platform that includes plate tectonics and continental drift. A period of intense bombardment by asteroids and comets was critical. If it had not been for cosmic intervention in the form of an asteroid impact that incinerated the dinosaurs, we might still be shrew-like animals picking up crumbs from the dinosaurs' table. The destruction of these predators led to an explosion of mammalian species and gave primates a chance to thrive (DeVore 2001).

Critics of the rare-Earth hypothesis point out that whereas a specific pattern of events did indeed lead to the evolution of life and intelligence on Earth, other patterns of events could have led to the evolution of intelligence elsewhere (Darling 2001). Think of the many different routes one might take to get from Montreal to Los Angeles! Besides, even if biological intelligence is rare and fleeting, it may be able to create synthetic intelligence that is capable of rapid and self-directed evolution (Shostak 2001). If nobody is out there in the biological sense, our galaxy could still be home to a multitude of all-but-indestructible communicating devices.

Satellites and probes have joined telescopes in the quest for life beyond Earth. Probes have flown by and orbited our neighboring planets. On occasion, robot craft have descended to the Moon, Mars, and Venus, where they take copious pictures and perform automated analyses. Despite representing the goddess of love, Venus is a complete hellhole utterly incapable of supporting surface life. Russian probes that landed there were briefly able to send back images and other data but were soon crushed (by the thick atmosphere) and cooked. Mars is much friendlier. Whereas we have long since abandoned the idea that it might be home to intelligence it remains possible that Mars was or is the site for microbial life.

As pictures from the Mars Global Surveyor rolled in, scientists found increased evidence that at one time Mars was a habitable planet. Where there is water there may be life, and water existed on Mars in the distant past. At some point back then an ocean may have covered the entire planet. Recent interpretations of Martian geology, based on new, high-resolution photographs, show effects that were most likely brought about by flowing water. In late 2000, Michael Malin, principal investigator of the camera on the Surveyor, unveiled pictures that contained layer upon layer of sediment (Malin and Edgett 2000). Layered sediments are favorable sites for finding fossils on Earth, so layered sediments on Mars are promising destinations for fossil-hunting robot explorers.

Attempts to conduct bioassays on Mars itself have led, at best, to equivocal results. NASA is in the process of planning missions that would return Martian samples to Earth for analysis. We already have some chunks of Mars: these arrived courtesy of asteroids that slammed into Mars spraying rocks spaceward with enough force that some reached Earth. In 1996, scientists released pictures of tiny worm-like structures found in ALH84001, a meteor that came to Earth from Mars. Visible only by means of a high-resolution scanning microscope, the unusual tube-like structures are less than 1/100th the width of a human hair. Critics, and they are in the majority, complain that the "fossils" are too small for organisms and that physical rather than biochemical processes account for these purported traces of past life. Advocates counter that we know of terrestrial bacteria of similar tiny scale.

The Stardust Mission, launched in 1999, sent a container on a seven-year round-trip through space. In 2004 it passed through the tail of Comet Wild 2, the right snowball at the right place at the right time. It returned to Earth in January 2006 bringing with it particle samples that have been distributed to approximately 150 scientists worldwide (NASA 2006). Preliminary analyses found iron, magnesium, calcium, aluminum, titanium, and materials reminiscent of Hawaiian beach sand and semiprecious gemstones. The lesson so far is that because different comets have different histories, individual comets are likely to be far more distinctive than earlier supposed.

Astrobiology should advance rapidly over the next few years as new research tools come on line. Kepler, an orbiting device once scheduled for launch in 2005, will explore a sample of 100,000 stars and give us an estimate of how many have Earth-sized planets orbiting within their habitable zones (J. Tarter 2001). It has no moving parts and will use transit-dimming to find extrasolar planets. The Space Interferometry Mission, with an expected launch date of 2009, should detect wobbles in stars up to thirty light years away, including minute jiggles caused by orbiting planets as small as Earth. If recently cancelled funding is reinstated, NASA's Terrestrial Planet Finder, once expected in 2011, will use four 8-meter telescopes to allow both direct imaging and spectrographic analysis of planets circling nearby stars. These analyses could reveal biosignatures and geosignatures, potential signs of life.

Still on the drawing board is the OWL (OverWhelmingly Large Telescope). If plans unfold, this would be located high atop a mountain, at five thousand meters, and would be operated from a base camp at three thousand meters. First choice is a mountain in the Atacama Desert in Chile, an exceptionally dry spot with little atmospheric and light pollution. With a main mirror more than one hundred meters across, the OWL will have forty times the resolution of the Hubble, and several thousand times that orbiting telescope's sensitivity. If all goes well, this telescope, with a mirror the size of a football field, will enter service in 2016.

SETI

SETI is the direct search for extraterrestrial intelligence, or more precisely, signs of technology that will allow us to infer intelligence (J. Tarter 2001). SETI refers to a set of search procedures undertaken by many organizations and investigators, including the SETI Institute in Mountain View, California; the Planetary Society; and the SETI League, a dedicated group of amateurs who use homemade search equipment and run over 130 search stations. The dominant procedure is to use radio telescopes to hunt for microwave emissions that are extraterrestrial and of intelligent origin. As of 2001, at least ninety-nine SETI observing projects had been mentioned in the literature, and there were at that time fourteen ongoing searches, some of them underway for decades (J. Tarter 2001). Of course, these searches can only find civilizations that use microwave radio. These may occupy a relatively brief window that opens when they gain microwave or laser technology but slams shut again when they become a "supercivilization" that advances to hypothetical quantum or other communication techniques that currently elude us (Ćirković 2004). This would severely restrict our opportunity to find them, but the only way for us to search is by means of technology that is available to us right now.

If astrobiology can be described as a "bottom up" approach assembling piecemeal evidence for simple or primitive life out there, SETI is a "top-down" approach that, if successful, can short circuit a tedious search process. Of course, SETI scientists applaud the achievements of astrobiologists, as the latter's findings tend to increase circumstantial evidence of extraterrestrial intelligence and in this way bolster confidence that their searches will someday bear fruit.

The microwave search process was illustrated with reasonable fidelity in the 1997 movie *Contact* starring Jodie Foster. Intercepted microwaves undergo analysis for evidence that they are not the result of purely natural processes. While static and other naturally occurring emissions tend to cover a fairly broad range of frequencies, deliberate transmissions are narrow band. Visual representations of these on laboratory equipment would display them as spikes. Then, it is necessary to show that these signals did not originate on Earth, or from some forgotten satellite or space probe. Other observatories must verify signals that pass these tests before their discovery is announced to the public. On occasion scientists have found some provocative candidates, but so far not one has survived the rigorous verification procedures

In the movie *Contact*, Earth's first indication of extraterrestrial intelligence is when radiotelescopes in New Mexico receive, some sixty years after it was first transmitted, footage from the 1936 Olympics in Nazi Germany. Might an actual extraterrestrial civilization acknowledge their presence by reflecting back one of our earlier broadcasts? In fact, since the 1920s some radio operators have wondered about "long-delayed echoes," transmissions that return to Earth a few minutes or even hours after they are sent. Careful research effectively eliminates the possibility that these echoes are rebroadcast to Earth via an alien spaceship. It's possible to estimate the location of the suspected spaceship, but astronomers who look there don't find one (J. Tarter 2001). Long-delayed echoes are not well understood but may result from the signals being bounced around by plasma and dust in Earth's ionosphere before they return to the surface.

A new generation of microwave observation began to take shape in 2005 when the Allen Telescope Array began to go on line. This consists of mass-produced six-meter (twenty-foot) microwave dishes erected at the Hat Creek Observatory near Mount Lassen National Park in northern California. Although the array started small, it may eventually grow to 350 to 1,000 dishes hooked together as one giant "ear." Researchers will be able to search for very faint signals among a million star systems containing on the order of seventeen thousand promising stars. The Allen Telescope Array is a multitasking system, meaning that it can conduct different types of astronomical research at the same time. In addition to SETI, it may be used to explore the very early universe, or to look for transient events such as supernova explosions. Discussing the Array, the astronomer Jill Tarter writes, "It is very satisfying to know that the array will be probing emergent cosmic evolution and the evolution of technology, two extremes on a continuum that stretches from primal matter to minds that contemplate their origins" (2003: 1).

OSETI

Pioneered by Stuart Kingsley and his associates at the Columbus Optical SETI Observatory, optical SETI (OSETI) searches for extraterrestrial laser communications. These could take the form of either continuous laser beams or powerful flashes or pulses measured in nanoseconds. Perhaps Earth is being "pinged" by civilizations that have detected terrestrial radio transmissions.

Lasers were developed at about the same time that radiotelescope searches began, and lasers, according to their proponents, offer a number of advantages over microwave radio for interstellar communication (Howard et al. 2004). Optical laser beams are more slender and focused than their radio counterparts. This makes them useful for transmitting large volumes of data at very fast rates over tremendous distances. The power of our radio transmitters has remained more or less constant for the last thirty years, but during this same period optical laser power has grown exponentially.

Microwave searches require sophisticated computers and complicated software to sift signal from noise, but laser transmissions are identifiable through the relatively simple process of counting photons. Whereas there is always the possibility of a false alarm, it is minimal in the case of OSETI. Pulsed optical lights—sparks, lightning, aircraft lights and so forth—are simply too dim to cause the "photon pileup" that is characteristic of sensing a pulsed laser. Detection devices are so powerful that OSETI searches can proceed in broad daylight. Relatively speaking, equipment costs are modest. Two large (ten-meter) telescopes could communicate over a distance of one thousand light years.

Unlike a sun or star, which emits a broad spectrum of light, lasers use monochromatic light; that is, light of a single pure color. A spectrographic analysis of an extraterrestrial laser transmission would show a disproportionate amount of light (the photon pileup) at one particular point on the spectrum, allowing researchers to infer that it is an intelligently controlled pulse. Thus, as in the case of radio SETI, OSETI seeks a narrow "spike" that stands out against a diffuse background.

The same sharp focus that enables lasers to transmit massive amounts of information over many light years also means that they take the form of pinpoints of light that are very difficult to find. (Indeed, months of searching may cover only one-millionth of the sky.) The problem is exacerbated in the case of pulsed lasers. That is, it is one thing to find a powerful continuous beam and another to find a brief "flash" that is visible on Earth we know not where and we know not when. Between 1998 and 2003, 2,378 hours of searching with the Wyeth Telescope at the Harvard/Smithsonian Oak Ridge Observatory yielded 15,897 observations of 6,176 stars (Howard et al., 2004). This included 274 interesting events, such as HIP 107395, which was noted simultaneously by two observatories. But this discovery was not repeated, so it's back to the telescope.

Could it be that the step-by-step approach of astrobiology, rather than the direct approach of SETI, will first find unequivocal evidence of a technologically advanced civilization? One way that the tortoise could beat the hare in this case is if astrobiologists discovered the spectral signature of industrial pollutants in a planet's atmosphere. Unlike the hare in the children's fable, who lost because its supreme confidence led it to take a rest, the hare in this case—SETI—is progressing at a relentless pace. Still, astrobiology is better equipped than SETI to detect societies that have not yet developed or have advanced beyond laser and microwave technologies but still leak signs of industrial activity.

Calling ET

Consider the excitement of an archaeological discovery, a long-delayed message finally reaching its destination, or, for that matter, finding childhood mementos in the attic. Such experiences prompt us to imagine that future generations would delight in learning about our lives and accomplishments. For this reason, people have prepared literally thousands of time capsules to inform future generations (Jarvis 2003). But in an era when we believe that we share the universe with other civilizations, why should we limit ourselves to our own descendents? If we were to herald our achievements far and wide, knowledge of our culture might survive long after a major asteroid impact or other event eradicated other traces of humankind. Furthermore, if every technologically advanced civilization is passively searching for transmissions from other civilizations, how could they ever communicate with one another? All civilizations would live in isolation unless at least one of them announced its presence.

During the closing years of the twentieth century a few scientists began active SETI—a highly controversial effort to send messages to the stars. "The profound need to conduct cultural and information transfer across vast spans of time," writes William Jarvis, "may well be a primal dynamic" (Jarvis 2003: 43).

Interstellar Transmissions

Microwave transmitters and lasers are appealing for interstellar transmissions, especially if their transmissions are powerful, systematic, and sustained. They can be developed using off-the-shelf technology, are relatively low cost, and are able to cover tremendous distances at the speed of light. The first deliberate interstellar radio broadcasts took place at the rededication of the Arecibo radiotelescope in Puerto Rico on 14 November 1974 (Drake and Sobel 1992). The pixels of this digital message, arranged into 73 lines of 23 characters, form graphic representations of hydrogen, carbon, oxygen, and phosphorous atoms; chemical formulas for sugars and nucleic acids; DNA; and line drawings of a single human figure and a microwave antenna. The transmission was aimed in the direction of the Hercules star cluster Messier 13 (M13), tens of thousands of light years away.

Beginning with "Cosmic Call 1999," a series of powerful transmissions were sent from the Evpatoria observatory radar in the Ukraine (Zaitsev 2002; Zaitsev et al. 2005). Yvan Dutil and Stephane Dumas of the Defence Research Establishment Valcartier in Quebec, Canada composed the initial message. Intended to be an "Interstellar Rosetta Stone," it built upon previous attempts to develop universal languages and depended heavily upon science and mathematics. Packed full of scientific notation, the message was put together like a textbook, starting with very simple ideas, such as the hydrogen atom, and then moving on to increasingly challenging topics. Since no communication is complete without a response it ended with an invitation for recipients to reply by telling us about themselves.

In August and September 2001, Alexander Zaitsev transmitted a "Message for Teens" that included a "Concert for ET" from Evpatoria to six nearby sun-like stars (2002). The concert included a solo instrument known as the theremin, which Zaitsev considered a good choice, because it produces a strong, clear tone that can whistle its way across vast interstellar distances. It is worth noting, however, that the theremin is considered quite differently in Russia and the United States (Wierzbicki 2002). In Russia, the theremin is an instrument of high culture and refinement, and welcome at classical music recitals. In Hollywood, theremin music sets the mood for horror and science fiction films. One can only guess what an audience in a distant civilization might make of it.

Then, in 2003, another Cosmic Call was broadcast to five Sun-like stars. This included the flags of 282 states, the song "Starman" performed by musician David Bowie, and drawings and pictures prepared by Ukrainian school children who were attending an educational forum in Moscow.

In 2005, Canadians submitted to the Discovery Channel messages that they hoped would be "voted off the planet"; that is, selected for transmission to a star fifty-six light years away. Contributors had only two weeks to prepare their entries, and these were reviewed by a "celebrity panel" that made the final selections. Entries for this "Calling All Aliens" contest ranged from the serious (trying to discover if the symbols of Earth's great religions resonated with extraterrestrials) to the humorous (leave a message after the beep). As summarized in a personal communication from anthropologist Kathryn Denning, approximately seven hundred entries were submitted from people of all ages and walks of life. She describes the contest as a useful "pulse-taking" exercise that revealed what Canadians thought about extraterrestrial intelligence. Some hoped extraterrestrials would pop down for a visit, others asked for help with everything from professional athletics to combating global warming and eliminating war. Many entrants made strong efforts to be multicultural and inclusive, urging the use of multiple languages and representing different animal species. Ultimately, more consideration was given to what to say than how to say it.

For a small fee, anyone can send interstellar e-mails or voice messages in the direction of extraterrestrials. In 2005, the Deep Space Communications Network transmitted more than 130,000 electronic messages, and enticed other customers with the prospects of a five-minute voice transmission for only $99. Messages were not to contain profanity or materials that (from a human perspective) were considered offensive or lewd. Another outfit, TalktoAliens.com, posted a 900 (toll) number where, for only $3.99 a minute, clients could talk to the stars. Some people interviewed for an MSNBC column on the topic thought that these were phone calls to oblivion (in the sense that they would never be intercepted) whereas others thought that callers would gain a sense of immortality just knowing that their images or words were in outer space, available for retrieval (Boyle 2005).

Probes and Markers

Probes offer certain advantages (Freitas 1983; Freitas and Valdes 1985). Once launched, there are no additional costs. Unlike a radio signal that loses strength, probes can continue indefinitely. Radio broadcasts race by at the speed of light, but probes can remain in orbit or on a planetary surface, awaiting discovery. If recipients of a microwave broadcast lack the equipment to respond or are uncooperative, we will never know that our transmission was intercepted. A probe can report back and even describe local conditions. Probes can be small and relatively inexpensive, and, as astrobiology progresses, they can be launched in the direction of promising destinations.

So far, four interstellar probes bearing messages from humankind are wending their way out of our solar system (Sagan 1978; Drake and Sobel 1992). *Pioneer 10* and *11* bear engravings of a man and a woman, and carry astronomical reference points indicating when and where the probes were launched. *Voyager 1* and *2* carry recordings of terrestrial sights and sounds, along with styluses and playback instructions not unlike the pictorial instructions that accompany globally distributed commercial products.

Pioneer 10, launched on 3 March 1972, flies toward the star that forms the eye of Taurus (the Bull). This star is sixty-eight light years from Earth, and the journey will take about two million years to complete. Its gold-anodized plaque shows our Sun's position relative to fourteen pulsars and the center of our galaxy, the planets of the solar system including Earth as its origin, and a silhouette of the spacecraft heading outwards. The best-known images are of a man with his hand upraised and extending outwards in what we consider to be a universal gesture of friendship. Intended to last twenty-one months, *Pioneer 10* sent back information for almost thirty years. In 2003 we lost its transmission, either because its power supply was then depleted or because our present reception equipment lacks the sensitivity to detect its increasingly faint signals. At that time it was 7.6 billion miles from Earth, eighty-two times the distance between the Sun and Earth, and proceeding outwards.

Voyager 1 and *2* were launched in 1977. They sent back a treasure trove of information and photographs as they progressed by the giant planets of Jupiter, Saturn, Uranus, and Neptune. These spacecraft are now billions of miles beyond Pluto. They will keep sending back information until somewhere around 2020 when their transmissions will no longer be powerful enough for us to receive them. Each *Voyager* contains plaques similar to those used on *Pioneer* and a golden record called *Murmurs of Earth* (Sagan 1978). This contains digitized photographs, greetings in fifty-five languages, and sound recordings including greetings from politicians, a baby's kiss, and assorted music. Samples of music include compositions by Bach and Beethoven, Peruvian pan-pipes, Navajo night chants, Azerbaijani music performed on two bala-bans that resemble bagpipes, a mother's lullaby, and Chuck Berry's rock classic "Johnny Be Good."

Other proposals would have us place markers in orbit, or on a planet or moon, to prove our existence to future explorers, terrestrial or otherwise. Although we have yet to create crystal cities on the Moon or carve huge sculptures on Mars, Gregory Benford and Jon Lomberg and their associates designed a tiny memorial to be sent to Jupiter's moon, Europa (Benford 1999). This intrepid group induced the DeBeers mining company to produce a thin, quarter-sized diamond disk to bear an inscription. Like the *Pioneer* and *Voyager* plaques, the disk would contain markings intended to convey where it came from and when it was sent. It was meant to be understood not only by alien visitors but also by humans who might reach the moon thousands of years from now.

The intended centerpiece was a painstakingly composed photograph with the working title "A Portrait of Humanity." This shows a group of men, women, and children from different races and generations. They are artfully composed on a Hawaiian beach, framed by palms. A young man and woman are in the foreground, and a calm ocean is in the background. To compose the picture, the artists had to wrestle with such issues as how to show that (in most cases) hair is a natural outgrowth from the body rather than an artifact that is manufactured for personal adornment. The image can be viewed in stereo.

Because of a falling-out among the collaborators, the project never reached completion. The probe left Earth with a holder for the diamond plaque, but without the actual plaque. It did carry a CD that had information of minimal value. Perhaps some day the celebrated diamond disk will make it to Europa. And perhaps many years after that an extraterrestrial explorer will stand on frozen slush that obscures it and ask a companion, "If they exist, why don't we see evidence of them?"

The Tiniest Messengers

The theory of panspermia proposes that simple forms of life—bacteria, germs, viruses, and spores—migrate throughout the universe, taking hold when they alight on planets that have supportive environments (Hoyle and Wickramasinghe 1993; Wickramasinghe 2004). Applied to our own origins, panspermia suggests that rather than emerging from primordial soup, our single-celled ancestors arrived from elsewhere and then evolved into the millions of species that inhabit Earth today. Germs may travel in stones or balls of ice, or as spores that like tiny solar sails, are propelled from one place to another by stellar light.

Panspermia could follow the flows and eddies of cosmic tides, or it could be directed; that is, deliberately sent on a specific course. If we allow our imaginations to roam, we may find our origins in cosmic flotsam that made its way to Earth, or that was sent here by a much earlier extraterrestrial civilization. This is not to be confused with ancient astronaut theory that, on the basis of bogus history and pseudoscience, claims that in the distant past extraterrestrial visitors willfully intervened in our biological and cultural evolution (Colavito 2005).

On Earth, DNA carries genetic information for bacteria and elephants, fungi and humans, goldfish, giant pandas, and every other living organism. Eventually, we may be able to communicate with off-world civilizations using tiny DNA messages. To deliver these we would have to assure the germs survived over interstellar distances and find ways to encode messages within the bacteria themselves. One research team embedded bacteria in lead pellets that were then shot from high-powered air guns (Mastrappa et al. 2001). Between 40 and 100 percent of the bacteria survived 2.5 to 25 times the estimated levels of acceleration and jerks that would be expected from planetary ejection, perhaps as the result of an asteroid impact.

Whereas dehydrated bacteria can survive almost indefinitely, the powerful vacuum of space does in fact deplete their ranks (Saffary et al. 2002). High levels of radiation are also lethal, and the combination of high vacuum and high radiation takes a particularly heavy toll. But even small amounts of protection (such as hiding in a nook or cranny of a spacecraft) increase survival rates. Given initially massive numbers of bacteria, panspermia can succeed even if the survival rate is low (Wickramasinghe 2004). Survival chances are improved when the bacteria are frozen within comets or clumped together in clouds. In these cases, some of the bacteria at the outer layers are sacrificed, but in the process they protect life closer to the center.

Pak Chung Wong and his associates took snippets of the children's song "It's a Small World" and encoded the information in artificial DNA sequences that were then inserted into the extremely hardy bacterial host, *Deinococcus radiodurans* (Wong et al. 2003). Later, the messages were retrieved using a polymerase chain reaction, based on amplifying the targeted DNA sequence with a series of heating and cooling cycles. They successfully stored and retrieved seven chemically synthesized DNA fragments in seven different specimens. Before long these techniques may be used to insert trademarks into genetically engineered seeds, thereby protecting the intellectual property. At some point, medical technicians may be able to encode a person's medical history in his or her genes. With the proper equipment, any physician who worked with this person could instantly access information useful for diagnosis or treatment.

Risks

Right now, microwave broadcasts intended for other worlds are racing through our galaxy while probes such as *Pioneer* and *Voyager* are lumbering along behind. Some broadcasters do have powerful equipment (Zaitsev's radar transmitter uses 150 kilowatts, about three times the strength of the most powerful commercial broadcast stations). Other broadcasters use unpromising low-power (500-watt) transmitters, and directed panspermia is closer to science fiction than to reality. Over time, we can expect our technology and techniques to improve. Many people will gain access to radio telescopes and powerful lasers, and as the costs of spaceflight decrease, an increasing number of governments and organizations will be able to launch interstellar probes. Slowly these attempts will make the transition from symbolic to functional and, as the sheer number of messages increases, so should the chances that one or more of these will be found.

The SETI Committees of the International Academy of Astronautics have worked over the years to encourage careful deliberation before revealing ourselves. The goal is to consult widely and then frame a message on behalf of Earth. But active SETI is under the control of freelance scientists and entrepreneurs. The first communications received from Earth may come from a special interest group, and any other effort based on careful consultation would lag behind. Since there is no way to control access to interstellar communication technology, many people may speak for Earth. If an extraterrestrial civilization is bombarded by different and sometimes conflicting messages, whom should they believe, and how could we maintain a rational dialogue (Michaud 2003)?

Another worry is that we will attract the attention of a civilization that chooses to exploit Earth, or eliminate humankind as a possible threat (Michaud 2005). For this reason, many SETI supporters prefer passive SETI—simply listening and watching—to initiating communication. Later, building on data from political science and history, I will argue that long-lived societies are likely to be peaceful, but this argument will be based on statistical trends, not absolute certainties, so even if it is correct we cannot be assured that the first contact will be with a civilization that wants to make friends. Apart from active SETI we may be discovered anyway, either by means of their sensors that detect Earth's own biosignatures and geosignatures, or through intercepting terrestrial radio activity such as *X-Files* reruns.

Hundreds, even thousands of years could pass between a transmission or launching of a probe and our receipt of a response. In the absence of a central registry, maybe nobody on Earth will remember the date and contents of the original message. The reply from extraterrestrials could be quite a surprise and catch our descendents completely off guard.

There are, however, ways to reduce the risks of active SETI. One is to develop technological fixes so that we can announce our presence in the universe, but without revealing our exact location. Another is to ensure that deliberate broadcasts are no more powerful than other broadcasts that have already been sent from Earth, and for this reason are not likely to attract unwelcome new audiences. And we could emphasize low-risk activities, such as placing markers on the Moon, Europa, and other places within our solar system. Any visitors that straggle into our solar system and discover these markers will have already found ample evidence of our presence.

Very low risk indeed is Allen Tough's "Invitation to Extraterrestrial Intelligence" on the Internet (Tough 2005). About one hundred scientists, artists, entrepreneurs, and students have joined Tough in extending this invitation. The goal is to initiate friendly dialogue in philosophy, science, and the arts. Any form of intelligence that has access to the Internet and discovers the invitation is encouraged to reply. This project, which rests upon the possibility that extraterrestrial probes are already within our solar system, costs practically nothing, and there are no annoying requirements for communiqués to travel light years to reach their destinations. Claimants are asked to answer questions about their culture, interests, intentions, and the like. Following their initial e-mail, they are asked to submit to authentication by answering a grueling set of questions. These questions focus on math and science and are very difficult for the average prankster to answer. So far, several self-proclaimed extraterrestrials (and their representatives) have stepped forward, but none of these has survived the preliminary rounds of the verification process.

As SETI astronomer Jill Tarter points out, we are in the midst of an experiment (2001). This experiment—to answer the question "Is there other intelligent life in the Universe?"—has been going on for about forty years. It could take another forty years, or four hundred years, or four thousand years, or it could be concluded tomorrow.

Given accelerating search procedures, a reasonable guess is that if there are any extraterrestrial civilizations that overlap ours in time and use technology similar to our own, confirmation of extraterrestrial intelligence should occur somewhere between 2025 and 2035.

—Four—

THE EXTRATERRESTRIAL HYPOTHESIS

One sunny afternoon in 1951, Deke Slayton was flying his propeller-driven Mustang fighter plane about twenty-five miles from Minneapolis and St. Paul (Slayton and Cassutt 1994). As he came out of a spin at ten thousand feet he saw a white object at about the same altitude. At first it looked like a large kite, but kites were rarely flown at that altitude. When Slayton flew closer, it looked more like a weather balloon, approximately three feet in diameter. After he turned and looked at it from yet another angle it appeared to be a disk on edge! He then discovered that his plane, which cruised at about 250 miles per hour, could not catch up with it, as one would expect if the object were in fact a weather balloon. Suddenly it streaked away at a 45-degree angle and left Slayton far behind.

Following his return to Holman Field, Slayton decided not to tell anyone lest they consider him crazy. Two days later at the Officer's Club, he relented and mentioned the incident to his superior who ordered Slayton to "get his ass over to Intelligence in the morning and give them a briefing" (Slayton and Cassutt 1994: 50). The intelligence officers took careful notes. Then they told him that a local company had launched a high-altitude weather balloon that they had followed with a light plane and a station wagon carrying two observers. These ground observers saw an object come along side the balloon, and then "take off like hell." They tracked the object with a then common surveying device and estimated its speed at four thousand miles per hour. Slayton concluded, "I guess they were trying to tell me that I was not exactly crazy; someone else had seen something unusual too. But I never heard another thing about it" (50).

Slayton went on to qualify as one of the original Mercury astronauts. He eventually became America's chief astronaut and flew aboard an American-Russian Mission in 1975. His UFO sighting, which he describes in his autobiography, shows that intelligent, educated, and socially aware people are among those who have reported UFOs. Slayton's firm grounding in reality and sensitivity to possible repercussions made him reluctant to reveal his experience. Ultimately (perhaps after being lubricated by a couple of beers) Slayton did inform his commander and his report was of interest to military intelligence at that time. He was reassured when the intelligence officers indicated that other witnesses had seen the flying object from the ground.

One important lesson is that many UFO reports come from people who, like Slayton, are honest and intelligent, people whose life and livelihood depend upon accurate observation and reliable reporting. Recently, Jerome Clark reviewed fifty years of sightings by aircraft pilots, sightings of objects that in some cases were as clear a car driving by and verified by other pilots, radar, and ground-based observers (2003). Richard Haines developed a catalog of over 3,400 reports from airplane pilots and helped form the National Aviation Reporting Center on Anomalous Phenomena (NARCAP) to document cases where UFOs posed risks to flight safety. Haines has also collected 242 cases where UFOs or their occupants responded to human-initiated activities; for example, when a pilot blinked his landing lights and a UFO flashed a light in return (1999).

Prominent scientists have seen UFOs but the number of such reports seems to have dwindled in recent years (Huyghe 2001). Early reports include a 1949 sighting by Clyde Tombaugh, the American astronomer who discovered the planet Pluto, and, in 1954, a sighting by British astronomer H. Percy Wilkins of silvery, plate-like objects moving against the wind. A triangular object spinning on its axis was seen by the entire staff of an observatory at Majorca, Spain in 1960, and a "white sphere" materialized near a truck carrying scientist/journalist John McPhee and a geologist in 1980. It is difficult to tell if today's scientists are less likely to see aerial mysteries or just less likely to report them. Over the years skeptics have become more vocal, so at the same time that the prospects for extraterrestrial life have grown brighter, the climate for UFO research has become more hostile. UFO sightings go unreported because the observer believes that the most likely result would be damage to their reputation. A survey of Canadian college students revealed that whereas 81 percent of the respondents would tell someone else about a sighting, less than half of them would be willing to report the sighting to the authorities and only a quarter of the respondents would mention it to the media (Patry and Pelletier 2001).

UFO lore, writes Daniel Wojcik, "is vast and divergent, ranging from familiar narratives about mysterious men in black suits, cattle mutilations and crop circles, to abductions by invasive grey aliens and reptilian beings, beliefs about alien life beneath the Earth and the ongoing conspiracy theories about massive government cover-ups, such as an alleged recovery of a crashed spaceship near Roswell, New Mexico in July, 1947" (2003: 274). UFO lore weighs heavily in contemporary life because UFOs mean many things to many people (Saliba 1995a). Physical scientists and engineers are intrigued by hints of advanced technology that might eventually become available to us. Social scientists are attracted by the psychological and sociological implications of UFOs, by their profound meaning in our culture. Government experts and military officials have worried on occasion about the level of threat that UFOs pose, if not to the nation's physical integrity then to its collective psyche (Swords 2000). UFOs offer adventurers and hobbyists an attractive mystery. Religious people see UFOs as signs of the times, bringing important messages to a deeply flawed humanity that stands poised on the brink of destruction (Wojcik 1997). UFOs present mystery, have spiritual dimensions, and in some cases offer salvation and redemption. Most avowed skeptics accept none of this; for them, UFOs represent fraud, error, and wishful thinking. UFOs strike a powerful chord, either resonant or dissonant, in just about everyone. Since UFOs began to weigh on human consciousness, writes Colin Bennett, "almost everything has changed from jokes to the color of socks but not the battle royal between believers in UFOs and scientists and skeptics" (2001: 13).

Slayton's report illustrates another crucial aspect of UFO sightings. Always, it seems, there is room for doubt. Were there really two objects above Minnesota that day, or was there only one? Could it have been that the "disk" was a misperception of the weather balloon? Were the intelligence officers sowing disinformation to distract attention from a secret weapons test, or could they have been having fun by "pulling Slayton's leg?" Could Slayton's memory have played a trick on him? Where there is room for doubt there is opportunity for controversy and UFOlogy is permeated by controversy galore.

UFOlogy

Throughout recorded history people have observed unusual aerial phenomena, but widespread public fascination with these awaited newspaper reports of Kenneth Arnold's 1947 sighting of glittery crescents flying at terrific speeds near Mount Rainier in Washington State. Almost immediately afterwards other sightings made national news, as did challenges to the accuracy of Arnold's clams. At first, most people thought that these were classified military aircraft or previously neglected natural phenomena. Over time, media publicity, UFO researchers and study groups, scientists, and skeptics generated multiple interpretations. UFOs have been construed as misperceptions of planets and military aircraft, mass hallucinations, and visitors from the past, outer space, or parallel universes. The list goes on, but as Erich Goode points out, for better or worse, it is the Extraterrestrial Hypothesis or ETH that has captured the greatest interest (Goode 2000). Although yet to be substantiated, the most popular explanation of UFOs (except among skeptics) is that they are extraterrestrial spacecraft.

According to the ETH, extraterrestrial spacecraft have been visiting Earth for thousands of years (Peebles 1994). These craft come in many sizes and shapes, ranging from huge mother ships adorned with banks of flashing lights to luminescent spheres about the size of basketballs. Some are cigar-shaped like a dirigible or blimp; some are triangular; some are spherical; some are shaped like bowls; some are ring shaped; and some are shaped like saucers. Some are amorphous balls of light; others are highly structured metallic constructions. UFOs fly independently, in formation, sometimes meld together and sometimes split apart. Occasionally they seem to materialize or dematerialize, to change color, or to change size or shape. Some look as familiar as Frisbees; others are so strange as to defy description. Some are silent; others make noises like a humming dynamo, the crack of a bullet, a whistle, or the rushing wind. Their very variety is problematic as it implies that either most reports are mistaken or that many different alien spacecraft are visiting us within a narrow window of time.

The strength of beliefs in the ETH is reflected in various surveys and polls undertaken over the years. These surveys are not strictly comparable because different investigators with different biases and expectations have conducted them. Questions have been framed in different ways, and have involved different samples of people ranging from physicists to tabloid readers. Nevertheless, responses to public opinion polls over the past fifty years have been fairly consistent, suggesting that almost everyone has heard about UFOs, roughly half the people believe that UFOs have visited Earth, and that somewhere between 5 and 10 percent of the population has actually seen one. Perhaps representative is a survey conducted for the Sci Fi channel (SciFi.com 2002). In this survey, 67 percent if the U.S. public believed that extraterrestrial life exists. Fifty-six percent believed that UFOs are real, and have visited Earth. Forty-five percent of the respondents think that we are being monitored. One person in seven reported that they, or someone they know well, have had a close encounter. Seventy-five percent felt prepared for the discovery of extraterrestrial life, and 55 percent believed that the government was not telling all that it knows about UFOs. Whereas there has been some variability over the years, the important point is that beliefs in UFOs are both widespread and stable (Barkun 2003).

UFOs can be studied scientifically, even though many researchers do not know how or choose not to do so. Thus, the relationship between UFOs and academia is troubled (Appelle 2000). On occasion, mainstream scientists drop into the arena, convinced that rational analysis and empirical procedures will soon put the matter to rest. Most of these adventurous souls disappear in the quagmire or rapidly return to their original interests where they are less likely to submerge from the sight of their professional colleagues (Moseley and Pflock 2002). UFOlogy and science, it appears, have never made comfortable bedfellows. The normal flow of events is for scientists to make a discovery and then try to "sell" it to the public. UFOlogy has largely been a grassroots movement, with an enthusiastic public trying to engage scientists in a topic that most scientists do not take seriously (Dick 1996). Scientists who are involved in astrobiology and SETI ignore or reject UFOlogy as amateurish and ineffective. Many scientists lump UFOlogy with other paranormal topics such as astrology, palm reading, ghosts, witches, and communicating with the dead (Goode 2000). Supernatural explanations, the growing dominance of alien abduction stories, and claims of government cover-up have done little to whet their professional appetites.

The psychologist Don Donderi wonders if science is actually the best tool for gaining reliable knowledge about UFOs (2000). Today's science, in his view, may not be up to the task of explaining them. Science is conservative, slow, and regulated by gatekeepers who divert attention from UFOs. He proposes two alternative models for assessing UFO evidence: the legal model and the military intelligence model.

The legal model requires adversaries, an impartial judge, and rules prescribing that the evidence must be relevant, material, and admissible. For example, two advocates might maintain very different "theories" about Deke Slayton's sighting described in the beginning of this chapter. (In law, a theory is simply an interpretation of the facts.) One might contend that Slayton saw an extraterrestrial spacecraft, and the other that he saw the weather balloon that was known to be in the vicinity at the time. In essence, there would be a trial. Advocates of the ETH might go first. They would establish Slayton's credibility as a witness, seek corroborative testimony from the balloon trackers on the ground, establish the professional competence of the engineers who were using the surveying device, and prove that the instrument was properly maintained and in good working order. Next, the skeptics would counter with cross-examination to shake the initial testimony and then present evidence in support of the weather balloon theory. Donderi suggests that, although the results of such trials might not establish that the object was an interstellar spacecraft "beyond a shadow of a doubt," (that is, with 90 percent certainty or better) some results might satisfy the criteria for a favorable judgment in a civil trial, which only requires a preponderance of the evidence.

Whereas scientists are slow, conservative, and reluctant to accept radically new ideas, the success of military intelligence depends upon speed and openness to outrageous possibilities (Donderi 2000). If we stick with the sober advice of "friendly" scientists we may be caught unawares. He points out that during World War II, British scientists considered it impossible for the Germans to bombard London by means of rockets. The powder-filled tubes that they could imagine were not up to the job, and, in any event, once they were launched there was no way to adjust their course in flight. The "friendly" scientists could not foresee a liquid-propelled rocket like the V-2 that could be controlled by moveable vanes. Military intelligence officers are able to assemble information from many different sources, sift through and evaluate the evidence, cut through deceit and subterfuge, and rapidly form a conclusion.

There are two types of explanations of UFOs whose very coexistence fuel partisanship and conflict. *Event-dependent explanations* focus on actual happenings in the real world out there. For example, is the bright light low on the horizon an interstellar spacecraft, the landing lights of a Boeing 737, the planet Venus, or something else? We think of event-dependent explanations as objective: the passage of the interstellar spacecraft (or, for that matter, the 737) occurs whether or not anybody happens to be looking upward. In an attempt to resolve the issue we might consider the light's apparent motion, the known location of Venus at the time of the observation, the presence and absence of nearby airports, flight logs, and many other pieces of evidence.

In contrast to event-dependent explanations that focus on "what really happened," *observer-dependent explanations* look to the people who report the UFO. The intelligence, experience, mental health, and motives of the observer are at the heart of the matter. Rather than emphasize the objective event, the explanation emphasizes the psychology of the observer.

Event-Dependent Explanations

Scientific UFOlogists study physical descriptions of UFOs, use tools such as radiation counters and magnetic flux indicators to look for environmental changes in the vicinity of a UFO sighting, interpret photographs of anomalous aerial phenomena, and do laboratory analyses of possible extraterrestrial artifacts. This kind of research includes in-depth analysis of individual reports as well as searches for statistical regularities across a large number of cases (Haines 1979).

Researchers hope for reports supported by multiple high-credibility observers and lots of other supporting evidence. This could take such forms as radar tracks that confirm the time and path of the object, photographs, or "trace" evidence consisting of measurable physical effects on the environment or on the observers, perhaps even some kind of material residue or (the holy grail in UFO research) an undisputable alien artifact. Physical evidence is crucial for people who argue that UFOs are "real" (in the same sense as weather balloons and spaceships) rather than mystical experiences, hallucinations, or socially constructed myths.

The Sturrock Panel

We can find an application, albeit imperfect, of Donderi's legal model to judge the best physical evidence pertaining to UFOs. The protagonists, antagonists, and jurors assembled at Pocantico, the Tarrytown, New York estate of the late Laurence Rockefeller (Sturrock 1999). This wealthy philanthropist shared many people's interest in the possibility of extraterrestrial life and suspected that UFOs could be evidence of this. In 1997 he sponsored a weeklong workshop at Pocantico chaired by the Stanford University physicist Peter A. Sturrock.

During this workshop, invited UFO researchers presented their best evidence to a panel of scientists who then evaluated it in terms of its scientific merit. It is difficult to find people who are not predisposed one way or another, so Sturrock composed the panel in such a way that, as a whole and following careful deliberation, it would have a chance of drawing fair conclusions. This is not a foolproof method, but should yield an outcome that is more trustworthy than one based on any individual's opinion.

Over the years researchers have assembled an abundance of still and moving UFO photographs, taken from many different distances and angles under different lighting conditions and using every imaginable grade of camera and film. An annoying percentage of UFO pictures are of the "blobs of light" variety, too small and grainy for careful analysis, but there are some notable exceptions (Haines and Vallee 1990). Richard Haines presented a 35 mm color negative to the Pocantico jury. (Negatives are considered more convincing than prints, because they are much more difficult to alter; thanks to products like Photoshop, digital pictures are all but worthless as proof that something actually happened.) The picture shows a mountain, evergreen trees, and a white cloud. A silver oval object stands against the blue sky. The photo was taken in a provincial park in British Columbia and the object, tilted slightly forward, appeared to be a disk with a small dome on its top. Alas, the photographer did not notice the object at the time the photograph was taken (and the people in the picture were facing away from it). In their discussion of the Haines picture the jurors expressed concern that since the disk had not been noticed at the time the picture was taken, it might be nothing more than a blemish on the film.

Earth is sprinkled liberally with radar stations that are used for such purposes as controlling air traffic, predicting weather, and detecting enemy intrusions. Radar sets include both transmitters and receivers. Transmitted pulses bounce off a target such as an airplane, ship, or cloud bank. The "radar return" or echo that comes back to the receiver makes it possible to paint a picture on a screen that shows the size, shape, location, and movement of the target. Aircraft carry transponders that send the aircraft's identification number and a certain amount of flight data to the radar receiver, so radar can identify and track known aircraft.

Despite the huge volumes of data, many radar stations save tracks for postmortems following aircraft near-misses and mid-air collisions. Careful analysis of these records allows researchers to determine which radar tracks correlate with visual sightings. In the United States, these data have not been made available to researchers, although French authorities have turned it over to qualified investigators. A few other European governments have eased up some since military security became less stringent following the dissolution of the former Soviet Union. Wealthy research groups have sought permission from their governments to operate their own radar sets. Authorities are reluctant to permit this since the freelancers could interfere with the operation of other radar sets, such as those that help assure aviation safety.

Pockets of warm or cold air—invisible thermal cells—can reflect radar transmissions, giving the false appearance of solid objects. Adjacent masses of warm and cold air create temperature inversions. Whirling air within these inversions collects dust that reflects radar waves and again gives the impression of a solid object. A transmitter operating from another radar station or an overhead satellite can generate mystery returns, as can steam arising from a lake or river after an environmentally insensitive manufacturer dumps tons of hot slag into it. When we factor in the differing skill levels of different radar operators and the varying levels of technical sophistication of the equipment there are many points of uncertainty.

Illobrand von Ludwiger (1998) reports an interesting incident on 5 June 1996 over Lake Constance on the eastern border of Switzerland. At that time six employees of the Swiss Military Air Surveillance group at Klothen observed from their military air traffic control center a big, silver rotating disk. This was just about one mile away and a little over one mile high. Believed to be a large, structured metallic object, the UFO moved from east to west and back, then accelerated and shot away at high speed. It was tracked by three radar sets. Still, to the Pocantico jury, multiple visual sightings confirmed by three radar sets were inconclusive. Jurors expect very little progress until air traffic control authorities are willing to release raw data for careful analysis by skilled professionals.

At crime scenes, trace evidence includes individual hairs and fibers, minute amounts of spittle or other human fluids that are amenable to DNA analysis, seeds or other vegetation that were imported to the crime scene (or exported to the perpetrator's automobile), footprints, tire tracks, and other ephemera. At UFO scenes, trace evidence includes electromagnetic disturbances that interfere with electrical devices: altimeters, compasses, radios, and automobile ignition systems sometimes malfunction, but typically return to normal after the UFO has passed. Other trace evidence includes alteration of the environment (compacted vegetation, indentations, burned areas) and physical effects on observers (burns, bruises, and scrapes).

Typically such environmental effects are ambiguous, open to multiple interpretations, or hinge on uncorroborated eyewitness testimony. Campfires and arson can create burned patches and vegetation is uprooted or mashed down by large animals and by sports utility vehicles.

Some observers may interpret a triangular pattern as indentations of landing gear while others behold the work of burrowing animals. Reports of elevated radiation levels and alterations in force fields are questionable unless obtained by credible technicians who are operating high quality equipment.

The Pocantico jury reviewed an incident that occurred involving a DC-10 passenger jet that was flying on autopilot from Buffalo to Albany, New York at 9:05 P.M. on 12 March 1977. At that time an intense light appeared and began pacing the jet, and there was a simultaneous unintended change in the setting of the autopilot. This resulted in an unexpected fifteen-degree turn to the left. The deviation from the flight plan was noted by a flight controller who radioed the pilot to ask what he was doing. At this point, the pilot noticed that three of the compasses in the cockpit were giving different readings.

Looking out the cockpit window, the pilot saw an immense bright light estimated to be two thousand feet across, but the air traffic controller could not confirm this by radar. The light seemed to pace the airplane, and then sped off. The jet safely reached its destination. When the captain reported all of this to his superiors he was told that "bad things" happened to the careers of people who made such claims. Still, the captain was nagged by the incident and went public after he retired. At the time he stepped forward the copilot and flight engineer were still commercial flyers, and refused to discuss the episode.

The Pocantico jury concluded that while the crew may have seen something unusual, and although the airplane may have had problems with its autopilots and compasses, this evidence had to be considered "anecdotal" in the absence of corroborating evidence from radar or the flight data recorder ("black box"). Furthermore, there was no proof that the bright light and the failure of the guidance system were somehow related to one another.

At Pocantico, John S. Schuessler presented the Cash-Landrum case, a spectacular incident involving personal injury (1998). During the evening of 29 December 1980, Vicky Landrum, age fifty-seven, Colby Landrum, age seven, and Betty Cash, fifty-two, were returning to their homes in Dayton, Texas. They were about fifteen miles from their destination riding in their new Oldsmobile Cutlass on a state farm road, about nine miles east of New Caney. As they drove down this road that was hemmed in by tall pine trees they noted a red glow on the horizon. Initially, it looked like a "streak of fire" but as they drew close they saw a grayish, diamond-shaped metallic structure, maybe two hundred feet tall. It was difficult to see the object clearly because it was embedded in a brilliant cloud of light and billowing flames obscured its bottom. Every now and then they heard a noise like a truck's air brakes, the flames would increase, and the object tentatively moved upward. All told, they watched the object for about fifteen minutes before it slowly rose to approximately eight hundred feet and then, now dull red, appeared to turn on its side and then drift south towards Galveston Bay. As they continued, they could see the object diminish in size and then disappear from the rearview mirror.

Betty was the first to leave the car to get a better look, and she stayed outside the longest. Before she re-entered the vehicle she discovered that the metal on the front of the car had become hot and the paint blistered. In only a matter of minutes Betty became nauseated. Her face was red and swelling, she had a terrible headache, and she suffered from an insatiable thirst. Later that night Vicky and Colby also felt ill, as if they had received bad sunburns. As the night progressed they developed other symptoms including extreme fatigue, a complete loss of appetite, diarrhea, vomiting, blisters, and in a short time, in Betty's case, delirium, severe weight loss, and hair loss. Eventually Betty's physician diagnosed radiation poisoning, and later she developed cancer.

Schuessler spent years exploring various aspects of the case: beating the bushes for other witnesses, interviewing doctors, seeking evidence that military helicopters seen in the vicinity had been deployed that particular evening (1998). The Pocantico jury expressed interest and concern, but in their view the big weakness in this case was the lack of independent supporting witnesses. Betty, Vicky, and Colby were the only people who saw the object in the remote Texas wilderness. The jury pointed out that the injuries could have come from some other source of radiation, but was hard pressed to identify what this source might be.

Any bona fide object, material sample, or debris that the UFO happened to leave behind would be most interesting. An authentic crashed saucer would resolve the underlying issue once and for all, as would a truly unusual artifact that could not have been manufactured on Earth. (Later we will consider saucer crashes.) On occasion chunks of metal or slag have been found in the vicinity of a UFO sighting. Could this metal be so unusual that it could not have been manufactured on Earth? Mysterious alloys are particularly provocative if they have unusual electrical or other properties that are consistent with a hypothetical interstellar propulsion system.

The problem is that over the years we ourselves have produced a tremendous range of alloys for all sorts of purposes. Persistent investigators may discover that mysterious substances are actually commercial products that only appear mysterious because in the course of their daily lives most people (including scientific investigators) never encounter them.

Another strategy is to check if the substance has a degree of purity that is unattainable with terrestrial technologies. That is, refining metals eliminates most but not all impurities, and if the sample's purity surpasses the best that we can achieve with available technology it did not originate in one of the world's laboratories. Usually, test results show that although unusually "pure" the UFO metal is not so pristine that it could not have originated on Earth.

A third strategy is to test for unusual radioisotopes. Radioisotopes are, in effect, the nuclear "signature" of a metal. Investigators expect metal from outside our solar system to show a different pattern of isotopes than the same metal from Earth. To be sure, copper is copper, but there are likely to be differences in the exact ways that metals get "cooked down" from hydrogen in different solar systems and this should show up as different radioisotopes.

At Pocantico, Jacques Vallee discussed several material samples, including molten metal that appeared near Council Bluffs, Iowa on 17 December 1977 (Vallee 1999). Two witnesses had seen a lighted object in the sky and eleven witnesses saw a flash followed by a flame. Police and fire personnel that rapidly reached the scene found a boiling orange mass. This turned out to be carbon steel. Other samples included tin, a mixture of tungsten carbide and cobalt, and an unusual carbon residue. The panel concluded that none of the samples fell outside present material science, but recommended stringent laboratory analysis of other credible samples as they are found.

What were the overall results of the Pocantico conference? Remember that this conference included UFO researchers who presented their best evidence, and a jury instructed to give these scientists a fair hearing. In effect, the jury did not find that any of the evidence posed a serious challenge to contemporary terrestrial science, nor did it provide unambiguous support for the ETH. Not one of the many pieces of evidence presented to the jury received its full endorsement; in each and every case the jurors were able to find a prosaic alternative, even if these alternatives were not particularly persuasive.

Jurors pointed out that there is always a possibility that scientists will learn something by investigating the unexplained, and urged UFO researchers to concentrate on cases that combine strong eyewitness testimony and physical evidence. Formal contact between members of the UFO community and science could be productive, they said, and it is desirable to provide institutional support for this kind of work. Thus, the panel left the door ajar for more UFO research. The jurors were under tremendous cross pressures—the expectations of the conference sponsor and the UFO researchers, the evidence itself, and the fear of ridicule by their conservative colleagues for participating in this unusual project. It is impossible to guess the exact mix of rational analysis, preexisting opinions, and social pressures to reach consensus that led to their conclusions.

Into the Driver's Seat

Despite the failure of sixty years of research to confirm the ETH, advances in our own science over the same period have made it just a little more difficult to exclude the possibility of interstellar visitors. The first challenge for UFO dispatchers is identifying Earth as a promising destination. Sure, spacecraft flitting about the galaxy might stumble across our solar system, but given billions of solar systems the chance of a random find is just about impossible. More promising, extraterrestrials could be attracted by radio waves from Earth, powerful broadcasts expanding outward from Earth at the speed of light and now comprising a sphere that extends about sixty light years outwards. Furthermore, if their civilization can match contemporary terrestrial technology, they should be able to use their own and perhaps more mature versions of Kepler, the Terrestrial Planet Finder, and the Overwhelming Large Telescope to locate us. Using remote sensing technology that will soon available to us, they could have found chemical indicators of biological processes well before the debut of *Homo sapiens*. This would allow ample time for a probe traveling at a small fraction of the speed of light to reach our solar system.

Astronomers, who have an appreciation of immense interstellar distances, are highly skeptical of travel between adjacent stars, never mind those that are hundreds or thousands of light years apart. The time and energy requirements would be enormous, and any ship traveling at an appreciable fraction of the speed of light could be battered to bits by cosmic dust. Still, some scientists are working on spacecraft that would use radically new types of propulsion that are comparable to those found in science fiction. As discussed by Marc Millis (2004), the purpose of the NASA Breakthrough Propulsion Program (BPP) initiated in the late 1990s was to find such amazing alternatives. This program sought to achieve three goals. First, reduce mass by eliminating the need for propellant, perhaps by discovering "fundamentally new ways to create motion, presumably by interacting with the properties of space, or possibly by manipulating gravitational or inertial forces" (2004: 1). Second, work around the limits set by the speed of light, thereby making deep space travel practical. Perhaps this could be accomplished by manipulating space-time itself to circumvent the limiting conditions of the speed of light. Third, find radical new power sources that would yield unlimited energy that could be used for interstellar travel. Of course, there would be false starts (many possibilities would prove unworkable) and progress would be slow and incremental.

Millis points out that although initially the concepts were considered too far from fruition to warrant any time, once discussions of them began appearing in peer-reviewed journals they deserved a closer look (2004). In his assessment of 16 breakthrough propulsion projects, of which half had been sponsored by NASA, six were found not to be viable, six remained unresolved, and four were deemed worthy of continued research.

Recently, physicist Eric W. Davis completed a "Teleportation Physics Study" for the U.S. Air Force (Davis 2004). In this he discusses several types of breakthrough propulsion possibilities, including wormholes: interstellar shortcuts or portals that make it possible to jump from one galaxy to another. Without minimizing the truly enormous engineering challenges, Davis believes that most of the underlying theories are sound and that experimental tests are possible. Even if we cannot withstand travel through wormholes, perhaps we could use them to reduce the distance that intergalactic radio signals have to travel, significantly cutting the time that they take to cover tremendous distances. Other options reviewed by Davis are reminiscent of *Star Trek*, or the movie *The Fly*. The troops, for example, enter a chamber, are dematerialized, and reassembled somewhere else. The energy and information-processing requirements could prove prohibitive: storing the information to reconstitute just one individual might require as many giant industrial hard drives as there are stars in our galaxy. The amount of heat that would be generated in the disassembly process might be comparable to that generated by the explosion of a hydrogen bomb. Experiments on quantum entanglement, where one subatomic particle acts on another instantly and independent of distance, hint that it may be possible to develop instant communication, even across many light years.

Naturally critics blasted Davis's Air Force research, arguing that some of the propulsion systems may not work in principle and others are impossible to engineer. Davis disagrees; after all, just fifty years ago computer chips were impossible to engineer; and it is doubtful that the Army Corps of Engineers could have constructed the San Francisco Bay Bridge in 1864. Explaining why the Air Force is interested in this kind of research, spokesperson Ranney Adams noted that, if they did not turn over stones, they would not learn what they had missed (Vergano 2004). Criticism seems to have done little to dampen Davis's enthusiasm, or, for that matter, dissuade the U.S. Air Force.

Scot Stride points out that since 1958 we have launched approximately 125 space probes (including lunar missions) to explore the solar system (2001). On the basis of these historical figures Stride develops various projections. For example, at the rate of 110 launches per hundred years and using probes that can achieve 10 percent of the speed of light, a civilization five thousand years into the space age would have 5,390 probes at selected star systems 10 to 500 light years away. Continuing in this vein—factoring in the possibilities that there may be many such civilizations, that some of them may have entered their space age a million years ago, that some probes may come close to the speed of light (and so forth), there is a nontrivial probability that one or more extraterrestrial probes are in our solar system right now. However, it could take considerable determination and time to actually find one of these, in part because extraterrestrial technology may make it hard for us to recognize them, and in part because they could be quite small.

Despite our current poor prospects for developing mother ships of the *Close Encounters of the Third Kind* variety, Brian McConnell envisions a probe the size of a medium bird, or even a butterfly (2001). Viewed edge-on, it could be only a few atoms thick, except for a delicate scaffold to support it. Attainable perhaps 20 years from now, its brain would be a one-square-centimeter device with up to 10 billion CPUs. Powered by solar wind or magnetic fields, these probes would adjust wing-like surfaces to control their flight. Nanotechnology would make this possible.

Writing in the *Journal of the British Interplanetary Society*, James Deardorff and his associates point out that given the improving prospects of interstellar travel and the possibility that advanced civilizations may prefer to silently observe us as an uncontaminated species rather than enter into direct communication with us, it makes sense to revisit "high-quality" UFO reports that have been particularly resistant to debunking (Deadorff et al. 2005). But even if all UFO reports are assumed false, it could still make sense to search for interstellar probes or artifacts in our solar system (Freitas and Valdez 1985; Stride 2001; Cornet and Stride 2003). Searches using astronomical telescopes have already taken place, but these were of limited duration and scope, so it is not surprising that they did not yield positive results. Today, there are many "off-the-shelf" technologies that could be applied to automated searches. We could search for obvious extraterrestrial constructions, anomalous radio or laser activity, visible signs of intelligent or autonomous behavior (mining), several signs of chemical emissions, and unexpected patterns of radioactivity (Stride 2001; Cornet and Stride 2003).

Calculations demonstrating the feasibility of interstellar communication helped move SETI from fantasy to mainstream science. Will advances in science and technology rationalize the search for an extraterrestrial presence in our solar system? Many of the scientists who propose this strive valiantly to differentiate their work from UFOlogy: for example, they frame the question as a hypothesis, and specify scientific methods for testing this hypothesis. But unless other scientists accept these arguments these researchers face an uphill battle to gain momentum.

Observer-Dependent Explanations

Observer-dependent explanations emphasize the psychological workings of the observer. Although it is possible to develop such explanations that are flattering to the witness (for example, positing that some people have special skills that help them glimpse hidden realities), positive spins are atypical. Observer-dependent explanations do not necessarily question the "honesty" of the reporter (after all, the person may accurately describe what it seemed like at the time), but still have pejorative overtones, emphasizing naïveté or lack of experience, suggestibility, emotional disturbances, memory failures, character flaws, and other psychological deficits. UFO events are transient in the sense that they disappear before scientists can study them. Although scientists do not have access to UFOs, they do have access to observers. It is partly for this reason that observer-dependent explanations are popular among scientists (Dean 1998; Denzler 2001).

Information Processing

We have limited abilities to process information. Even honest and intelligent people can be mistaken in their impressions. Since the 1940s we have known that people's motives influence their perceptions, and although we have long known that memories are subject to distortion, only recently have we begun to appreciate the extent of their frailty (Schachter 2001).

Eyewitness accuracy rides on many factors, including the acumen of the observer and the nature and speed of unfolding events (Wells and Olson 2003). Research on eyewitness testimony in courts suggests that in comparison to young adults, children and the elderly tend to be less reliable. Studies involving police line-ups reveal that intelligence has at best a modest effect on eyewitness accuracy. In children, disabilities do not necessarily lead to inaccuracy, but less intelligent interviewees may be more likely to change their stories when challenged or interrogated repeatedly (Henry and Gundjonsson 2003).

Early research found little relationship between people's level of confidence and the accuracy of their testimony. More recent research suggests a modest correlation between confidence and accuracy, but some supremely confident witnesses are extremely inaccurate. People that try to regulate the impressions they make on other people, feel a lack of control over their own lives, or are anxious to be liked and accepted are more easily swayed by their interviewers' biases (Wells and Olson 2003). People who are suggestible are more likely to falter, especially when the interviewer gives them misleading or false information (Liebman et al. 2002). And, of course, it is always possible for an interviewer to ask biased questions and to bully or "lead" a witness. Intimidating behaviors may shake the testimony of observers who lack self-confidence or view themselves in a negative light. Warning witnesses that they may be exposed to false information and urging them to report only what they "really remember" increases their accuracy.

Further complications come from verbal foreshadowing effects (Bower 2003). The very act of describing what one has seen or heard reduces the accuracy of the memory of the event. Once we put something into words we tend to remember the verbal description of the event rather than the event itself. This can be a particularly large problem if the event is unusual and difficult to describe, or if the claim meets with strong approval or disapproval. The implication is that a person who immediately tells friends about a UFO sighting may be less accurate than someone who waits to be debriefed by a skilled investigator. If the friends interject their thoughts, or propose words and phrases to help the tongue-tied observer, they inadvertently shape content of the report.

Where does this leave us? UFO reports (like other reports) depend on a complex interplay of the event, the viewing conditions, the witness, and social influence processes. It is too simplistic to think of eyewitnesses as reliable or unreliable; accuracy is a matter of degree. Pro-UFO researchers may be predisposed to overrate the accuracy of eyewitness reports, but skeptics are predisposed to underrate them. If for no other reason than this, the pro-UFO researchers assign more weight to eyewitness reports and anecdotal evidence than do skeptics.

Personality

Half a century ago strong beliefs in UFOs were seen as the product of primitive thinking or a disturbed personality. In Washington, DC at least, people who claimed to have personally met an extraterrestrial were whisked off to a mental hospital (Goldberg 2000). Troy Zimmer estimated the number of people who have seen UFOs at somewhere between 9 and 18 percent of the North American population—in other words, tens of millions of people (1984). Sighters were likely to be men, relatively young, more educated, and more likely to come from a rural area than were nonsighters, but these differences were slight and UFO observers come from a wide variety of demographic and social backgrounds.

Zimmer also compared 75 college students who claimed to have seen UFOs with 398 college students who had never seen a UFO (1984). The two groups did not differ in terms of cultural alienation, malevolence of worldview, or personal well-being. The sighters and nonsighters were equally likely to be science majors, and each group contained the same proportion of high academic achievers. This ran counter to the social marginality hypothesis, that UFO sightings were linked to status deprivation, that is, low-status people could break out of their place in the social order and gain recognition by reporting UFO phenomena (Warren 1970). Still, the social marginality interpretation reappears from time to time (Clancy 2005). Quite possibly, socially marginal people choose to discuss their unusual experiences while their better-educated counterparts choose to remain silent to preserve their integration in mainstream society.

In comparison to people who had never seen a UFO, sighters were more likely to know other people who had seen a UFO (Zimmer 1984). Perhaps knowing someone else who has seen a UFO increases confidence in one's own observation; perhaps sighters network with one another to share insights and compare emotions. Sighters were more likely to be drawn to science fiction, but this was a very weak result. Furthermore, they were more likely to believe that at least some UFOs were extraterrestrial spacecraft, that the government was suppressing information about UFOs, and to express interest in the paranormal or occult.

Investigators look in vain for a relationship between interest in UFOs and indicators of poor mental health. In a later paper, Zimmer found that people who believe in UFOs were not likely to have "disturbed psyches" but were more likely to believe in "alternative realities" (1985). This particular finding has been repeatedly verified (Ring 1992; Clancy 2005). June Parnell administered the Minnesota Multiphasic Personality Inventory (MMPI) and the 16 Personality Factor Questionnaire (16PF) to 225 people who had experienced UFOs (Parnell 1998). The MMPI is a standard tool for spotting psychiatric disorders, and the 16PF is an established test for selected personality traits. There were no signs of overt pathology.

Berthold Schwartz, a psychiatrist with a keen interest in the paranormal and a dedicated UFO hunter, reports that of thirty thousand hospitalized mental patients in New York not one had been institutionalized because of hallucinations or demented beliefs about UFOs (1988). In psychiatric jargon, in none of these cases were UFOs either the "presenting" or "secondary" symptom. Schwartz interviewed scores of UFO witnesses and their families and has, in many cases, administered psychological tests such as the MMPI that was used by Parnell.

Almost invariably, Schwartz describes witnesses as honest, sincere, trustworthy, and free of psychiatric blemish, although in a few cases he found "unrelated" psychiatric problems. Robert Baker, a psychologist who is strongly identified with the skeptical position, also places little faith in efforts to link UFO sightings to psychopathology (1997). People who report sightings are in most ways similar to the general population, again with the exception that they are likely to have exotic beliefs including "alternative conceptions of reality," which allow for mystical events, mysterious planes of existence, hidden dimensions of reality, and other ideas that teeter on the wall that separates science and myth. Other reviews of psychological research point to similar conclusions—people who report seeing UFOs are not dumb, crazy, or social outcasts, but may have somewhat unconventional takes on reality (Saliba 1995b, 2003).

One possibility is that people who see UFOs are already predisposed to accepting paranormal phenomena. People who are not similarly inclined are more likely to "see" Venus, a weather balloon, or an experimental aircraft. Alternatively, people who have seen UFOs may start out like everyone else but discover that the UFO challenges their sense of the possible. No matter how honest, sincere, and well intentioned, skeptical explanations do not do justice to their personal experiences, so they question science's depiction of reality.

Almost everyone, "believer" and "skeptic" alike, acknowledge that many UFO reports are fraudulent. Human desires to demonstrate superiority over other people, sheer greed, and a perverse sense of humor lead to hoaxes of many kinds, including those of the UFO variety. UFOlogy has many colorful and headstrong adherents, and in the history of UFOlogy there has been good reason to doubt people's veracity (Hansen 2001; Moseley and Pflock 2002).

Still, it is not wise to engage in "if-then" thinking on the order that "if this claim strikes me as unbelievable, then the person who made it must be telling a lie." Many people who step forward know that rather than earning the accolades of an admiring public they are more likely to earn ridicule, rejection, and even the loss of employment. Certainly there may be some unabashed publicity-seekers, but it is unlikely that many claims of UFOs can be attributed to a search for fame and fortune.

Before reaching a snap judgment on someone's honesty and accuracy it is worth noting that jurors do poor jobs of assessing the accuracy of eyewitness testimony (Wells and Olson 2003). Consider, for example, the increasing number of prisoners who were convicted on the basis of unambiguous eyewitness testimony and who were later freed on DNA evidence. We rely too heavily on the content of what other people say—sure to work against people who report something unusual—while ignoring nonverbal cues of honesty and deception (O'Sullivan 2003). Investigators who focus on body language may misunderstand it—oftentimes it is the honest person that has a shifty look while the accomplished liar makes a good impression because he or she understands the value of maintaining eye contact. Some honest observers are penalized by the "Othello" effect: their fear of being disbelieved makes them appear nervous and their jitters are misinterpreted as evidence of lying. In general we tend to distrust people who appear unconventional or deviate from prevalent norms. There is a tendency to distrust the new and unusual, without giving it fair hearing. As the sociologist Erving Goffman pointed out years ago, many people reject "the astounding" and want simple explanations that eliminate the mystery and restore their faith in our consensual view of reality (Goffman 1986).

The distinction between event-dependent and observer-dependent explanations is more than an exercise in classification. A person who learns about someone else's UFO sighting and the actual observer are likely to be drawn to very different explanations. People who are caught up in an event focus their attention on the event itself. They are more sensitive to the situation that confronts them than their inner psychological workings. An anomalous experience—one that doesn't square with the scientific and skeptical worldviews that so often serve us well—may grow in importance over time.

People who observe UFOs strive to understand what happened and in the course of this become immersed in UFO literature, which tends to underscore the legitimacy of their experience but also moves them further and further from conventional thinking. People who have unusual experiences learn rapidly who will listen to their story and who won't. They are more likely to gain support from people who are pro-UFO with the result that the significance of the experience snowballs. Uncovering the truth becomes a personal mission and the person who actually saw the thing may develop the attitude "whatever it takes."

Other people who learn about the sighting are more likely to focus on the witness than on the event. This is one of the fundamental biases in human perception, and it is particularly pronounced in Western cultures where we think of behavior as the unfolding of personal dispositions rather than as a complex interplay among the person, the event, and the physical and cultural contexts (Norenzayan and Nisbett 2000). Thus we might expect UFO sighters to favor explanations that revolve around the external event, while people who were not in the same situation are drawn to observer-dependent explanations. In other words, while the observer sees the UFO as existing out there, other people see it as a figment of the observer's imagination.

The ETH—Not Proven

Almost sixty years of energetic research has failed to convince scientists that UFOs transport visitors from our own future, carry beings from another dimension, or bring us aliens from outer space. Researchers of all opine have interviewed observers, poured over piles of photographs, scrutinized hundreds of landing sites, consulted physicians and medical textbooks, and studied mysterious substances. Summarizing the state of scientific UFOlogy at the end of the twentieth century, Peter Sturrock wrote, "Concerning UFOs, we are not sure whether they are hoaxes, illusions, or real. If real, we do not know whether the reality is of a psychological and sociological nature, or one that belongs in the realm of physics. If the phenomenon has physical reality, we do not know whether it can be understood in terms of present-day physics, or whether it may present us with an example of twenty-first century (or thirtieth century) physics in action" (Sturrock 1999, 42).

More recently, Colm Kelleher and George Knapp reported on research conducted by the privately funded National Institute for Discovery Science (2005). This included analyses of purported extraterrestrial artifacts and even tissue. Without exception the results of these difficult and oftentimes expensive physical, chemical, and biological analyses yielded only terrestrial signatures. All examined artifacts, pieces of metal, and DNA came from Earth. To their knowledge not a single piece of metal or artifact acquired in nearly sixty years of research has survived scrutiny and is still regarded as genuinely anomalous. Both Sturrock and Kelleher were open to the possibility of UFOs but their findings point to the same conclusion that has been drawn by many skeptics.

Whether or not even one UFO sighting is an extraterrestrial spacecraft, people's beliefs about UFOs are very real. Widespread, firmly entrenched views about UFOs already affect expectations of intelligent life in the universe, and will impact worldwide reactions if such life is discovered. Like it or not, UFO lore overtly and covertly structures many people's thinking about our place in the universe, as well as influences politics, and it will continue to do so in the foreseeable future.

Five

OF GODS AND SPACEMEN

In the movie *Oh God*, an assistant grocery store manager (played by John Denver) is instructed by God (George Burns) to renew America's faith and spirituality. Although Denver's character claims to be in contact with God, no one else can see Him. Eventually, Denver is brought before an inquisitorial panel that (with the exception of one hesitant rabbi) dismisses Denver's thoughtful and scholarly answers to their tough questions about God, the Bible, and the meaning of it all. At exactly that point when all appears lost, God enters the room. At first, seeing only an old man, the panel remains skeptical. Mostly, God urges faith and humility, but at the end of his remarks he asks, what is reality? To underscore his point, he turns day into night, then, admonishing the panel to look once again, he turns night back into day. The inquisitors exonerate Denver, but agree never again to mention the episode.

There is only one science, but there are many religions. Although a handful of major religions together provide the basis of faith for huge numbers of people throughout the world, there are countless variations on each theme. There are twenty-two thousand denominations of Christians alone (Webb 2004). Each year 270 new Christian denominations appear worldwide, while an unspecified number disappear. For any individual, religion can be intensely personal, involving idiosyncratic views and rituals that don't neatly mesh with the textbook descriptions. Social critic Francis Wheen has referred irreverently to the "do-it-yourself" faiths of many Westerners as "hybrids comprising elements from Christianity, Hinduism, geomancy, the teachings of the Dalai Lama, the religions of Atlantis, and much else" (Wheen 2004: 121). Still, religion offers a source of wisdom and strength that helps people cope with the explosion of new knowledge.

According to Loyal Rue, religion serves an important adaptive function (Rue 2005). Religion gives people cosmological ideas and a set of moral principles. The former lend a perspective on reality and a sense of what is required for human fulfillment. Religion tells us where we came from, our place in the universe, and what really matters. The moral principles help us get along with one another. The Ten Commandments illustrate religion's moral component. People need to look to their Creator for guidance and treat each other with love and respect. Ethical principles that we associate with Christianity are found in many other religions, too, and in secular humanism, a moral philosophy that does not depend on God. Secular humanist Paul Kurtz lists four basic moral decencies (1988). These are: integrity (honesty, sincerity, keeping promises), trustworthiness (dependability and faithfulness), benevolence (civility, good will, and a lack of malfeasance) and fairness (tolerance, patience, cooperation, justice).

Together, the ideas and principles build a sense of personal wholeness and promote social harmony, and for these reasons religion is important for both the individual and the society. Religion's failure is revealed in fear and anxiety, psychiatric illness, divorce, social upheaval, criminal activity, and war.

Cosmological ideas and morality are integrated into central myths or "root metaphors," such as: there is but one God, love is all that matters, and that Jesus died on the cross for our sins (Rue 2005). These narratives excite the imagination and promise deep insights. To succeed, they must appeal to a wide range of people who differ considerably in terms of background, age, interests, and level of sophistication. Successful religious stories convey subtle and complex ideas in straightforward, concrete ways and are easy to learn and remember. They leave room for discussion and interpretation and are flexible enough to stay believable despite technological and cultural change. For a religion to survive, it must continually express, transmit, and revitalize its myth. "One of the great achievements of Christian theology," Rue writes, "has been the success of the tradition in demonstrating that it was systematically consonant with the best knowledge of the day" (2005: 209).

Religion is both inside the person and a part of society. Thus, religion like science can be viewed as a social institution that structures the relationships among people. Organized religions have social hierarchies or pecking orders: pope, cardinal, archbishop, bishop, and priest in one well-known church. Gatekeepers decide which ideas and people are acceptable, and depending on the "strictness" of the church there may be strong pressures to conform. Both religion and science have specialists to convert outsiders—in the case of religion, religious educators and missionaries, and in the case of science, science educators and skeptics. Senior clergy, like senior scientists, provide a strong counterweight to innovation and change.

Religious denominations include church, sect, and cult (Hood et al. 1996). Established churches, such as the Roman Catholic Church or the United Church of Christ, have huge memberships and their views are highly consonant with those of the host culture. Sects are smaller groups that have split off from churches, and their views tend to be less consistent with those of society at large. Cults march to their own drummers. In a sense, cults are to churches what fringe science is to mainstream science. The most extreme cults do not meet the basic requirements of religion and are analogous to pseudoscience.

The term "cult" is almost entirely pejorative. When asked to name cults it is often the most horrific that comes to mind. How many people would first name the defunct but benign Church of Jesus the Saucerian (Partridge 2004)? More likely, they would think of Charles Manson's cult that reveled in depravity and is remembered for a series of gruesome and senseless murders. Or perhaps they would mention Jonestown, where hundreds of people committed suicide (in some cases "assisted" suicide) under the direction of charismatic pastor Jim Jones; or Heaven's Gate, whose members' murky thinking about UFOs triggered a mass suicide (see Chapter 7). But not all cults are dangerous and for this reason sociologists prefer the more neutral appellation of "new religious movements" (Palmer 2004). Sure, there are authoritarian, coercive cults that brainwash their members, but many do not attempt to do this and widespread beliefs that cults have adverse psychological effects on people are not supported by the data (Aronoff et al. 2000).

Rue acknowledges that many of the world's religions have lost supporters in recent years because worshippers no longer find their stories believable (2005). The advance of science, which casts doubts on religious claims such as miracles, is one reason for this. Another is a growing awareness of cultural relativity; recognition that a religion that holds sway in one culture has almost no adherents in another. Given that there are so many competing central myths, how can we select one as true? Finally, conflicting activities, such as spectator sports, running errands, and strolling around the mall are drawing people away from church.

Religion in an Age of Science

William Sims Bainbridge points out, "Historians have argued that the modern emergence of science was facilitated by a religion of a particular kind, either Protestantism specifically or monotheism more generally. The belief that the Universe was created by a single God embodying his laws provide a religious basis for the scientific assumptions that there are natural truths capable of being discovered through research" (2004: 1009). Furthermore, science and religion have coexisted for hundreds of years, both are going strong, and it is unlikely that either one of them would collapse as the result of a "surprise" coming from the other one.

Still, skeptics marvel that in an age of science interest in religion remains as high as it is (Shermer 1999). For some people who are exemplars of the scientific worldview, religion represents nothing more than wishful thinking, a doomed quest for immortality (Kurtz 1991). Those of us who give in to religion's blandishments let wish and imagination define reality in such a way as to make us feel better than if we relied on rational analysis alone. Other skeptical explanations suggest that religion is a form of cultural adaptation that was functional once but has now outlived its usefulness, or that religion offers the elite yet one more convenient way to control the masses.

Carl Sagan deplored spiritualism and mysticism as expressed in everything from New Age beliefs to religious fundamentalism. People who refused to be rational in an age of science bothered him, and his coauthored book, *The Demon-Haunted World: Science as a Candle in the Dark* warns of the dangers of accepting these ideas (Sagan and Druyan 1997). "The reader" comments Joel Achenbach, "could sense a note of frustration, as though Sagan was astonished that there remained people who rejected science in favor of myth, superstition, and the paranormal" (1999: 174). This book, one of many by Sagan, is devoted to refuting pseudoscience such as astrology and dismissing reports of UFOs and alien visitors. Still, many of the chapters attack religion, especially in its popular forms.

Sagan's novel *Contact* and the 1997 movie based upon it, comments Ian Barbour, convey Sagan's sense of awe and wonder and his commitment to science and discovery (2000). Barbour is less happy with Sagan's portrayal of institutional religion, "represented by such dubious figures as fundamentalist protesters who think all space travel is the work of the devil and a handsome TV evangelist who is more open to science but has no education past grade school" (2000: 12). Describing Sagan as a new kind of high priest—a high priest of science—Barbour praises him for bringing astronomy to the public, and for his great ethical sensitivity and deep concern for world peace and environmental preservation. However, he questions Sagan's unlimited confidence in the scientific method, and criticizes his focus on demons, witches, faith healers, and psychics as central elements in religion today. "Apart from one brief comment," Barbour continues, Sagan "nowhere considers the writings of well-informed, university-based theologians who might be the intellectual counterparts of the scientists he admires" (2000: 13).

In *Darwin's Cathedral: Evolution, Religion, and the Nature of Society*, David Sloan Wilson proposes that evolution occurs at the group level including churches and sects (Wilson 2002). To survive, a religion must attract and retain members. The utilitarian function of membership in religious groups includes opportunities to make friends and find a mate, get social support, and perhaps obtain material assistance—welfare of sorts—to ease the faithful through life's rough spots. Religions serve as blueprints for action, and these affect people's motivation and behavior. The key may be more what this blueprint does for the person right now than in some imaginary future. Wilson writes, "Even massively fictitious beliefs can be adaptive, as long as they motivate behaviors that are adaptive in the real world…. Supernatural agents and events that never happened can provide blueprints for action that far surpass factual accounts of the natural world in clarity and reasoning power" (Wilson 2002: 41–42). And, indeed, research reviewed by Ralph Hood and his associates (1996) shows that religion offers many benefits, although skeptics might attribute these to expectations, self-fulfilling prophecies, and social support networks rather than to divine intervention.

Over forty-six thousand adults responded to one Internet-based survey, and about half of these answered the open-ended question, "Imagine the future and try to predict how the world will change over the next century. Think about how the world will change over the next century. Think about everyday life as well as major changes in society, culture, and technology" (Bainbridge 2004: 1010). Over twenty thousand responses to this question yielded two thousand distinct ideas, including one hundred visions of religion in the year 2100.

Views of the future of religion fell into three categories. First, there were visions of religion changing independent of science. Scenarios included a revival of conventional faith, a proliferation of religious movements, and an explosion of New Age ideas. Second, there were visions of religion with science. This included the possibility that religion and science would support one another over the next century. The third prediction involved the ascendance of science with religion withering and dying. Under this scenario, "Religion will start to die a slow death, as people become more informed and start thinking for themselves. The Christian Church will become increasingly irrelevant. Christian beliefs will fade from the political agenda" (Bainbridge 2004: 1017). At present, secularization is undercutting religion in most countries, but not the United States. How this all plays out is one of the crucial issues for the future.

Hidden Realities

Is there more to the universe than can be revealed by science? Religious scholars such as Huston Smith are convinced that science gives us only a narrow glimpse of reality (Smith 2001). When we look at the world through the lens of science we peer through a tunnel that restricts our vision. The floor of the tunnel is scientism, "which refuses to admit the validity of all forms of knowledge other than those of the positive sciences, and ... relegates religious, theological, ethical, and aesthetic knowledge to the realm of fantasy (Shermer 1999: 138). The left wall of the tunnel is higher education. For centuries, universities and colleges offered well-rounded curricula in science and religion. While they still offer courses in religious studies, the number is dwindling and these courses are increasingly crowded out by specialized science courses. The right wall of the tunnel is law, which prohibits religious instruction and ritual in school while allowing atheism and secular humanism to roam freely. The tunnel's roof is the media, science's ally. The media works in concert with government, the military, and business, which fund science and technology for near-term practical results.

Smith discusses multiple different planes of existence that are not always accessible to us through our senses and for this reason are home to "hidden realities" (2001). We are most familiar with the "Terrestrial Plane" where we live. This is the physical realm that we know through our senses, the realm of everyday life, and the only plane that most scientists find comfortable and acceptable. Up one notch we find the "Intermediate Plane," which is partly material and partly spiritual. Further up come the "Celestial Plane" and the "Infinite Plane," reserved for the most spiritually advanced, such as God. It is in the higher planes, not the Terrestrial plane, that myths are enacted (Armstrong 2005).

The Intermediate Plane is also known as the "Third Realm" and most closely resembles the "alternative realities" that enter into discussions of the paranormal, including UFOs and alien abductors (Ring 1992). Teetering at the boundary between the material and the mystical, the Intermediate Plane is the region of angels, demons, leprechauns, fairies, and other entities that seemed real or half-real at various points in history. Also known as "the realm of the imaginal" and "daimonic reality," many people regard events there just as real as those that occur in the physical world (Harpur 2003). In earlier times—Shakespeare's day, for example—people would not have drawn such a sharp distinction between natural and supernatural phenomena; ghosts and angels would have been seen as right and natural. Because the Intermediate Plane intersects with the material world, events like these seem real and convincing. Because they are not entirely anchored in the material world, these events defy the known laws of Newtonian physics and elude proven tools of science. By placing an encounter with an alien in the Intermediate Plane, one makes it "real" without having to excuse the lack of corroborative physical evidence. This invites treating the incident with greater respect than if it occurred only in the person's head, but incurs the wrath of skeptics because such fantastic claims are impossible to disprove.

It is very unlikely that we will abandon the idea of hidden realities and the fact that some people believe that they have glimpsed these realities is only one reason for this. In fact, we are surrounded by hidden realities that have been later illuminated by science. Could ancient humans understand that whistles that are inaudible to us could be used to summon dogs? That someday we would be awash in radio waves that are completely undetectable to our unaided senses, but can be transformed into accessible information? That x-rays could enable us to see the skeletons of living beings? Scientific discussions of higher dimensions, hyperspace, membrane or "brane" worlds, and the like do little to discourage faith in hidden realities (Greene 2004; Halpern 2004; Radin 2006).

Subjective Knowledge

Unlike science, religion contends that intuition, emotion, and other subjective experiences are honorable paths to enlightenment. These experiences, often deemed mystical, involve direct knowledge, a sense of oneness with nature, and communion with God. They are powerful, ineffable, and difficult to express. Religious rituals, like pregame pep rallies, help move people out of their isolated reality and connect them to something much larger than themselves (Newberg et al. 2001). Ritual helps connect people to "the source" and interpret themselves as embedded in a grand matrix, connected to all living things (Shlain 1998).

Dean Hamer distinguishes between spirituality and religion, and his research suggests that spirituality is rooted in biology (2004). In his view, spiritual people are able to become so absorbed in ritual, prayer, and meditation that they lose their sense of self and feel connected to other people, places and things—in other words, the source. Spirituality, he shows, is "hard-wired" into some people but not into others.

Religion, a cultural phenomenon, may shape the content of a mystical experience, such as a Christian's sense of having seen the Blessed Virgin Mary or connected in a real and personal way with Jesus. Yet, Hamer points out, even agnostics and atheists can have mystical experiences. Psychologist Abraham Maslow was an avowed atheist and scoffed at people who believed in big daddy in the sky. Maslow nonetheless wrote of peak experiences that Hamer describes as "strikingly similar to ... spiritual revelations reported by both Western religious figures and Eastern meditators" (2004: 18).

God

Most religions look to God, a supernatural agent, for understanding, meaning, and solace. Archaeological excavations show that interest in superhuman beings has been with us for millennia. These digs, coupled with later historical records, show that so far, religion has developed in phases (Armstrong 1993, 2005). In one of the earliest of these, animism, nomadic tribes saw nature as sacred and endowed in every natural object, such as birds, streams, fishes, trees, lightning, and snowstorms. Gradually, their spirits took the form of deities that required worship and sacrifices to act in ways that would allow human survival. This transition led to polytheist (many-god) religions, such as those that prevailed in ancient Mesopotamia, prior to the arrival of Judaism and Christianity. Some polytheist religions embraced hundreds of gods with varying degrees of power and authority that performed specific functions. During that era there were so many different gods that "live and let live" was the only workable policy.

Knock-down, drag-out conflicts awaited monotheistic (single-god) religions (Shlain 1998). Adherents to monotheistic religions, including Islam, Judaism, and Christianity, believe in one creator. In some religions the creator is supported by lesser supernatural and quasisupernatural agents such as angels and saints that perform functions similar to those performed by "lesser" gods in the polytheistic religions.

Conceptions of God have varied over the past four thousand years, fitting in with different periods and cultures (Armstrong 1993). Sometimes God is distant and aloof and sometimes close and personal. Sometimes God is vengeful and sometimes loving. Sometimes He gives us great latitude and other times He is a merciless micromanager. Still, there are certain recurring themes such as mind, purpose, and morality.

John Jungerman points out that throughout history we have had different models of the universe (Jungerman 2000). These include the Platonic model, which depicted the heavens as permanent and inalterable, and the current dynamic model based on the Big Bang and cosmic evolution. He writes: "These are models of the universe with a small u. They are our feeble approximations of the actual Universe with a capital U, which is not fully knowable. Similarly, we have human models for the divine in all cultures and we should remember ... that these are models of God are with a small g. God with a capital G is surely beyond our grasp, just as the actual Universe" (Jungerman 2000: 187).

Origins

Science, as most of us understand it today, looks at the Big Bang as the origin of the universe, a singularity that triggered cosmic evolution. Evolutionary theory insists that we are the product of blind forces, or purely natural events. For many people, life seems too complex, too important, too purposeful and too special to be the result of scientific laws. Of course, attempts to find empirical support for the literal Biblical story of creation have failed miserably. Thus, for most contemporary theologians, the Biblical story of creation is not taken at face value; rather, they favor the idea of "a dynamic universe created over a long period of time by a God who is immanent in nature, but also transcends nature" (Barbour 2000: xiii). God "might act in ways that do not violate known laws of science, in which case evolution is not inconsistent with the idea of God (xiv)." Of course the Bible is built on myth and metaphor. One can imagine not only the impossibility but also the uselessness, for audiences thousands of years ago, of a Bible framed in terms of physics, biochemistry, evolution, and DNA (George 2005).

Current debate over the issue of our origins includes the theory of intelligent design. This theory contends that the universe is too "fine-tuned" for humans to have occurred by chance. An ever-so-slight tweak, for example, if Earth did not have the Moon, or if Earth's axis had been ever-so-slightly different, would mean that we would not be here (Ross 1989; Behe 1996). Intelligent-design theorists marvel at the complexity of life. They cannot see how life could result from nothing more than chance variation and natural selection.

Evolutionists stoutly maintain that life's complexity is in fact a result of blind and impersonal natural forces and that evolution does in fact account for our presence (Darling 2001; Shermer 2006). They insist that intelligent design is an illusion in the eyes of the beholder, a consequence of people's abilities to discern patterns even when there is nothing there. Intelligent design theorists present themselves as scientists who are trying to forge ahead in an exciting new research area but who are fought every step of the way by close-minded evolutionists who refuse to give them a fair hearing. Evolutionists, on the other hand, represent intelligent design as a sneaky form of creationism, a disingenuous attempt to ease God into science.

Could the discovery of extraterrestrial intelligence resolve the issue in favor of evolution once and for all? Eric Chaisson proposes that SETI is "driven by a fierce anti-anthropocentrism," an earnest desire to show that we do not depend upon a Creator or intelligent designer (2001:143). Discovery of intelligent life beyond Earth would constitute unassailable proof that intelligence is the result of purely natural rather than divine processes. It would be the capstones for the Copernican and Darwinian revolutions—the final nails, so to speak, in God's coffin.

In fact, many theologians are enthusiastic about the idea of extraterrestrial life as they believe that this would expand God's provenance and provide even greater testimony to his glory (Dick 1996, 2000b; Hoffman 2004a, 2004b). Surveys of priests, rabbis, and ministers suggest that the discovery would not conflict with their views of creation, nor would it upset members of their congregations (Alexander 1998). In her review of Catholic dogma, scripture, and scholarship, Marie George finds nothing that precludes the discovery of extraterrestrial life (George 2005). This discovery, in her view, would not challenge the special relationship between God and humankind: whether or not God also maintained a special relationship with other intelligent creatures would remain an open question. Indeed, the idea of life on many worlds is compatible with many religions, including that of the Mormons. It was during the years that it was headed by a Mormon that NASA supported SETI (Noble 1999).

Sjörd Bonting, a priest and scientist, argues that Christ atoned for the sins of all intelligent life everywhere (2003). He points out that each and every one of us is, in effect, "cooked down" from the same material that, following the Big Bang, gave birth to the stars. Because of this, humans and extraterrestrials would, in a sense, be related and have certain similarities. Intelligent beings throughout the universe will develop moral awareness. Like us, their development will depend upon a slow process that involves God's progressive self-revelation coupled with evolving self-understanding. Like us, they will be imperfect and suffer from a certain "brokenness" that requires God's intervention to correct. In short, they, too, will need redemption.

Jesus incarnate, Bonting continues, descended physically (not just metaphorically) from the stars. Cooked down after the Big Bang, he too was a relative of life throughout the universe. Relying on scripture and his knowledge of ancient Greek, Bonting concludes that Jesus is the "Cosmic Christ." This one act of sacrifice is sufficient; there is no requirement for Christ to be crucified on each and every world. Bonting writes: "The incarnation, death, and resurrection of Jesus Christ taking place in Palestine two thousand years ago, are of cosmic significance and lasting validity. These epochal events bring salvation to us, who live two thousand years later in other parts of the planet, yes, to all humans who ever lived on Earth at any time and any place ... Why not, then, to creatures on another planet?" (2003: 599).

Ascent of the Astronauts

Whereas we tend to think of space exploration as a scientific endeavor, a closer look reveals strong religious and spiritual themes. David F. Noble evokes parallels between the ascension of Christ and the flight of astronauts to the heavens (1999). Even as Christ walked on Earth, the Apollo astronauts walked on the Moon. For centuries, observes Noble, religious thinking has permeated visions of spaceflight. We move beyond our imperfect planet to find salvation above. Jules Verne implied that the closer we get to the stars, the closer we come to immortality. Actual spaceflight marked the dawn of a new millennium, our entry into the space age.

The astronauts of the 1960s were known as the best and the brightest and in the eyes of the public had god-like qualities. Part pilot, part engineer, part explorer, and all hero, they underscored the superiority of America and the American way. Courageous, cheerful, and unanimous, they revealed no sign of need, greed, or blemish—NASA saw to that. These heroes—the men that walked among the stars—gave Americans the heavens. Although the astronauts seemed to be free of emotion, their wives provided balance and made the space program seem like a real human endeavor as they showed anxiety, fear, ambivalence, and exhilaration (Dean 1998).

Given today's philosophical, political, and legal efforts to separate science and religion, it is hard to imagine that less than fifty years ago space exploration, one of the great achievements of the twentieth century, was orchestrated by scientists and technicians who were quite open about their faith. General John B. Medaris, whose military rockets performed better than expected, believed that he could not have achieved consistent success without God's assistance. Later, with less success, he sought to establish a Chapel of the Astronauts on NASA property (Noble 1999).

Many people who were alive at the time remember Apollo astronauts, in flight or on the Moon's surface, reading excerpts from the Bible. But how many remember that before Neil Armstrong and Buzz Aldrin left their landing module to first set foot on the Moon they used a small kit, provided by a pastor, to take communion? Apollo astronaut Charlie Duke found God and announced: "That walk on the Moon lasted three days but my walk with Jesus lasted forever" (Noble 1999: 141). Later, a shuttle astronaut commented that the interior of the *Columbia* reminded him of a miniature cathedral.

A liberal number of astronauts and cosmonauts have been transformed spiritually by their flights. Traveling in space they experience "overview effects," a sense of awe, majesty, and wonder, accompanied by a sense of connection with God and oneness with all humanity (White 1987). Looking down from on high, spacefarers see a beautiful blue sphere, unmarred by political boundaries. They feel a surge of protectiveness of Earth, her ecology, and other people. The problems of everyday life seem insignificant in comparison to the sense of grandeur and opportunity of space. Trying to find words to express these feelings, astronauts have thanked God and praised Allah. In space, near-mystical experiences and humanistic thinking can overpower, at least temporarily, a worldview forged in science and the military. After his trip to the Moon, Edgar Mitchell developed a new philosophy and went on to found the Noetic Institute so that his experiences could benefit many other people (Mitchell and Williams1996).

There were few atheists among the German rocket scientists who provided scientific and technical leadership during the early years of NASA. Some of these men had weak religious affiliations during the Nazi era in their homeland, but became born-again Christians after they relocated to Alabama, Texas, and other parts of the U.S, Bible

Belt. Wernher von Braun, who oversaw rocket development from the German V-2 that bombed London to the American Saturn V that carried the Apollo astronauts, believed that the universe was the product of an intelligent designer. The laws of nature, he thought, must have been laid down by a conscious, willful being. In 1975 he said during an interview with the Southern Baptist Radio and Television Commission "I just can't envision this whole universe coming into being without something like a divine will. I cannot envision the concept of creation without the concept of a creator" (Peters 1977: 117).

Biblical stories, such as the tale of Noah's Ark, inspire scientific visions, such as the use of spacecraft for storing back-up copies of terrestrial life (Freitas 1983).

Gregory Benford proposed archiving genetic material from Earth's rapidly depleting species (Benford 1999). This he sees as a way of perpetuating the rich biological diversity on Earth, but such materials could be sent forth—either as frozen samples or as DNA encoded into computer programs—to distant stars. Given millions of species on Earth, we may have to resort to sampling to give some indication of the range and diversity of Earth's plants and animals.

Exomissiology

As Tom Hoffman points out, a mission is a ministry commissioned by a church or some other organization for the purpose of propagating its faith or carrying on humanitarian work (2004a, 2004b) Acts 1:8 reads "You will be my witnesses in Jerusalem, in all Judea and Samaria, and to the ends of the earth." Today, missionaries still serve in areas that were once known as Judea (present-day Jerusalem) and Samaria, and although reduced in number, still carry their missions to the ends of the Earth.

Discipleship is a central theme in missionary work, but there is also a strong humanitarian element. Contemporary missionary work includes healing and promoting a sense of wholeness and joy in the world. Missionaries counsel young gang members, perform lifesaving operations, and sponsor safe houses for girls who have been sold into prostitution. Unlike earlier missionaries who helped European explorers claim new territories, today's missionaries are expected to soft-pedal dogma and prophecy.

Missiology is the study of the church's missionary work. According to the American Society of Missiology, the field has been defined variously as "the science of the cross cultural communication of the Christian faith," as "preeminently the scholarly discipline understanding the task of world evangelization," and "the field of study which researches, records, and applies data relating to the biblical origins and history of the expansion of the Christian movement to anthropological principles and techniques for its further advancement" (American Society of Missiology). This field has been characterized as an applied science: a distinctive interdisciplinary effort that draws upon theology, anthropology, and history, liberally dosed with communication theory, psychology, and sociology. In the Society's view, missiology comes into its own when it is enriched by ecumenical views and non-Christian religion. Or, as Hoffman points out, for missionaries, it pays to adopt a broad perspective, listen carefully to diverse viewpoints, avoid ethnocentrism, and be good guests in foreign lands.

Hoffman, a Methodist minister and missionary who serves in Russia, points out that SETI scientists have brought disciplines such as ethics, religion, and theology into their discussions. He proposes a field of exomissiology that would focus on the histories, theologies, and futures of Christian missions as they relate to issues of space settlement and alien contact. He explains that the Church has consistently been present and involved during intercultural contacts and exchanges, even when initiated by nonreligious governments and organizations. Exomissionaries could play key roles communicating religious ideals and ethics, and serve as brokers that help interpret extraterrestrial theologies and religions to humans.

Hoffman accepts that exomissiology will be a tough sell to contemporary scientists, many of whom are professed agnostics or atheists, tend more towards cultural relativism than the absolutist views of some Christians, and have a limited view of missionaries as nuisances who distribute pamphlets door-to-door and who may best "serve humankind" after having been spooned out of the cooking pots of cannibals. He proposes high standards for the exomissionaries that will accompany astronauts in space or work alongside SETI engineers. They will be engaged in a ministry of risk: "practicing at the edge of society, the edge of the church, and off the edge of the planet" (Hoffman 2004a: 61). Still, he argues, carefully overseen by the World Council of Churches, highly qualified exomissionaries could bring many strengths to the interstellar bargaining table: purpose, dedication, awareness of history and cultural differences, ability to work with openly hostile populations, and, in the case of space exploration, readiness to go almost anywhere on a moment's notice.

Angels, Demons, and UFOs

"Very few people," writes Huston Smith, "are able to subscribe to either the scientific or traditional [religious] worldview without [unconsciously if not consciously] smuggling in some features of the other outlook" (2001: 33). Indeed, when it comes to looking for intelligent life beyond Earth, it is all but impossible to keep science and religion separate. Karl Guthke characterizes the idea of extraterrestrial life as a religion or quasireligion that may play an important role in how we define ourselves (1960). As quoted in Denzler, Paul Davies suggests that the belief in super-advanced aliens somewhere "out there" gives us some measure of comfort and inspiration. "This sense of religious quest may well extend to scientists themselves" (Denzler 2001: 153). SETI is science, not religion, and whatever the satisfactions they may or may not experience, SETI scientists work hard to dispel the idea that the search has religious overtones.

Many of the world's great religions are based on visions of prophets (Shlain 1998). According to biblical accounts, superior beings including angels and Jesus descended from the heavens with challenges or reassurances for Earth. Sometimes these visitors from afar are accompanied by startling visual displays such as large unusual clouds, pillars of fire, strange mists, and bizarre light patterns (Downing 1997). Yahweh—the god with no followers—appeared to Abraham and promised that if Abraham pledged unswerving loyalty then Abraham would become a great landholder with a multitude of children. Fealty (and, it turned out, circumcision so that Yahweh's male devotees would always be recognizable) was demanded in return for these gifts. Later, Yahweh gave Moses the Ten Commandments. "Unlike the distant Marduk, Amon and Baal" notes Leonard Shlain, "Yahweh operated on the plane of everyday life, and He was not above intervening in the affairs of everyday people. He [spelled out] in excruciating detail exactly what he wanted from every Israelite" (1998: 77). Many centuries later, the angel Moroni showed Joseph Smith the gold tablets that would provide the basis for the Church of Jesus Christ of Latter Day Saints—the Mormons.

Sometimes visitors from above appear to be of flesh and blood and as real as a next-door neighbor. Other times they appear as apparitions to people who are in a trance or in a dream state. Angels revealed the Hebrew faith to Moses in ways that biblical scholars viewed as real and objective, but most revelations occurred in a dream or in the fogginess of a vision (Downing 1997). While sleeping in a cave Mohammed was approached by the Angel Gabriel. The angel ordered Mohammed to read some words that were written on a silk coverlet. Mohammed protested that he could not read, but Gabriel pressed him tightly with the coverlet and repeated his command. Mohammed did read, and Gabriel departed. Later, after Mohammed had left the cave and was midway up a mountain, he heard a voice from heaven saying "O Mohammed! Thou art the messenger of Allah and I am Gabriel!" (Shlain 1998: 280).

The first flurry of UFO sightings led to speculative reinterpretation of biblical events. This is one of the basic foundations of ancient astronaut theory (Colavito 2005). The idea is that extraterrestrial astronauts visited Earth at various times in the distant past, perhaps seeding our planet with intelligent life and occasionally intervening in human evolution and culture. Rather than reflecting imagination or myth, perplexing ancient accounts of strange beings and implausible events demonstrate our ancestors' inability to describe extraterrestrials and their technology. If this is so, then maybe the miraculous phenomena reported in the Bible were the works of alien spacemen, rather than God or the devil.

Barry Downing argued that in the 1960s most Christian fundamentalists viewed UFOs as deceptive and demonic (Downing 1997). This view persists today in claims that UFOs are demonic manifestations originating in other dimensions but that are revealed to people whom inadvertently or knowingly engage in the occult. Downing himself proposes that UFOs are angelic, "an expression of the divine force that guides the Universe, agents of the one that the Bible calls God. They are in fact responsible for the development of life on Earth as we know it and responsible for the religion of the Bible" (1997: xv). Neither extraterrestrial visitors nor myths, "UFOs are a manifestation of the force that has created and now directs life on earth ... it is time that we explore the possibility that UFOs carry the angels of God" (xix).

In her discussion of a religious movement known as the Raellians, sociologist Susan J. Palmer casts an interesting light on whether or not extraterrestrial interlopers can be considered gods (2004). The group's founder, Rael, reports that he met the "Elohim," members of an advanced extraterrestrial race that was influential in our distant past and is destined to play a role in our future. The Raellians are concentrated in the Canadian province of Quebec. When they applied for tax-free status as a religion, Canadian authorities turned them down. The official reasoning was that whereas the Raellians worshipped superhuman beings, the Elohim were material entities with physical bodies. Real gods, according to Canadian authorities, had to be immaterial and spiritual.

The Raellians had better luck in the United States where authorities took a more relaxed view of religion and granted them tax-exempt status.

Religion and UFOlogy are linked also by themes of spirituality and ethics that appear in accounts of people who claimed that they had been in contact with entities from other planets (Denzler 2001). In the 1950s, "contactees"—the precursor of today's abductees—reported encountering "space brothers," benevolent teachers from other worlds. The titles of some of these space brothers at once command respect and suggest that their governments have yet to move beyond bureaucratic forms of organization: "Commander Gyeorgos Ceres Hatonn ... Commander in Chief, Earth Project Transition, Pleiades Sector Flight Command, Intergalactic Federation Fleet—Ashtar Command, Earth Representative to the Cosmic Council and Intergalactic Federation Council on Earth Transition" (Barkun 2003: 148).

Typically, these human-like beings wore flowing white robes and had long blond hair. They were very good looking and bore a remarkable resemblance to Jesus as portrayed by northern European and American artists. Their message was straightforward and consistent with the religious tradition. They urged humans to be agreeable, get along with one another, be tolerant and forgiving, and show optimism about the future. Religious themes are so prominent in parts of UFOlogy that parts of the field can be construed as a new religion tailored for an age of science. As Downing writes, "Religion is the process by which we invent a set of beliefs that give our life 'meaning' in this hostile world. What about UFOs? We invented them because in our scientific age we no longer believe in angels, so we instead believe in visitors from outer space, high tech angels" (1997: viii).

Two assumptions make it tempting to attribute extraterrestrials with god-like qualities (Harrison 2005). The first assumption is that any extraterrestrial civilization that we will find is likely to be older than our own. The basic idea is that our Sun is relatively young. Other Sun-like stars began much earlier than ours and have had a generous head start for cooking up life. Ray Norris assumes that stars like our Sun have been forming since our own galaxy began ten billion years ago (Norris 2000). For the first five billion years there would not have been enough time for a civilization to evolve. During the next five billion years, the number of civilizations would increase in a linear fashion. Now, however, some of the first Sun-like stars are dying off at about the same rate that new Sun-like stars are forming. According to his calculations, the average civilization began about 1.7 billion years ago. Some of these will have succumbed to nuclear wars, asteroid impacts, and other cataclysmic events. Because of these limiting factors the first extraterrestrial civilization that we will discover—or that will discover us—will not necessarily be two billion years older than our own, but they will be vastly older.

The second assumption is that extraterrestrial civilizations will be benign, even benevolent. Rather than fearing space invaders, we hope for representatives of a cosmic peace corps. Political scientists provide us with four lines of evidence that justify this hope. First, cosmic evolution, the shift in the direction of larger communal and sociopolitical units, has been accompanied by increases in the number of people who have been defined as "like us" and hence accorded "insider" treatment (Shermer 2004). For the greatest part of human existence biological factors controlled moral sentiments and the overriding goal was to protect one's family. Later, favored treatment was extended to the entire community. Modern society further expanded the circle of people who should be accorded fair treatment, and the end of the Cold War sparked a new wave of liberal internationalism and inclusiveness. This new wave looks beyond sovereign rights to human rights, beyond national security to human security, and beyond national interest to planetary interest (Michalak 2004).

The second relevant discovery is that totalitarian regimes are being replaced by liberal democracies (Ray 1998). For example, in 1840 there were two democracies populated by 44 million people, a mere 4 percent of the world's population, while today 3.467 billion or 57 percent of all people live under a democratic form of government (Modelski and Perry 2002). It should take about 228 years to shift from 10 percent to 90 percent democracies, the saturation level to be achieved in 2113.

This transition in the direction of liberal democracies has implications for interstellar affairs because in comparison to subjects of totalitarian states citizens of democracies are less likely to be subject to repression and political violence, more likely to have their basic needs for food and shelter satisfied, and more likely to develop economic surpluses that encourage trade. Most importantly, democracies are less likely to get embroiled in wars, a finding that is so robust that one scholar concluded that the link between democracy and peace is the strongest empirical law in international relations, and led another scholar to propose that other research on conditions of war and peace might as well be consigned to the scrap heap (Ray 1998).

Third, mathematical modeling shows that nations that practice collective security, that is, do not initiate war that but do go to one another's defense, survive longer than states that follow more aggressive foreign policies (Cusack and Stoll 1994). The more states that join a collective security pack, the longer the members survive. Thus, aggressive, berserk, fang-and-claw societies put themselves out of business.

Finally, historians foresee, within maybe two hundred years, a world without war. This trend prevails despite the recent carnage of two world wars: we are in the midst of a long-term shift towards stability and peace (Shermer 2004). If these trends reflect deep, underlying principles, and I suggest that they do, then statistically speaking, we should expect peaceful civilizations to outnumber warlike civilizations that pursue selfish ends (Harrison 1997, 2000). Stated less formally, those civilizations that survive their period of technological adolescence (where they have highly destructive weapons but lack the cultural tools to control them) are likely to achieve great age and overlap our own civilization in time.

Allen Tough proposes that extraterrestrials may remain elusive until we prove ourselves worthy of contact (Tough 2000). This demonstration of worthiness does not depend upon ritual and prayer. Rather, we may have to achieve a certain level of intellectual proficiency and moral attainment as evidenced in demonstrations of freedom, peace, and humility. If extraterrestrials are monitoring us—perhaps by means of a probe no larger than a fly on the wall, perhaps by tapping into the Internet—there is no hiding from them, even as there is no hiding from God.

SETI is not to be confused with religion and myth, so any superficial similarities among extraterrestrial radioastronomers, God, ancient astronauts, and space brothers have to be taken with a huge grain of salt (Harrison 2005). God, if He exists, is supernatural. Extraterrestrials would be the product of biological evolution. God is everywhere; extraterrestrials may be scattered here and there throughout the universe. God is omniscient; extraterrestrials would have to use surveillance technology to watch over us. God is eternal; extraterrestrials may be very old, perhaps kept alive by advanced biotechnology or within the electronic circuits of robots and computers. God communicates in mysterious ways; extraterrestrials communicate in mysterious ways, too, if crop circles and cattle mutilations are attempts at this. Most importantly of all, for religious people God is a given, but for scientists extraterrestrials are hypothetical, at least pending empirical verification.

Christopher Partridge reminds us that while the "angelic" interpretation of flying saucers has gained ascendance, Christian demonology continues to influence perceptions of UFOs (2004). The "reptilian" or "reptoid" alien is an example. Supposedly these ugly creatures have been on Earth for time immemorial. They have joined forces with evil governments throughout the world. Some of the world's most influential people are in on the plot. Reptilians walk among us: unrecognizable, because as "shape shifters" they can give the impression that they are humans. They work alongside humans in secret, underground laboratories and military bases. Demons, of course, are known for their ugly appearance and deceptive behavior. Signing a pact with the reptilians is like—just like—signing a pact with the devil. What seems like a good idea at the time turns out not to be so in retrospect. Remember, it was a reptile—a serpent—that tempted Adam with an apple from the tree of knowledge. And both secret alien bases and Hell are underground. Partridge traces how these evil, manipulative demons appeared first in the Bible and then in science fiction before making their debut in UFO lore.

Brave New Religions

In recent years, scholars and theologians have proposed brave new religions to accommodate real and anticipated scientific discoveries (Hoffman 2004b). The historian Steven J. Dick has outlined "cosmotheology," a new way of understanding God that accommodates a universe full of life. "Cosmotheology... means using our ever-growing knowledge of the universe to modify, expand, or change entirely our current theologies, whatever they may be" (2000b: 200). This new approach to religion requires us to take into account our growing understanding of the cosmos and to use nature to inform a much broader range of discussion.

Cosmotheology rests on the principle that humanity is neither physically nor biologically central to the universe. Humanity is, at best, somewhere midway in the great chain of intelligent beings, and we must adopt a reverence and respect for all life everywhere. This moral dimension, Dick notes, may be very difficult for a species such as ours that comes to blows over such superficialities as differences in race and nationality. Cosmotheology fosters a conception of God that is rooted in cosmic evolution. It is intended to be a God that is compatible with science. He writes "With due respect for present religious traditions whose history stretches back four millennia, the natural God of cosmic evolution and the biological universe, not supernatural God of the Near East, is the God of [our new millennium]" (Dick 2000b: 208). God will persist, but adjusted to reflect cosmic evolution, space travel and—

quite possibly— communication with extraterrestrial intelligence. The trend towards greater inclusiveness may extend to all life everywhere. Cosmic grandeur also typifies Diarmuid O'Murchu's quantum theology (O'Murchu 2004). Mystics, in their search for light, have abandoned pilgrimages to holy shrines in favor of finding sacred places within themselves. Their search is at once personal, interpersonal, planetary, and cosmic. Each religion may be right for its own time, but people's quest for spirituality is continuous and important for cosmic evolution. Formerly, we identified Earth as the world, now we marvel at the entire universe.

Quantum theology explores the metaphorical, mystical, and philosophical implications of the quantum vision. A defining characteristic of quantum physics is that everything is connected and interacts, thus giving rise to a dynamic whole that is greater than the sum of its parts, a living universe. "Quantum theology," O'Murchu writes, "calls for a more expansive understanding of our universe and our role within it ... in the ensuing millennia or billennia, we humans will be outgrown by other species, as yet not even vaguely imagined in the thought forms of our time" (2004:103). We should not consider ourselves the summit of evolution and interpret everything relative to ourselves—we are not in charge of the universe, we only play a part in its development. We will eventually be eclipsed if we are not overshadowed already. "Our universe is so vastly complex and mysterious," he observes, "that no one species (no matter how enlightened) and no one religious system (no matter how sophisticated) could comprehend and understand" it. (64). For many people, human religious categories do not do justice to the universe; only through recognizing our participation in something much greater than ourselves can we discover and rediscover spiritual awakening. One of Dick's comments about cosmotheology also applies to quantum theology: "it may be that religion in a universal sense is defined as the never-ending search of each civilization for others more superior than itself" (2000b: 205).

Six

VISITOR EXPERIENCES

Captain Joshua Slocum, the first man to circumnavigate the globe, once looked out of the tiny cabin of his sailing ship and saw that a stranger had grabbed the wheel. This seaman, who maintained his iron grip, claimed he had served on the crew of Christopher Columbus's ship *Pinta* hundreds of years earlier, and that he had rematerialized for the express purpose of helping Slocum. In another eerie incident a man standing in the doorway of an Alaskan hotel beckoned to a musher who was driving by on a dogsled. The musher entered, registered, and went to bed. Later, another musher found this "guest" not in the hotel, but almost frozen to death in a pile of snow. And, discussing his monotonous solo flight across the Atlantic in 1927, Charles Lindbergh acknowledged that he was assisted by phantoms that slipped in and out of his airplane, providing him with reassurance, advice, and insights that were not attainable in normal life. After describing these episodes linked by solitude, monotony, and a sensed presence, Peter Suedfeld concluded that when the brain is deprived of stimulation it interprets memories and fantasies as external events (Suedfeld 2001).

Throughout history and on every continent people have reported encounters with mysterious visitors that appear to be in this world, but not of it. Some of these beings have immense powers, trigger strong emotional responses, transform individual beholders, and alter the course of civilization. Visitors include God and his messengers, the Blessed Virgin Mary, little people (elves, fairies, and leprechauns), beings of light, and, in our current era, extraterrestrial entities. Do claims of encounters with extraterrestrials tell us more about outer space, the varied creatures that inhabit the universe, or inner space—the workings of the human mind?

Inner Space

At the close of the nineteenth century Vienna's Sigmund Freud was developing an intricate theory of personality and mental health based on levels of consciousness and the power of the mind. Harvard's William James was busily analyzing religious experiences in exquisite detail. A separate group of academics who were charting the course for modern psychology proceeded down a very different path. To affirm psychology as a science they sought to pattern themselves after physical scientists and be as objective as possible. Although they considered it perfectly acceptable to analyze observable stimuli and then record how people reacted to them, these psychologists did not consider it fruitful to dwell on mental processes since they are invisible and not amenable to scientific study. Another reason for disassociating themselves from mental activity was to avoid confusing the public. At that time the public knew about spiritualists who conducted séances and psychic readings, and about religious visions. Early psychologists wanted to keep these topics separate from their newly emerging field. Very few credentialed psychologists ever would conduct scientific studies of psychic phenomena and as a field the psychology of religion was slow to take off (Hood et al. 1996).

At the beginning of the twenty-first century, professional opinion is divided on the nature and role of consciousness. For some scientists, consciousness is a nuisance that should be avoided or explained away. They consider it a by-product of evolution and believe that it plays only a minor role in our lives. According to psychologist Merlin Donald, this "minimalist" or "hardliner" position is in fact supported by a substantial amount of research (2001). Findings suggest that we are largely under the control of "background programs" that are built into our genes. We attend to only a fraction of the information that is available to us, and often miss critical pieces. We make crude assessments and sloppy decisions. We begin to take action (for example, reaching with a foot for the brake pedal) before we issue ourselves a conscious command (STOP). And, despite the best of intentions, we nevertheless reach for that smoke, have another beer, or gobble down too many candy bars.

Donald contends that the "hardliner's" research is competent and informative but too limited in scope. Scientists seek accurate, reliable evidence. Today, if we want to apply rigorous procedures, we have to study consciousness under carefully controlled laboratory conditions, and even then in small bites. This means observing people in contrived settings where they perform fixed tasks such as choosing between two pictures or pushing a button in response to a light. The laboratory is impoverished compared to our normal environment where we have many ways to do things that require extended thought. Discussing a movie, he notes, people must remember the movie's characters, cast, scenes, and plot. They have to shift rapidly from topic to topic, taking other people's intellectual levels and emotional states into account, weighing and evaluating different opinions, and finding the right words to express themselves. Compared to the laboratory, the real world forces us to organize and understand information; to plan, act, and respond to feedback; and to stay "on target" for extended periods of time.

Furthest removed from the hardliner position is the contention that consciousness is all that matters. After all, everything we know about the outside world we know because of consciousness. We can only assume that the material world exists independent of our experience of it. Still, there are three reasons that this is a good assumption (Russell 2005). First, reality imposes limits upon us. If it did not exist we could fly at will, eat as much of anything that we wanted without gaining weight, and enjoy limitless sex without fear of disease, guilt, or social condemnation. Second, our experiences generally follow well-defined principles and laws. If we let go of a glass it crashes to the floor. The Sun rises and sets on time. Do someone a favor, and they are likely to do a favor for you. Finally, other people have the same pattern of experiences and thus confirm them. The easiest way to explain this similarity of experience is in terms of objective, external reference points.

Despite (or perhaps because of) its elusive nature, consciousness plays a major role in discussions of our place in the universe. Consciousness allows us to imagine the unknown. Who could guess what levels of awareness and mental powers are available to the immensely old and wise beings that might inhabit other planets and what their capabilities could mean for us?

Mystical Experiences

Mystical experiences differ in fundamental and important ways from ordinary conscious awareness and give people the impression that they have encountered a reality that is different from—and in some crucial sense, higher than—that of everyday life (Wulff 2000). They convince people that they have risen above material existence and confer a sense of uplifting unity with something much larger than the self (Newberg et al. 2001). During a mystical experience, everything seems to have "cosmic significance" and confers a sense of having achieved a fundamental insight into the true nature of the universe (Ramachadan and Blakeslee 1998).

Mystical experiences are not hallucinations nor are they based on mental illness (Newberg et al. 2001). They are coherent, rich, and textured, seem very real and are usually described in positive terms. Hallucinations are frightening and fragmented and usually accompanied by a sense of unreality. Mystics may never be convinced that their experiences were not real, but they can easily navigate conventional reality and fit in with society. Although in other societies people may welcome and enjoy mystical experiences and treat them as real, in Western society many people tend to distrust them.

From the religious worldview divine inspiration may explain mysterious visitors, but from the scientific perspective, biological and cultural factors are explanation enough. Our ability to have such experiences may not be a gift from God, but a product of evolution. External and internal events trigger biochemical and electrical activity that result in sensed presences and other mystical phenomena. The form of the visitor is determined by personality and culture. Mohammed interpreted his visitor as the Angel Gabriel. In today's highly technological society, where astrobiology, SETI, science fiction, and many other factors prompt us to think in terms of a populated universe, visitors are aliens from outer space.

Neurotheology

Coined as a term in the 1990s, neurotheology refers to the role of the brain and nervous system in mystical experiences. As noted in the last chapter, it now appears that we are "wired" for spirituality, while environmental factors, such as culture and upbringing, shape religious belief. There is a genetic component as evidenced in studies of twins, and there is an identifiable gene associated with the ability to experience transcendental states (Hamer 2004). This may have survival value, perhaps by encouraging optimism that overcomes adversity, or it may be an accidental byproduct of evolution. It's just not possible to ignore the intricate relationship between brain (body) and consciousness (mind). Injuries to the brain affect the way we see, understand, and remember things. Stimulation of the brain, by scalpel or electrode, triggers memories—sometimes real, sometimes false—influences moods, and gives rise to visions. Recordings of events within the brain correlate remarkably with people's mental states.

The human brain operates electrochemically, and by using an electroencephalograph (EEG) researchers can monitor subtle electrical activity. Several electrodes are pasted onto the subject's scalp and the electrical activity that they detect is fed into a device that identifies and analyzes different patterns or "brain waves" and creates a visual record of how they change over time. Norman Don and Gilda Moura studied thirty Brazilians who reported UFO contacts and abduction experiences (1997). Each of these volunteers claimed that, as a result of their abduction experiences, they spontaneously gained the ability to enter into a trance. Indeed, analyses of their EEGs showed that all were able to voluntarily enter a mental state characterized by muscle relaxation, immobility, and brain waves suggestive of a superconscious state. This state, which is rare, usually requires many years of initiation by yogic adepts to achieve. There was no brain activity (or clinical indicators) of schizophrenia or other psychopathology. According to the researchers, the subjects gained advanced meditative skills after the encounter.

In recent years, the EEG has been joined by functional magnetic resonance imaging device or fMRI. Rather than analyzing brain waves, this implement allows direct observation of the relative amounts of activity of the different parts of the brain itself. In essence, when a particular part of the brain (which has a characteristic function) goes to work, it "heats up" in a way that can be monitored by the fMRI. The output in this case is a picture of the brain that is reminiscent of an x-ray except that it is in colors that are keyed to the amount of activity in the different structures (lighter and brighter colors are indicative of greater levels of activity). With fMRI we can, in a very real sense, watch people think.

Most of the time we live in our normal stare of consciousness. However, conditions can alter this state and hence the way we perceive reality. Environmental forces include persistent monotonous conditions, an indispensable prerequisite for the visitor experiences described at the beginning of this chapter, and the amount of oxygen in the brain, which is diminished, for example, at high altitude. (The person who is oxygen deprived is usually the last to understand this.) Drugs, rituals, and meditation facilitate altered states. Psilocybin, derived from "magic mushrooms" used in religious rituals by some Native Americans in the Southwest, provokes powerful transcendental experiences that permanently alter users' perspectives, leaving them far more spiritual than they were before (Hamer 2004). LSD reliably prompts mystical experiences, and in the early 1960s was seen as a potentially powerful agent for positive change. The early promise of LSD as an aid to psychotherapy is important to remember when evaluating complaints about its purported role as a mind-altering drug used in evil ways by manipulative governments.

We experience altered states daily when we get tired and go to sleep. We are so used to six-to-eight-hour periods of oblivion punctuated by unpredictable and sometimes intricate and bizarre dreams that, in the absence of insomnia, we hardly ever give this state a second thought. It is not too surprising, then, that for time immemorial a preponderance of visitor experiences have occurred at night. The form of these visitors has varied across history and culture: demons intent on forcing themselves sexually on unwilling victims; witches; ghosts; imaginary aliens of many different types; wise and compassionate beings of light.

Visitor experiences are likely during sleep paralysis, which occurs just before going to sleep or waking up. At these times the person is aware (apart from the visitor, everything seems normal, but it isn't) yet is unable to initiate voluntary action. Thus, he or she cannot fend off the invader, or flee the bedroom. Sleep paralysis affects maybe 15 percent of the population, but not every episode of paralysis is accompanied by a sensed presence. By some estimates as many as half of all cases of alien abduction are linked to sleep paralysis (Randle et al. 1999; Clancy 2005).

In his laboratory, psychologist Michael Persinger uses "the octopus," a cap that is fitted with many electrodes, to stimulate different parts of the brain (Persinger 2000). This creates experiences that are real to the research subjects, even though they know on an intellectual level that they were artificially induced. In one instance a woman seated in a laboratory chair who was told that her brain would be electrically stimulated kept referring to "the entity." Another person became fearful and sensed someone nearby, then distinctly saw a person who seemed to be standing in the sun. A man reported that some people were talking behind him: although he could hear their voices he could not understand what they said. Still another subject reported seeing an angel. "Nearly every basic element of mystical, religious, and visitor experiences," writes Persinger, "has been evoked with direct electrical stimulation" (2000: 270).

Science writer John Horgan was skeptical of the octopus and it had little effect upon him (2003). Coverage of Persinger's research, he says, implies that the effects are profound religious visions such as those of Abraham, Mohammed, and Jesus. In Horgan's personal experience there were no demons or deities; the only voice he heard was that of the researcher after the electricity had been shut off. He proposes that skeptics who are eager to find a materialistic explanation of mystical phenomena overstate the strength of Persinger's findings to bolster their own arguments. He adds that because skeptics like Persinger's scientific explanation of supernatural events, they are willing to overlook his research on extrasensory perception (ESP).

Still, there is enough research to show that the brain's right temporal lobe is the home of many mystical experiences and paranormal events. Pediatrician Melvin Morse, who studies near-death experiences, considers the right temporal lobe the "God spot," an area of unlimited potential where God lives within us (Morse and Perry 2000). Morse, who considers himself as a body within a soul rather than the other way around, claims that this area of the brain is not just a storage bin but a receiver and transmitter that ties us in with a "universal memory bank." Could it be that some of what we interpret as memory exists outside of our bodies and is tapped into in some mysterious way by the brain? Preposterous—but if it weren't, the brain structure would be, in effect, a previously unknown mechanism for connecting ourselves with the universe, allowing us to directly perceive reality, unfiltered by the limits of the five senses. Americans, Morse notes, worship logic even when it is wrong and deny intuition even when it's right. By ignoring or dismissing skills associated with the right temporal lobe we cut ourselves off from the universal memory bank, or, in spiritual terms, God's grace.

Superminds

Hidden dimensions of reality, parallel universes, quantum mechanics, and other mainstays of the new physics have given rise to a new generation of group mind theories that are cloaked in space-age trappings. These suggest that consciousness transcends time and space and could be responsible for instantaneous communication over vast distances, although at our present stage of evolution we are not particularly well equipped to understand the messages. In these theories, consciousness exists—to some extent—either independently of or above and beyond its biological foundations. We are enmeshed in an invisible net or web that constitutes a greater consciousness or awareness, and from time to time this net impinges on individuals. This matrix of consciousness goes by many names: the noosphere, the vacuum-based holofield, the universal living memory, and the Cosmic Internet (Radin 2006).

Psychologist Jenny Wade offers a rather complex theory that depends upon on two streams of consciousness (1996). The first of these, transcendent consciousness, is part of the universe's order and independent of human nervous systems. Transcendent consciousness exists prior to birth and after death. Evidence of this, she explains, is found in studies that demonstrate conscious memories at the beginning of life, before the nervous system is sufficiently mature to perceive and remember events, and near the end of life (for example, during near-death experiences) when unconscious patients or victims give accurate reports of events that take place in the presence of their comatose bodies. (She describes these reports as accurate because they come from independent witnesses, but because they involve paranormal events most scientists would ignore or reject them.) The second type of consciousness, brain-based consciousness, is individual consciousness as understood in contemporary mainstream neuroscience, cognitive science, and psychology.

According to her theory, transcendent consciousness does not require a mature or healthy nervous system and this is the reason that it can register before birth and after death. After birth, as the nervous system develops, brain-based consciousness gains strength and crowds out transcendent consciousness. Occasionally material from the transcendent consciousness slips through, but parents (and mental health experts) interpret this as magical thinking, regressive behavior, and pure fantasy. As the environment, brain, and nervous system play larger and larger roles, children learn to separate the imaginary from the real. Later, through religious ritual and meditation, some people can once again access the transcendent consciousness. Their insights cannot be understood by a vast majority of people, who are so dominated by brain-based consciousness that they cannot access the transcendent consciousness that was available to them in infancy.

In his book *The Planetary Mind,* astronomer Arne Wyller seeks a scientific rationale for the idea that we are embedded within a higher level of consciousness, even as we are embedded in an atmosphere and gravitation (1996). He rejoices in a level of beauty and design in the universe that seems unlikely to have resulted from evolution alone, and complains that science has not made much progress understanding consciousness. Evolution, in his view, lacks mathematical rigor, ignores too many major gaps in the evidence, and glosses over too many unresolved issues. In his opinion the original thinking of the great master Darwin has become dogmatized and codified. On the other hand, "everything falls into a meaningful pattern if we look at evolutionary developments within the framework of a creative intelligence that is growing, experimenting, learning and developing" (Wyller 1996: 97). In a sense, he revives vitalism—the idea that matter is shaped and dominated by a life principle—and pantheism, the idea that God (or at least an intelligent designer) is revealed in all of nature.

To Wyller, the Planetary Mind Field coexists with the energy fields of physics. This Field affects us largely at the unconscious level, but (as in the case of transcendent consciousness) some people occasionally glimpse its workings. Consistent with ideas about cosmic evolution, he contends that the Mind Field is moving in the direction of increased cosmic awareness. As a part of the Planetary Mind Field we are contributing to our own evolution, and, in the process, reaching out to the rest of the universe. He adds: "In light of humanity's emerging awareness of the possibilities for life elsewhere in the universe, it would not surprise me if a ... powerful goal of the Planetary Mind Field were to establish contact, through the development of human beings, with other Mind Fields in the cosmos" (Wyller 1996: 246).

Are ideas about transcendent consciousness and the Planetary Mind Field important advances in thinking or more eruptions of new-age ideas? Do they forecast the next step in cosmic evolution, or are they needless explanations of nonexistent phenomena? Are they old ideas, such as daimonic realities, appropriated from religion and myth, or is there a solid basis for them in the new physics (Radin 2006)? Whatever else they may or may not be, they reflect a conviction that contemporary science bypasses many important questions and gives inadequate answers to others.

The Great Alien Invasion

Accounts of humans abducted by aliens drew national attention in October 1966 when *Look* magazine published an article on the experiences of Barney and Betty Hill (Matheson 1998; Randle et al. 1999; Jacobs 2000a). Five years earlier, while driving late at night through the repetitious and monotonous forests of Northern New Hampshire, the couple spotted a light in the sky. Repeatedly they stopped their car to get a better look at it. Through binoculars the object looked like the fuselage of an airplane, and colored lights flashed along the rim. It seemed to follow the Hills, and, as it grew closer, it glowed white. As they sped down the road, the mysterious light followed them. When it caught up with them the car vibrated, they heard two electronic beeps, and they became drowsy. The next thing they knew they were several miles down the road. Their watches had stopped, and when they got home they discovered that the trip had taken about two hours longer then usual. What might account for this missing time? Betty noticed some unusual shiny marks on the trunk of the car and began having nightmares. Barney became agitated and refused to discuss the matter. In early 1962 the couple sought the help of Benjamin Simon, a Boston psychiatrist and hypnotist (Fuller 1966).

Initially their reports were garbled and the incident itself had a dream-like quality, but gradually, under hypnosis, the Hills remembered that after the UFO landed six men approached, reassured them, and then escorted them aboard the spacecraft. The abductors were short with gray metallic skin, and had oversized bald heads and little slit noses. On board the UFO Betty and Barney underwent physical examinations that included taking hair samples and inserting needles under their skin. Through telepathic communication Betty tried, in vain, to explain Barney's false teeth while the aliens in turn struggled to describe where they were from. Dr. Simon concluded that the Hills were not telling lies. However, he noted that rather than reporting factual events they were recounting a fantasy that was embellished over time. The Hill case became the subject of John Fuller's *The Interrupted Journey* (1966), and then aired as a television movie a few years later.

The Hill case was followed by other high-profile abduction cases that became the subject of popular books, movies, and TV shows. In 1967, the family of Betty Andreasson Luca, a New England housewife, entered a state of suspended animation (Fowler 1979). Four aliens led by "Quazgaa" then escorted her to their ship where she underwent a medical examination. She was taken to a shrine and shown a huge bird, known as "The One," that was consumed by fire. The ashes were transformed into a large worm, and after she expressed faith in Jesus Christ a voice explained that her faith was the reason that she was chosen. Like many of the people who had met Space Brothers a decade or so earlier, she was told that because of her faith she would be entrusted with information to be shared with humanity. The entire experience was profoundly spiritual for this "born again" Christian, and few other accounts include such vivid religious symbolism (Denzler 2001).

In 1973, Charles Hickson and Calvin Parker, who were fishing on the banks of the Mississippi, reported being abducted by a large UFO (Lorenzen and Lorenzen 1977). Under hypnosis Hickson became terrified. He passed a lie detector test but the results were later disputed. Shortly thereafter, Travis Walton reported that while cutting trees in Arizona he was immobilized by a beam of light (Walton 1978). Then Travis was confronted by large-eyed humanoid beings that eventually lifted him on a table, placed a mask on his face, and rendered him unconscious. Walton returned to civilization five days later. Later, the public learned of five women from Tujunga Canyon, California who had undergone numerous abduction-like experiences over a period of several years (Druffel and Rogo 1980). Their encounters were not as extreme or bizarre as those of some of the earlier abductees, and there was a strong spiritual component.

From the mid 1980s on, a stream of books appeared that presented multiple case histories that bore similarities to the Hill case and to one another. Among the most influential of these were Budd Hopkins's *Missing Time* and *Intruders* (Hopkins 1983, 1987), David Jacobs' *Secret Life* and *The Threat* (Jacobs 1992, 1998), and psychiatrist John Mack's *Abduction* and *Passport to the Cosmos* (Mack 1994, 1999). In 1987, Whitley Strieber launched a series of best-selling books that recounted unusual personal experiences as well as discussed extraterrestrial life and abduction reports in general (1987, 1988). A 1992 survey hinted that as many as 3.7 million Americans had been abducted (Hopkins et al. 1992). A later poll conducted in 1999 by the same sponsor showed that either the rate of abductions decreased in the 1990s, or that these earlier estimates were too high, reflecting, in part, methodological difficulties. Worldwide, most abduction reports come from North and South America, with fewer reports from England and Australia, a handful from Europe and the former Soviet Union, and almost no reports from Asia or Africa (Bynum 1993). Thus, to some extent, alien abductions are culture bound.

Abduction reports share common themes, largely (but not entirely) established by the Hill case (Matheson 1998). These include spotting strange lights or mysterious aircraft in the skies, and contact with humanoids that communicate telepathically. In the early accounts these entities would escort the abductees to the UFO; later (perhaps reflecting *Star Trek* technology) they would "beam" their captives through walls or ceilings to the interior of the craft. There, he or she—usually she—undergoes a sometimes painful and usually humiliating examination that includes inspection of the genitals and perhaps the collection of sperm or ova. Some abductees are shown unpleasant pictures of the future: a desolate and dying planet ravaged by nuclear war or runaway ecological disaster. Some claim that they were taken to a shipboard nursery where they see, or even hold, frail and sickly babies that appear to be human-alien hybrids. After being returned home, abductees may have fragmentary and confused recollections of the event, and, like Barney and Betty Hill, be perplexed by "missing time." Some abductions are followed by strange physical symptoms: a false pregnancy, a tiny cut of unknown origin, a previously unnoticed scar that appears to cover a hole where a small amount flesh was scooped out, evidence suggestive of an "implant" perhaps used by the aliens to keep track of abductees. One recent study shows that when abductees recollect their highly improbable abduction experiences they show strong emotional responses, as if they had in fact been traumatized (McNally et al. 2004).

David Jacobs tells how, in an early workshop on abductions, the participants rapidly devolved into two factions. His group, the realists, took a "hard-edged view of the subject: beings from somewhere else were coming to Earth to fulfill an unknown agenda of which the abduction of humans was central" (2000c: 205). As recounted in his own book *The Threat*, Jacobs warns that aliens are coming to Earth to participate in a breeding program with humans (Jacobs 1998). Like scientists, the realists take a materialistic view of reality, seek standardized interview and reporting techniques, try to disentangle conflicting recollections, and look for evidence to corroborate the validity of the their reports. Perhaps where they differ from most scientists is a certain blindness to the strength of competing interpretations and insufficiently vigorous efforts to disprove their own hypotheses.

Researchers in the second tradition, the positivists, move beyond the consensual scientific view of reality. Positivists—principally the late Harvard psychiatrist John Mack—suspect that other realities or higher dimensions coexist with the materialistic reality of the scientists and pragmatists, and that abduction and other visitor experiences may involve tapping into events in this higher reality (Mack 1994, 1999, 2000). Unconvinced, Jacobs writes, "Astral travel, past lives, future lives, religious experiences, and messages of spiritual enlightenment—all could be part of a 'world' in which the aliens also dwelled. Who was to say, in this new universe, what was reality and what was not?" (2000c: 206). Jacobs complains that occult and metaphysical interpretations are unscientific and detrimental to UFO research and obscure the possible danger that we are being taken over by aliens.

Realists

Realists propose four main types of evidence that Earth is under siege by little gray aliens, but skeptics counter that each type withers under critical analysis. Realists point to: (1) large numbers of cases which suggest that "something" is going on; (2) a lack of psychiatric illnesses, which implies that abduction reports are not based on delusions and hallucinations; (3) high consistency among different reports indicating that the reports must be anchored in factuality; and (4) corroborative evidence in the form of multiple witnesses and physical traces.

Simply because large numbers of people hold the same belief does not mean that they are correct. In fact, millions of people from many different lands and times can and have been wrong. The pre-Copernican view of the heavens, the idea that witches applied supernatural powers to make other people get sick and die, the belief that cigarette smoking offered health benefits, and, more recently, convictions that thousands of babies were abused and even murdered during satanic rituals were all widespread and incorrect.

An apparent lack of psychiatric problems among abductees is a second finding that realists find congenial with their position. Certainly, space aliens may enter into hallucinations or paranoid fantasies, but keep in mind that we cannot explain away abduction reports by attributing all reports to emotional problems. That admitted, it is all but impossible to prove that one particular group does not differ from another, because methodological and procedural shortcomings and sampling vagaries could mask real differences between groups. But the biggest weakness in this argument is that overruling one explanation—psychiatric disturbance—does not prove that another explanation—they're here—is correct.

Third, realists suggest that similarities among different abduction accounts prove their factual basis. As Jacobs explains, "Most accounts independently share an extraordinary critical mass of common details" (2000b: 3). Given the many different types of aliens featured in science fiction, why do the same we find the same kinds of aliens involved in the same repetitive plot?

Essentially all abduction elements appeared in science fiction films before they began to appear in case histories. In a 1908 movie the "man in the Moon" levitated or floated a bride up from Earth. Images of bug-eyed monsters examining women strapped to tables appeared in the 1930s and 1940s and by the 1950s movies included alien implants. Almost daily, it seems, TV viewers are greeted by a new show (and many reruns) depicting UFOs and abductions. Millions of people have seen the archetypical, classic alien face that dominated the cover of Whitley Strieber's book *Communion* (1987). Because of all of this, two decades ago psychologist Robert A. Baker could claim with fairness that the abduction fable is known to every man, woman, and child, every newspaper reader or moviegoer in the nation (Baker 1987). The idea that the alien script is widely known in our culture has been reinforced by Kevin Randle, Russ Estes, and William P. McCone (1999) and by Harvard abduction researcher Susan Clancy (2005).

A literary analysis by Terry Matheson questions the consistency among abduction reports, at least those described in major books (1998). Matheson starts from the position that, like many other works, abduction books are advocacy documents, intended not only to engage the reader's interest but also to convince them of the reality of the phenomena and build support for a cause. To do this, authors bring certain literary devices into play. He points out, for example, that an abduction book typically begins with a strong endorsement by a prestigious scientist or physician, who, by lending his or her name, adds to the credibility of the work. The book's author claims that he or she is a hard-nosed pragmatist, not given to silly beliefs or easily fooled by other people's fantasies. After many years of study the author reluctantly concludes that the story is true and feels he must warn the public.

Abduction writers, Matheson states, avoid the pitfalls of many of the contactees of the 1950s who identified alien visitors as coming from nearby planets including Mars and Venus. Such details make stories too easy to refute. Abductees learn little from their abductors; at least not much can be evaluated scientifically and rejected if untrue. In these books Matheson also sees a forced convergence of detail, so that the different accounts seem to validate one another. Interesting psychological characteristics of individual abductees—such as a history of mystical or psychic experiences—are shoved into the background. Implausible ideas, such as blatantly Christian themes that seem too likely to have originated on Earth, drop out. Thus, there are indeed striking consistencies in the high-profile abduction books that he studied, but these are the product of interviewing procedures and editing rather than consistency across reported experiences. More recently Susan Clancy states that the accounts that she heard from many abductees were similar only in broad strokes, that there was little or no convergence of detail (Clancy 2005).

Finally, realists point to physical evidence that supports their interpretation. This includes corroborative eyewitness testimony, multiple abduction cases, photographic evidence, physical marks on abductees' bodies, and physical traces on the ground. These are the kinds of evidence surveyed and discounted by the Sturrock panel, described in Chapter 4 (Sturrock 1999). Is the corroborating witness reliable or unreliable? Was the scar present before the abduction or only afterwards? Is the implant of extraterrestrial manufacture or something prosaic, such as small shard of glass that was stepped on years ago? Such evidence tends to evaporate under close scrutiny or create even more mystery, dragging investigators ever deeper into the quagmire.

The Positivists

A rather bleak assessment of the realists' position comes from the late positivist psychiatrist John E. Mack (1994, 1999, 2000). In his second abduction book, *Passport to the Cosmos*, Mack wrote that the physical evidence offered in support of the realists' position does not satisfy scientific criteria (1999). Whereas there is enough of this evidence to maintain the support of believers, it is woefully inadequate to convince skeptics. Furthermore, he cites disconfirming evidence, for example, family members watching the "abductee" sleep at the time of the supposed abduction. Even if we ignore the likely effects of the mass media and assume that individual abduction reports are independent and convergent, Mack writes, we cannot take them as evidence of life on other worlds, at least not the physical worlds that are familiar to astronomers, physicists, and biologists.

Mack focused on the nature and meaning of abduction experiences: the thoughts and emotions that the encounter provokes, how they are interpreted within the framework of our present-day culture, and their possible implications for the future of humanity. Compared to the realists, scoping out the nature and implications of the experience are more important than establishing its "reality." For Mack, abduction phenomena reflect culture, human potential, and the evolution of higher levels of consciousness. Real or not, abduction experiences have psychological and cultural meaning.

Attempts to link physics, consciousness, spirituality, and paranormal phenomena make frequent references to energy and light, and both of these are prominent elements in abduction accounts. Mack reports that "extraordinary energies are involved" and a sense of "higher vibratory frequency appears to be directly related to the feeling of a shift of consciousness itself to higher levels" (1999: 63). One person reported that, during the experience, every cell in his body was vibrating. Others reported playful luminescent orbs or lights so bright that they turned night into day. Occasionally abductees feel as if they are glowing, or have been transformed into pure light. There is a sense of acceleration, of moving faster and faster (not unlike an adrenaline rush). Claims that these energies affect nearby electrical appliances dovetail nicely with earlier reports that UFOs interfered with automobile ignition systems and avionics.

Positivists attach significance to reported visions of a devastated Earth. These visions show a dying planet, perhaps wracked by nuclear war, perhaps stripped of natural resources by unmitigated overpopulation, perhaps slowly dying as a result of ozone depletion, rising temperatures, and hopeless pollution. "Carlos," reported Mack, was shown "scene after scene depicting mankind's destructive ways and its impact on the environment," accompanied by the telepathic message that Earth is dying. Carlos learned that "if we can't take care of ourselves and our planet, how can we expect to join the galactic neighborhood?" (Mack 1999: 91).

Certainly some abductees are terrorized by their encounters with mysterious entities that seem able to move people through solid walls, levitate them aboard a spaceship, force a humiliating medical examination upon them, show them pictures of death and destruction, and perhaps impregnate them, then rob them of their children. Yet the positivists point out that some abductees gain profound insights about the nature of the universe and their place within it and overcome fears of their finiteness. This includes a heightened sense of ethics and responsibility to the planet. Some abductees sense that they have encountered something greater than themselves. If abductees run at the forefront of human evolution, the rest of us who lag behind the first wave could not begin to understand them. Rather than a sign of chaos, positivists portray the experience as one of order and progress that, repeated often enough, could transform humanity. It is another step in cosmic evolution.

Can we reconcile the contrasting images of victim and growth as maintained by the realists and positivists, respectively? Only a few abduction researchers have training in psychology, psychiatry, and mental health. Of these, John Mack, with almost fifty years experience as a psychiatrist, was the most prominent. In his work he stresses peoples' potentials rather than their psychological weaknesses and shortcomings. He carefully selected the people with whom he worked—referring some unsuccessful candidates to mental health services if necessary—and, I strongly suspect, ran his research and support groups to move participants in positive directions. The potential to get well and progress to higher levels of existence is within the person. Mack's role was not to provide magical solutions but to facilitate the process of self-exploration. Therapists' expectations are very important. The expectation that someone is a victim who must fight to overcome a deficit is very different from the expectation that someone has had a unique opportunity to grow psychologically. The main difference between victimization and enlightenment may very well depend on the attitudes and techniques of the professionals who work with them.

Psychotherapist Carl Goldberg reminisces that when he began working at Washington D.C.'s Saint Elizabeth Hospital in the late 1960s, mention of a contact with an alien was rewarded with a quick ticket to the psychiatric ward (2000). Generally, both statistical studies and clinical experience suggest that abductees do not fall into standard psychiatric diagnostic categories and that they are free of disorders that are associated with hallucinations (Appelle et al. 2000). Their responses to major tests of mental health generally fall within the normal range. Research shows certain characteristic personality differences between abductees and nonabductees although these differences in no way explain all abduction accounts. Abductees do tend to be suggestible, imaginative, open to unusual experiences, and susceptible to dissociation: a sense that one is absent from one's body, a feeling that whatever is happening, it is not happening to oneself (Appelle et al. 2000). Perhaps tellingly, these personality variables correlate many anomalistic or paranormal experiences, such as out-of-body experiences and ESP (Cardena et al. 2000). More recently "schizotypy" entered the mix (Clancy 2005). Not to be confused with schizophrenia or mental illness, this refers to magical thinking and eccentric beliefs. People who score high on schizotypy do not think the same way as scientists and skeptics. Rational arguments, data, probabilities, and parsimony are overpowered by anecdote and feeling.

Goldberg proposes that illness and health aren't the real issue; rather the issue is how people cope with stress and conflict and find meaning in their lives (2000). He points out that many of Mack's cases had undergone a personal crisis before their abductions. In Goldberg's view, "people who experienced troubled lives and/or a lack of purpose for their existence desperately seek a way to explain their troubles and give meaning to their lives" (2000: 319). For people who have had an unusual experience, perhaps during sleep paralysis, conviction that one has undergone an alien abduction may accomplish this. Results of a recent study of seventy-five women who had "peculiar beliefs" (including about aliens) are compatible with Goldberg's hypothesis (Boden and Berenbaum 2004). With some qualifications, the women considered their beliefs important, because they clarified their understanding of themselves and their place in the world and had an overall positive effect on their lives.

The Skeptics

Skeptics distrust abduction reports and seek explanations based on what we already know about mind and culture. One of the most scathing and incisive critiques of abductions comes from Kevin Randle, Russ Estes, and William P. McCone who argue that many abduction reports are, in effect, fictitious memories that are manufactured by misguided investigators and therapists who feel an intense need to "do something" to control their own anxiety (1999).

Many people who believe that they were abducted have inferred this and have no recollection of the actual event (Clancy 2005). Or, as in the case of Barney and Betty Hill, recollections are fragmentary, vague, and have dream-like qualities. The terrifying episode is repressed—that is, shoved out of awareness and locked up in the realm of the unconscious. On occasion there may be leaks—a special feeling at a certain location, a sense of resonance with a magazine article or television show, recurrent elements in dreams.

Eventually, as a result of personal volition—or in response someone else's urgings—the person seeks a therapist. Through inexpert questioning, therapists can, in effect, "plant" false memories in people. Later these memories are indistinguishable from real memories. Hypnosis is not necessary for false memories to form, but some of the richest material is brought forth under hypnosis. The controversy over the use of hypnosis as an investigative tool is detailed and complicated but much of it boils down to whether or not the investigator leads the witness (Baker 1987, 1997; Hopkins 2000). Hypnotic procedures frequently elicit inaccurate reports and amplify the effects of suggestion. As an investigative tool, hypnosis is not likely to increase accuracy of what people remember, but it is likely to increase the subject's confidence in the validity of her report (Schachter 2001). Whereas abduction researchers deny that they "lead" their subjects, skeptics remain that these researchers play a powerful role in shaping their subjects' responses (Randle et al. 1999).

A potent demonstration of the fallibility of human memory is found in historian Timothy Ryback's *The Last Survivor* (1999). Mingled throughout his discussion of the Dachau concentration camp is Ryback's quest to understand the life of Martin Zaidenstadt, who claimed to have been incarcerated there during parts of World War II. Zaidenstadt recalls witnessing the gassing of thousands of victims. This particular style of genocide didn't happen at the Dachau concentration camp, but none of the current residents of the town of Dachau choose to correct Zaidenstadt as he portrays these ghastly events to horrified tourists.

Zaidenstadt, a Polish Jew, was indeed a victim of the Nazis. A member of a valorous regiment that held out against the Wehrmacht, his wife and daughter presumably died in a packed synagogue that was deliberately set on fire. But Zaidenstadt's memories of Dachau do not square with the facts. Ryback unraveled the mystery when he realized that our memories reflect a combination of personal experiences, our friends' experiences, and material that we have read about and seen on TV. As far as we ourselves are concerned, all of our memories are factual and it is hard to convince us otherwise, even in the face of inconsistent facts. Contrary to Zaidenstadt's claim that Dachau was an extermination camp like Auschwitz-Birkenau (where millions of people were systematically gassed) and despite his recollection of shrieking victims crammed into Dachau's small death chamber, the chamber was constructed late in World War II, and was never used. Ryback found other false victims of concentration camps, including some who remember incarceration even though they were born after the camps were closed following the Allied victory in 1945.

It takes very little, notes Daniel Schachter, for spurious memories to form and take hold (Schachter 2001). In one study, Dutch psychologists asked people if they had seen a television film of an airplane crashing into a building in Amsterdam (Crombag et al. 1996). More than half of the respondents said that they had seen the airplane strike the building even though there was no such film (the crash was real enough). During a follow-up interview, the number of people who remembered the film rose to two-thirds and many of these could "recall" details. Other research cited by Schachter found that as a result of nonhypnotic suggestion, people recalled fictitious episodes such as overturning a wedding cake, getting lost in a shopping mall, or being attacked by an animal. The implication for us is that the mere suggestion that a person has been abducted can set in motion a chain of events such that the person concludes that the abduction actually occurred. Recent laboratory research shows that in comparison to people who have not reported an abduction experience, those who believe that they were abducted were more likely to "recall" and "recognize" words that had not been shown to them before (Clancy et al. 2002).

Therapists' expectations and support groups mold and reinforce people's beliefs that they have been abducted. Randle and associates suspect that many researchers investigate abduction accounts in such a way as to make them consistent with the investigator's preconceptions and biases (1999). Although nobody ever admits to leading their witnesses, analysis of filmed and taped interviews and hypnotic regressions shows that this does occur. The researcher or therapist responds favorably when the subject or patient utters something that is consistent with his or her pet theory, and remains quiet or responds negatively when the subject says something that the researcher doesn't want to hear.

Most likely the researcher and the subject have certain expectations regarding the course of the sessions and each plays a part in bringing the expected results about. For example, the investigator may ask the subject if he or she remembers anything about a bright light in the sky, being transported through walls or ceilings, seeing small humanoid creatures, undergoing a gynecological exam, and so forth. Slowly, or perhaps not so slowly, this interaction stimulates recollections that conform to the research hypotheses. The subject, who may have had no clear ideas about what happened along the lonely stretch of road or during a mysterious dream slowly develops a picture of what "really happened" that is validated by the therapist or researcher.

Finally, their beliefs become even more firmly entrenched if the person joins a support group (Randle et al. 1999). Historically the idea behind a psychotherapeutic support group is to bring together people who discover that they are not alone in their problems and personal suffering. Under the guidance of a skilled therapist, participants learn about each other and in the process learn about themselves. As this occurs, perhaps in conjunction with individualized therapy, they build strength. The goal of a standard psychotherapy group, then, that deals with real and identifiable issues—bereavement, impending divorce, loss of employment, illness—is to help people work through issues, speed them on the path to recovery, and get them out of therapy and on with their lives. The function of support groups for people whose problems lack independent verification is to validate and bolster the idea that they are victims. The stars of the group are not those who are making the best progress towards readjustment but those who claim to have been abducted the most times and who are subjected to the most outrageous violations. Some abductees who were initially shy and prefer anonymity eventually appear at conventions and give media interviews. Rather than dismissing them as publicity hounds, perhaps we should think of them as seeking other people's agreement to bolster their confidence in their own imperfect memories.

—Seven—

TRICKSTERS

Within a month of Kenneth Arnold's June 1947 sighting of UFOs, Fred Crisman and his accomplice Harold Dahl sent *Amazing Tales* editor Ray Palmer fragments of material that "might" have been shed by a flying saucer. Palmer, who realized that UFOs were a goldmine for his magazine, offered Arnold $200 (a significant sum of money in those days) to fly to Crisman and Dahl's home city of Tacoma, Washington and investigate the matter. On his way, Arnold experienced two unnerving events—he sighted more UFOs (twenty-five brassy objects that looked like ducks) and discovered when he arrived in Tacoma that some unknown person had made a hotel reservation in his name. These two events, explains UFO historian Jerome Clark, convinced Arnold that "dark forces were shadowing him and common sense would desert this ordinarily commonsensical man" (Clark 2003: 43).

Crisman and Dahl claimed that they were harbor patrolmen who had encountered six doughnut-shaped objects at Maury Island, three miles off the Tacoma coast. They stated that five of the craft hovered around the sixth, which was losing altitude and descended to about five hundred feet above their workboat. Substances resembling lava and white metal rained down on the boat, breaking one worker's arm and also killing his dog. Dahl maintained that he had taken some snapshots during the incident. Later, Dahl said, he was approached by a mysterious man in a dark suit who warned him not to discuss the matter.

The mysterious substance was actually slag from a local smelter. When Arnold was shown samples of the material he recognized that it was nothing special. Still, his most recent UFO sightings, the unexpected hotel reservation, and new UFO reports (including another UFO that dripped an ash-like substance) that appeared in the newspaper were a source of concern. So, Arnold continued to believe that

Crisman and Dahl's fabrication was at least somewhat true, even when Dahl explained that he had given the undeveloped film to Crisman who in turn swore that he had lost it. Arnold suggested that military intelligence should be brought into the investigation and soon two Air Force officers flew up from California to investigate. They rapidly concluded that the Maury Island story was a hoax, then in a bizarre twist perished when their airplane crashed on its way back to California.

Years later, a reporter who was working on the story interviewed Dahl on the latter's back porch. An enraged Mrs. Dahl flew out the back door and ran towards them, brandishing a knife. The reporter was relieved when she brought the point up to her husband's nose. "I am tired of being embarrassed by your lies" she shouted, "Tell this man the truth" (Clark 2003: 47). At that point, Dahl confessed the hoax.

George P. Hansen points out that all of the areas that touch upon the paranormal, including UFOlogy, are tainted by suspicion, confusion, controversy, secrets, and lies (Hansen 2001). Such phenomena are characterized by instability, ambiguity, uncertainty, and transience. This lack of structure and order opens the way for "the trickster," whose activities are tinged by treachery and deceit. Tricksters have been with us since antiquity and share several notable qualities, including disrespect for the establishment, a penchant for disruption, and an affinity for deception. Tricksters come in unending variety ranging from primitive buffoons to deceitful gods. They love to work at the margins of inquiry where the lines between reality and fantasy are unclear, at the intersection of science and religion, at the fringe of science, during periods of cultural upheaval, and on the cusp of paradigm shifts. Their deceptions may result from delusions, incomplete knowledge, flawed assessments and faulty decisions, or deficient communications skills. Or, they may be willful, deliberate, and intentional.

Tricksters, continues Hansen, annoy authorities, muddy the water, throw serious investigators off track and, when they are unmasked, create turmoil and anger. They discredit the areas that they work in and may leave an indelible taint, but often evade the harsh condemnation that they have earned. Although specific individuals may repeatedly act as tricksters, it is more appropriate to think of the trickster as an element within everyone's personality that surfaces from time to time. Who among us has never lied or played a practical joke?

UFOlogists are certainly aware of deceit, but Hansen argues that most do not take the risk of treachery seriously enough. In UFOlogy the status of operatives is unclear, fact and fiction are mixed, and deception and conspiracy thinking abound. Hansen adds that UFOlogy's "entire history is permeated with fraud and con artists, and it makes the physical mediumship of nineteenth-century Spiritualism pale by comparison" (2001: 249). As a researcher in parapsychology Hansen reports that he has never encountered an area where it is so difficult to obtain reliable information as in UFOlogy. Colin Bennett comments that, thanks to such shenanigans, the picture of reality that emerges in UFO discussions is shot through with more holes than a Swiss cheese (Bennett 2001).

Why do people listen to half truths and even accept lies? Tricksters play into people's sense of the possible: while the story seems preposterous, just maybe there is an element of truth. The trickster helps us maintain pet views even in the absence of supporting evidence: the reason that the UFOs are so elusive is because conclusive evidence is kept hidden from us. Furthermore, outrageous false claims may make more modest fictions seem believable. All of the conditions that Hansen identifies as conducive to prevarications and dirty tricks—working at the fringe of science, the intersection of science and religion, the eve of a paradigm shift—are prominent in our era of burgeoning knowledge.

Tricksters will flourish in any area that rests 20 percent on evidence and 80 percent on personal belief. One of the greatest accomplishments of science is agreed-upon procedures and reference points (methods and data) that allow us to gauge the accuracy of a claim. Tricksters do appear in science, but scientists have effective tools for culling tricksters from their ranks. For this reason, SETI has an edge on UFOlogy. From time to time someone reports that a radiotelescope has intercepted an extraterrestrial signal. Astronomers who train their telescopes in the direction of these purported broadcasts rapidly debunk such false assertions.

Hoaxes

Hoaxers, like Crisman and Dahl, may deceive other people for notoriety and personal gain, to demonstrate a sense of superiority over the gullible fools who believe them, or maybe just for fun. In the seventeenth century one of the greatest scientists of all time, Sir Isaac Newton, alarmed his neighbors by launching a hot air UFO made of wax paper and candles (Shlain 1998). In the closing years of the nineteenth century, people made up stories about huge airships that flew around North America, shining bright spotlights on the terrain below (Vallee 1993). Occasionally they landed, and their occupants looked and acted a bit peculiar. An informal "liar's club" in Texas claimed that one of these airships had crashed. Nobody can be sure of the origin of all of the mysterious objects and lights that were sighted just before real airships were invented, but in later accounts the tricksters' handiwork is clear. A good hoax is difficult to disprove and therefore feeds confusion for years. Although the weight of evidence mounts against the hoax, there remains some element of doubt, which leaves latitude for bitter argument. A person retracts an amazing claim. But exactly when did the person lie: in making the initial claim, or later, during the retraction? Someone takes convincing up-close photographs of UFOs. Later, models that resemble these UFOs are found in the man's garage or barn. Does this mean that he faked the pictures, or that someone else placed the models there in order to discredit him? A person is caught in a lie, confesses, and then offers an even more outrageous story that he claims is the "real" truth, an even more stunning revelation that somehow regains the audience's confidence. What can we make of such situations? How do we identify the truth? Is it worth trying?

In *Passport to Magonia*, Jacques Vallee describes how visitors themselves sometimes act in trickster-like ways (1993). In his view human interaction with UFO crews and other mysterious entities takes on the qualities of a theater of the absurd. These unusual strangers often act in improbable, silly ways, speak in riddles and conundrums, give misleading statements, make false promises, and in general treat people as suckers. *Magonia* develops Vallee's theme that visitors from outer space bear a certain resemblance to the "little people" of myth and folklore: trolls, hobgoblins, leprechauns, fairies, genies, gnomes, and imps. Because of this resemblance, the extraterrestrials that people claim to encounter may be part of broader, ongoing phenomena, rather than hailing from outer space.

The idea that certain themes remain stable in myths while their manifest content varies across time and culture is appealing. In essence, yesterday's demons and fairies appear to us as today's UFOnauts. In olden times, people were thought to have had sex with demons; now the claim is that alien abductors artificially inseminate women. Flying objects themselves have made the transition from dirigible-like airships in 1897 through nuts and bolts craft in the 1950s and 1960s to the varied craft that people report today. However, there are some invariants: the little people, the airship captains and the iconic grays are mysterious and somehow superior to us. Vallee writes, "the entities' reported behavior is consistently absurd and the appearance of their craft is ludicrous. In numerous instances of verbal communication with them their assertions have been systematically misleading ... This absurd behavior had the effect of keeping professional scientists away from the areas where that activity was taking place" (1993: 161).

Scientists, like everyone else, have certain ideas about how "real" aliens would act, notes astronomer David Grinspoon, and get "huffy" when imagined rules are violated (Grinspoon 2003). Real aliens would not travel interstellar distances, lie to people, speak in riddles, play practical tricks, abduct people from their cars and homes, and collect sperm and ova. Yet, we are profoundly ignorant of what a real alien might be like. Grinspoon does not argue that real aliens—if they exist—would do such things, only that they are not obligated to act in ways that make sense to us. From the human perspective, a radically different culture may appear to be fraught with absurdities. What would our ancestors of two centuries ago make of someone playing a handheld game of Tetris while sitting on a flush toilet? Or what might someone from Alpha Centauri think when they notice that Earthlings pull down the "start" menu to shut off their computers?

Prophets

Prophets entered into UFOlogy very early on and this had the effect of throwing the spotlight on people who "believed in" UFOs rather than on the UFOs themselves (Dean 1998; Denzler 2001). Typically, UFO prophets see humanity as rapidly approaching a crossroads and that they must take drastic action to prevent a cataclysmic millennial event. They and their followers must warn the world, or take specific steps to save themselves. The scientifically and morally superior beings that control UFOs will then come to the rescue, perhaps by descending to Earth to evacuate the faithful, or perhaps by using their vast powers to force some other favorable resolution.

Susan Palmer provides an insightful analysis of the Raellians, a group concerned about nuclear Armageddon and other social ills (2004). Raellians believe that in 2035 a vast armada of flying saucers will bring the "Elohim" to Earth, ushering in a new age of science, wisdom, and peace. Their prophet, Rael, was told this by occupants of a flying saucer that was marked with a swastika inscribed within a Star of David. Rael has been in mental contact with the Elohim for decades and his missions are to spread the word and construct an embassy to welcome them. At one point the preferred site for the embassy was Israel, but the saucer's emblem made the embassy a hard sell.

It is too early to tell for sure about the Raellians but past prophecies of this type have failed. Prophets have a good bag of tricks to evade or at least postpone disconfirmation (Palmer 2004). Prophets can be vague or imprecise with respect to timing. The drawback here is that promoting a sense that the event is imminent may be necessary to sustain the group's interest and morale. Another strategy, useful as the designated hour draws nigh, is to find some reason that the occurrence has been delayed or even put off entirely. Perhaps the fervent efforts of the faithful have assuaged the wrath of God. Then again, the prophet can complain that the prophecy has been fulfilled, but in an unanticipated way, for example, by transpiring on a spiritual rather than physical plane. James R. Lewis concludes that if a particular worldview and lifestyle are maintained by ongoing conversations within a group, and that group continues to address the concerns of its members, then the leader's hypocrisy, failed prophecies and other potential wake-up calls are unlikely to diminish faith (J. R. Lewis 2003).

Many people who are drawn to such movements look like the varied group of college students who show up at class, rather than like kooks and zombies (Balch 1995). Palmer describes the Raellians in predominantly favorable terms: young, attractive, educated, largely successful, and fun loving (2004). They are dedicated to improving society, and, apart from occasional run-ins with the Catholic Church (for example, when passing out birth control literature at Catholic schools), tolerant of others. People may be drawn to such groups because they believe that their philosophy will help them grapple with troublesome questions about human existence. Once they join, social influence processes nudge their beliefs ever closer to those of the prophet. In some, not all cases, the group may exert increasing amounts of control over its members although it may be extreme to refer to this as brainwashing.

The press tends to treat cults harshly. UFO groups can be somewhat secretive (the Raellians are a notable exception) so that the press relies on cult-bashing organizations for information. For the most part such groups are harmless, and it is difficult to find adverse consequences (Aronoff et al. 2000). Members may realize many of the satisfactions that are associated with mainstream religions and gain a new sense of identity. Some black Americans found comfort in the United Nuwabian Nation of Moors, a movement that reflects the black cultic milieu of Harlem and mixes occultism, Christianity, Judaism, and Islam. According to its founder, writes Theodore Gabriel, the movement creates new identities based on a mix of extinct cultures (such as ancient Egypt) and extraterrestrial mythologies (2003). This helps eradicate a sense of oppression and boosts self-esteem.

But in some cases, such as Heaven's Gate, the consequences can be disastrous (Balch 1995; Steiger and Hewes 1997; J.R. Lewis 2003).

Since the 1970s, Marshall Herff Applewhite and Bonnie Lu Nettles, known at various points as "Bo" and "Peep," "Do" and "Ti," and "The Two," had been espousing strange mixtures of UFOs and religion. Applewhite, for example, had mystical interests, and at one point he was debriefed on the nature of the universe by a being of light, and concluded early on that UFOs were transportation to heaven. At one point "The Two" propounded "Human Individual Metamorphosis" that would allow believers to proceed to a higher evolutionary level. The faithful would be taken to the "Kingdom of God" aboard a cloud of light that we would call a UFO. There they would be able to change their "vibration rate" and appear and disappear at will. The world was coming to an end. Because people had failed to evolve properly, humanity was about to be recycled or, in more graphic terms, "spaded-under" (Balch 1995). Through faith and taking appropriate action, Heaven's Gate members could "graduate to the next level," a process that is equivalent to resurrection.

The size and wealth of their group fluctuated from year to year but by 1997 Nettles had died and Applewhite was leading a small but thriving group in San Diego. At that point fortune was, in a sense, smiling upon the group because members were gainfully employed (designing Web pages) and they were well fed, clothed, and housed. This was a far cry from the early days when Applewhite and his followers lived under the stars and rummaged in garbage cans for food. Still, Applewhite was lonely without Nettles, and worried about the future of his flock. More and more, suicide—followed, of course, by resurrection in a higher kingdom—seemed like the best option to him. Early that year, Applewhite concluded that the UFO to transport them to the next Kingdom would follow the then-approaching Hale-Bopp comet. After careful preparations (including a last supper of chicken pot pies) thirty-nine members of Heaven's Gate—including Applewhite—willingly took poison and died. They were found nicely dressed and with their possessions packed to accompany them to the great beyond.

Even more horrific but less well known is the apocalyptic mass suicide of the Solar Temple. In 1994, fifty-two members of this group living in Canada and Switzerland committed suicide simultaneously to bring about transit to the star Sirius. Within another year twenty-one more members died, including fifteen who committed suicide during the spring equinox of 1995 (Dein and Littlewood 2005).

Evil Empire

Although we hope for a world united in peace we still live in a world of intrigue and danger. For self-protection we maintain military and intelligence organizations whose work sometimes requires clandestine activity. In intelligence and police work, secrecy protects key sources of information, minimizes embarrassment for the unjustly accused, and reduces undue alarm. Secrecy also cloaks conspiracies, including coordinated undercover efforts on the part of some people who seek advantage at the expense of others. And, it promotes beliefs in real and imagined conspiracies. Michael Barkun identifies three characteristics of conspiracy theories: nothing happens by accident, nothing is as it seems, and everything is connected (2003).

Daniel Pipes traces conspiracy theories back to the time of the Crusades and shows that such theories have always played a role in American politics, including the colonists' decision to break away from England in the eighteenth century (Pipes 1997). Historically and globally, the "villains" in such thinking have been Jews, Freemasons, and the British. Since World War II the United States has gained prominence, taking over for the British. Halfway through the twentieth century, Americans' trust in its own government began to decline, so that by 1994 less than 20 percent of the respondents to a Gallup poll trusted the U.S. government to do what was right (Harrison and Thomas 1997). It was no longer unthinkable that government or its institutions could act in ways that were contrary to the common good. Can we expect much improvement in an era where illusory weapons of mass destruction provide justification for military action?

These days, very few people seem startled by allegations of government duplicity or cover-up. A quick Google check on the Web for the phrase "government cover-up" on November 2006 yielded 148,000 hits (up from 120,000 in October 2005). Aspartame, the downing of TWA Flight 800, AIDS, tobacco, asbestos, air pollution, medical malpractice, and germ warfare are just a few of the areas in addition to long-standing accusations concerning the John F. Kennedy assassination and UFOs. Pervasiveness of beliefs that the government is not telling all that it knows about UFOs is revealed in an April 1999 Roper Poll commissioned by the National Institute for Discovery Science. When asked how they thought the U.S. Government would react to the discovery of extraterrestrial life, more than two-thirds of the respondents thought that the government would suppress the information. This included 48 percent who believed that the government would "classify the information and not allow it to be released to the public," and 23 percent who believed that the government would "classify all aspects and move to suppress civilian sources from obtaining or disseminating information about the topic." These reactions were not limited to the uneducated, poor, and disenfranchised. Suspiciousness was higher among respondents that the Roper organization defines as "influential" with 51 percent and 29 percent (a total of 80 percent) endorsing the two "cover-up" options. Only 9 percent of all respondents believed that the government would immediately apprise the public of its findings.

Harold Relyea describes how the U.S. government's proclivity to classify information has varied over the years (2003). Since World War II, some presidential administrations including that of Harry Truman (1945–1952) and Ronald Reagan (1980–1988) have moved towards increased secrecy, while other administrations including those of Dwight Eisenhower (1952–1960), Richard Nixon (1968–1974), and Bill Clinton (1992–2000) favored a more relaxed approach. During the George W. Bush administration, in part in response to terrorist attacks, the pendulum swung back in the direction of increased secrecy. Today in the United States more information is classified and less is released in response to Freedom of Information Act inquiries. Government Web sites have been cleared of information that might somehow benefit terrorists.

In a democracy, Relyea insists, officials may temporarily impose secrecy for the good of the nation. However, officials must remember that the secrecy they impose is only momentary and that the shrouded decisions and policies that they make, once revealed to the citizenry, must be acceptable to them. The public accepts such secrecy only on a limited and temporary basis because they want to know that their representatives are making decisions and policies that are for the public good. A government failing to honor these arrangements, we have been warned, may well be one "not worth the cost of preservation" (Relyea 2003: 412).

Government files in the United States, United Kingdom, Russia, and many other countries certainly do contain secret (and formerly secret) material, but keep in mind that intelligence work requires collecting information about anything that might affect national security. Official UFO reports go back at least as far as 1915 when the British Admiralty investigated reports of floating balls of light, then classified their findings (Redfern and Roberts 2003). Government files also contain information on sea monsters, spontaneous combustion, Noah's Ark, crop circles, and cattle mutilations.

UFOs and the Cold War

To understand the government's interest in UFOs we have to turn the clock back to 1947, when the United States was easing into the first years of the Cold War and UFOs gained national prominence (Peebles 1994; Hoyt 2000; Jacobs 2000a, 2000b, 2000c; Swords 2000). At that time there had already been sightings of "foo fighters," mysterious spheres of light that accompanied allied airplanes during bombing runs over Europe, and unidentified "ghost rockets" that had flown over Sweden. Scientists and military experts of that day could envision military satellites circling the globe and intercontinental ballistic missiles bearing atomic warheads. An iron curtain separated Soviet bloc and Western nations, and the United States and her allies were understandably concerned about the Russian military.

While there was a good chance that UFOs were harmless—rarely encountered natural phenomena, misidentified weather balloons, our own top-secret airplanes and rockets—it was unsettling that many of the reports came from highly qualified observers, including Air Force pilots, and that UFOs were attracted to military installations. Some members of the military foresaw the necessary technology to develop workable flying saucers even though the United States had not achieved this. UFOs just might be Soviet secret weapons, perhaps developed by captured Nazi scientists. Skies filled with strange lights could make it difficult to discern a Soviet attack. Thousands of panicked citizens swamping the telephone lines could frustrate officials' efforts to respond effectively to any true emergency. "During the Cold War," writes Michael Swords, "what perhaps should have been an idealistic venture into scientific research and discovery became possible evidence of danger. Strange phenomena in the skies were wonders to the naïve, but were portents of threat to the armed service personnel who grimly watched over a world of building tensions. UFOs were *never* viewed benignly by those who first began studying them, nor for those who set policies for handling evidence about the UFOs... This attitude had a powerfully distorting impact on UFO research that lasted through the twentieth century... (2000: 82-83). A secretive phenomena, he adds, was coupled with "a secretive human activity (military intelligence) at a time of maximum concern and confusion."

The government was faced with two problems—establishing the level of threat posed by UFOs and calming an anxious public. To some extent the strategies required to address the two problems were incompatible. Assessing the level of threat required careful scientific investigation. Reassuring the public required suppressing potentially alarming news and telling everyone that that there was nothing to worry about. It also meant controlling people who might spread alarm, if not by dropping their strangled bodies in the desert, then at least through strict admonition and robbing them of their credibility.

Several governmental agencies were involved in studying UFOs, but the primary responsibility went to the Air Force. The twin assignments led to some interesting paradoxes that could only fan suspicions of government chicanery. From the very beginning, writes Diana Hoyt, the Air Force would "publicly debunk and treat the matter lightly, and privately investigate, and take the matter seriously" (2000: 12). When, during Project Twinkle, the Air Force was secretly setting up cameras to conduct photographic surveillance of a UFO hotspot, they were dismissing UFOs as airplanes, weather balloons, meteorological phenomena, and other natural events (Moseley and Pflock 2002).

Between 1947 and 1969, three major Air Force projects—Sign, Grudge, and Blue Book—researched UFOs and their impact on the public. According to Hoyt, each project was formed in response to a wave of UFO sightings. Each involved serious attempts to understand UFOs, each was intended to "settle the matter" in the eyes of the public, and each was viewed with ambivalence by high-level Air Force officers (Hoyt 2000).

Project Sign, initiated in the closing days of 1947 at Wright Patterson Air Force Base, recruited a highly talented group of officers and engineers who had divergent opinions about UFOs. One camp thought that UFOs were top-secret aircraft; another thought that they might be extraterrestrial spacecraft and a third group thought that the public was suffering from mass hysteria. Project Sign explored about two hundred cases, and whereas most were "resolved" some remained perplexing. At one point, project personnel prepared an "estimate of the situation" which stressed the extraterrestrial hypothesis. General Hoyt S. Vandenberg rejected the assessment on the grounds that it was not supported by sufficient evidence and ordered the report destroyed.

In February 1949 Project Sign was classified as and became known as Project Grudge. While standard military intelligence procedures were to be used, everything was evaluated from the perspective that UFOs do not exist. The goals were to explain away UFO sightings, a tactic that never deflated public interest but certainly did discourage scientists. This was achieved by suppressing disturbing evidence, ridiculing the very idea of UFOs, and discrediting UFO observers. "Official explanations for UFO sightings" notes Jodi Dean, "focused on witnesses' unreliability, either on their moral failings (dishonest and drunk) or on their failures of judgment (lapses in sanity or perceptual skills)" (1998: 39).

In March 1952, following yet another wave of sightings, Project Grudge was upgraded and renamed Project Bluebook. This remained in force for seventeen years. Captain Edward Ruppelt, who was chief of Project Blue Book from 1951 to 1953, estimated that during his time the Air Force received reports on only 10 percent of the UFOs sighted in the United States. He was dissatisfied with the Air Force's negative approach that emphasized discrediting witnesses and falsely writing off cases that had yet to be solved. Ruppelt in fact solved many mysterious cases but remained curious about the 20 percent or so of unsolved cases that remained in Blue Book files (Ruppelt 1956).

By the 1960s when the Air Force sought to divest itself of the UFO business, there was another surge of sightings, again increasing pressure on the government (Hoyt 2000). The Air Force's solution was to send the problem elsewhere. At first they tried to transfer responsibility for UFOs to other governmental agencies and private research centers, including NASA and the Brookings Institution. None of these organizations would get entangled with UFOs since by that time the mere mention of them was stigmatizing (Denzler 2001).

Eventually, the University of Colorado accepted a large grant for taking on the responsibility (Hoyt 2000). The principal investigator was a reluctant Professor Edward U. Condon, a fearless defender of science with a sparkling record of accomplishment. Both the University and Condon were well aware of the political and public relations nightmare that they had embraced. They accepted the project more to perform a public service than to answer a scientific question. The specific question that the Condon Commission studied was whether or not continuing research on UFOs would be of scientific value.

As reported by Roy Craig, an investigator on the project, the 1969 report concluded that nothing of scientific value had come from governmental investigations and that further studies were unlikely to extend scientific knowledge (1995). The report went on to recommend (tongue in cheek, I suspect) that granting agencies should approach the topic in an open-minded fashion and evaluate research proposals fairly, on an unprejudiced basis.

The efforts that led to the Condon Commission Report, as well as the report itself, have now undergone years of scrutiny, and the problems are legion (Sturrock 1999; Hoyt 2000). Many of the key people whose names were prominently associated with the project played a minimal role. Among the staff, there was dissension between those who maintained that a serious study should be undertaken and those who thought that since UFOs were so much bunk the study could be superficial. By the time the research was concluded, twelve of fifteen top staff members disagreed with Condon and he fired the two who disagreed with him most vocally. Former project members spoke out against the project and the university and some went so far as to issue a counter-report. Critics complained that bias permeated the study. And the report itself was disjointed and grotesquely bloated. The summary and conclusions did not seem to follow from the research. The overall impression was that one group did the work and another group did the writing.

The Condon Commission Report, then, did not provide any new fundamental insights to ameliorate the UFO controversy. It did disengage the Air Force from UFO research, and discouraged lingering interest on the part of scientists. Despite its flaws it was rapidly validated by the National Academy of Sciences. A subsequent subcommittee of the American Institute of Aeronautics and Astronautics questioned the report to no avail, and Peter Sturrock found that it was impossible to publish his critique of the report in a scientific journal (1999). Not one of the six editors that received his submission sent his article out for peer review.

Commission investigator Craig points out that people were less interested in studying the scientific value of UFOs than in discovering their real nature (Craig, 1995). In his view, people were looking for confirmation of their beliefs, which were based mostly on desire. They wanted proof that we are being visited by beings from another world. He also felt that "unnecessary Air Force secrecy from 1947 to 1968 regarding UFO matters played a significant role in the distrust of American people in their own defense establishment" (xiii).

Quite possibly it was never in the Air Force's interest to explain away all UFO sightings. Once fears of mass hysteria receded, a "UFO sighting" became a convenient excuse for sightings of spy planes, clandestine rocket launches, and top-secret satellites plummeting to fiery deaths. Many formerly unexplained UFO sightings in the United States and Russia coincide with satellite reentries and other classified events. Thus, in addition to wondering about the nature of UFOs and trying to calm the public, the government took advantage of interest in UFOs to camouflage its own secret activities.

Crash Retrievals

Certainly the most startling claims are that the U.S. government has crashed UFOs and alien bodies in its possession, or has even signed a secret treaty with creatures from outer space. One hears claims of mysterious underground bases, off-limits hangars at U.S. Air Force Bases, and of Nevada's mysterious Area 51. All of this would be highly classified, but is revealed through rumors and people who come forward and break their security oaths to warn the public of government treachery and impending danger.

Attempts to uncover a conspiracy are time consuming, frustrating, and fraught with error. Most likely, information about extraterrestrial visitors would be compartmentalized as well as classified, so that even people with high-level security clearances would see only a tiny piece of the picture. We might expect the government to sow disinformation as well as to harass, intimidate, and threaten people who get out of line. Disinformation could be based on mixing truth and falsehood, and "bait and switch" tactics that promise researchers and media interviewers interesting documents and films but then deliver worthless materials. People who leak information would be ignored or derided—throwing them in prison for violating their security oaths would only verify their claims of access to secret information. When we factor in such possibilities as mind control experiments, paranoid thinking, honest mistakes, people who are in it for the money, and reporters looking for sensational stories, sifting fact from fiction becomes all but impossible.

Astronomer David Grinspoon was part of a large, diverse, and enthusiastic audience that attended one of many rallies intended to force the government to come clean about UFOs (2003). He found the principal speaker attractive and likeable and heard him give articulate, moving descriptions of extraterrestrial involvement in human affairs and government cover-up. Whereas initially governments were forced to suppress information about extraterrestrial life to prevent panic, the speaker said, this is no longer necessary today when people are already used to the idea of extraterrestrials. However, governments are interested in building their power, willing to prosper at the expense of the people and engage in cover-up to maintain the economic status quo. The few benefit over the many. And bungled human-extraterrestrial relations put us on the brink of an alien invasion.

Such rallies include a parade of witnesses who profess high credentials and are willing to reveal top secrets. Some of these witnesses claim to have access to information denied to the Director of the CIA and even the President of the United States. The strategy seems to be that if enough people reveal small parts of the overall picture and reinforce one another's claims, audiences will conclude that they are learning the truth. But some of the anecdotes raise credibility issues. Grinspoon found that his open-mindedness crumbled when a former Air Force sergeant claimed that someone had beat us to the Moon and built structures on the back side. "I know the Moon," reflected Grinspoon, "Assuming the soundness of my basic frame of reality, which I do assume, the giant structures on the Moon are not there" (2003: 365). Another credibility issue arises from the wholesale violation of security oaths. Professionals who sign security oaths are not the same as children playing games, drunks participating in a bull session, or movie actors—they consider themselves morally as well as legally obligated to abide by them. Background investigations, lie detector tests, and interrogations must be useless indeed if people who are given such important information feel free to discuss it on stage.

Claims that the government had in its possession a crashed UFO surfaced very early in the history of UFOs. In his 1950 book *Behind the Flying Saucers*, Frank Scully announced that crashed flying saucers were found on 12 October 1949, by coincidence the anniversary of Columbus's arrival in America (1950). Scully said that through an oil millionaire he met a mysterious "Dr. Gee," an engineer who had accompanied seven other scientists to New Mexico to examine a trio of crashed saucers. For several days they studied the first saucer and through the portholes they saw a crew of sixteen tiny humanoids dressed in blue jumpsuits. The crew was free of dental cavities, and had a radio about the size of a pack of cigarettes that contained no tubes or wires. They also inspected a second large saucer that also carried a crew of 16, and a much smaller third saucer that carried only two crew members. An Air Force UFO investigator who later spoke with Scully got "the definite impression he doesn't believe his own material, but is getting a big kick out of the public's belief in it" (Moseley and Pflock 2002: 82).

By far the most widely publicized crash occurred in Roswell, New Mexico in 1947. Following an initial inspection of materials found at the crash site in the desert the Army Air Force issued a press release indicating that they had recovered a crashed UFO. Pictures were taken showing high-ranking military officers inspecting the wreckage, which was strewn about an office floor. Soon, the press release was retracted, and the Air Force indicated that all that they had found was the remnants of a weather balloon. The episode receded from sight until Charles

Berlitz and William Moore published their book *The Roswell Incident* many years later (1980). Interviews of people in Roswell who had to think back decades implied that perhaps a real UFO did crash in the desert, and that the government's denying that all that had been found there was a weather balloon was simply a convenient cover story.

Other books followed, some pointing to the conclusion that a UFO had crashed, others suggesting that this was nonsense. A review of this voluminous literature is far beyond the scope of the present work, but suffice it to say that the elements of ambiguity and uncertainty, and blurred the lines between fact and fiction, provided a fertile ground for error, deception, and fraud. Not too surprisingly over the 33-year period between crash and publication many witnesses had died and others' memories were faltering, perhaps hopelessly contaminated by what they had read or heard.

Members of opposing camps interpreted the same evidence in different ways. Were the hieroglyphic-like marks found on part of the wreckage extraterrestrial markings, or simply decorative tape that was manufactured on Earth and used for many purposes, including toy manufacture? Were there alien bodies and if so, what had happened to them? Could they have been photographed? Randall Fitzgerald summarized the situation nicely when he wrote "A combination of human foibles coalesced to create the modern myth of what happened near Roswell, including a contagion of rumor mongering, miscommunication, misperception, exaggerations, self-aggrandizing behavior, lies for financial gain, and a psychological condition called false memory" (1998: 90). Once again, a lack of hard evidence coupled with uncertainty and confusion allows many theories to flourish.

A highly detailed and meticulously documented book by Karl Pflock strongly suggests that whatever crashed at Roswell, it was not a craft from outer space (2001). Initially he thought it might be a spacecraft, but his investigation pointed to a different conclusion. Although when it comes to Roswell, Pflock is a skeptic, he also believes there was a window of time between the late 1940s and mid 1970s when authentic extraterrestrial spacecraft visited Earth. They are gone now, and there is no hint of when, if ever, they will return.

Pflock favors the theory that it was a secret military balloon that crashed at Roswell in 1947. Pflock, who worked for a New Mexico congressman, was instructed to get the inside story from the U.S. government. When Pflock tried to do this, he discovered that the government was less than forthcoming. Eventually the Air Force allowed that what had actually crashed in 1947 was a super-secret Project Mogul balloon that was intended to spy on the Russian A-bomb program. Later, in an attempt to explain reports of alien bodies, the Air Force issued another report stating that the bodies were in fact dummies used in tests in the 1950s. Spokespersons pointed to memory distortions to explain why witnesses might remember seeing something in 1947 that had not actually occurred until 1955. That may have been true, but because it seemed far-fetched, it did little to bolster the public's confidence in the Air Force's credibility.

Perhaps the most sensational conspiracy theory of all is that artifacts recovered from a UFO serve as the basis for much of modern technology. In the late 1990s this gained widespread exposure with the publication of Philip Corso and W. J. Birnes's book *The Day After Roswell* (1997). This assisted autobiography presents a fascinating account of Corso's top-secret activities to transfer extraterrestrial artifacts to major American corporations. On assignment to a very real General Trudeau, Corso would be given an artifact from the Roswell crash retrieval. Dressed in civilian clothes he set forth to companies such as IBM, Dow Corning, and Bell Labs where items would be studied and serve as models for such inventions as night vision, Kevlar armor, integrated circuit chips, and fiber optics. Summarizing Corso's self-proclaimed successes, Pflock wrote, "Corso's work made it possible for the West to win the Cold War while keeping our kids entertained with video games" (2001: 205).

Can we accept this history of modern technology? Since Corso's work was "secret" there was no paper trail, and fifty years later, when Corso got around to telling how he spread alien technology, the senior scientists and business executives who might have been able to confirm his claims were dead. Corso's account was riddled with mistakes and inconsistencies, and despite his much earlier achievements in the military and government there were growing concerns about his credibility. Corso's arguments had a strong ring of implausibility, and apart from some tired old documents that had been circulating for several years he had no backup. But Corso's claims did fit in with some people's suspicions of government cover-up.

The biggest problem for Corso's story is that we have a competing history of modern technology, one that is supported by a huge paper trail, personal reminiscences on the part of the inventors, and corroboration by independent eyewitnesses. Work on many of the inventions began long prior to Roswell and some of them, such as the transistor and the integrated circuit, were already in use before Corso began his furtive missions. *Crystal Fire: The Birth of the Information Age*, published the same year as *The Day After Roswell*, offers a meticulously researched, painstakingly recounted history of the transistor, an account that has been verified by other authors (Riordan and Hoddeson 1997). We know how the transistor and integrated circuit were invented. Alien technology is not the key to today's electronic marvels: the credit goes to scientists such as William Shockley, not to crashed space invaders.

Conspiracy Thinking

"Conspiracy theories" writes Daniel Pipes, "have three basic elements: a powerful, evil and clandestine group ... dupes and agents who extend the group's influence around the world so that it is on the verge of succeeding, and a valiant but embattled group that urgently needs help to stave off catastrophe" (1997: 22). Although Pipes's primary concern is political conspiracies (such as the supposed conspiracy of the nineteenth-century English to engineer potato famines in Ireland) these three elements are easy to identify in discussions of UFO cover-up. In the case of UFOs they are: (1) a secret elite group high within the U.S. government, (2) Air Force and CIA agents that carry out this group's directives, and (3) independent investigators and political action groups that are intent on prying the truth from the government. The conspirators are organized, treacherous, and up to evil, while honest and decent people seek enlightenment.

Conspiracy theories have a way of growing on people. Evidence of the conspiracy appears everywhere, and some people find themselves devoting more and more time to understanding and exposing the conspiracy (Pipes 1997). It is impossible to read too much on the topic, and the obsession may force family and career into the background. There is cross-fertilization of conspiracy theories so that people who suspect that the government is suppressing information about UFOs may also believe that it is lying about the John F. Kennedy assassination (Barkun 2003). Different conspiracy theories may be taken as providing independent support for each other.

Not everyone who subscribes to a conspiracy theory is paranoid, but paranoid thinking may strengthen some people's beliefs in conspiracy. A lack of community encourages paranoia, as does a sense of powerlessness (Alper 2005). This leads to rigid, narrow, rule-bound thinking. Everything is black and white—for example, other people are either loyal or treacherous—there is no in-between. The paranoid is bedeviled by innocuous detail, and has a gift for thinking small. Coincidences are seen as intentional. (If we do not know Prince Phillip's whereabouts on the day of a UFO landing in Scotland, then it goes without saying that he was negotiating with the aliens.) The paranoid is ever on guard, and, once triggered, paranoia assumes a life of its own. Since paranoia is a stain or blemish, nobody wants to admit to paranoia. Remonstrating the government represents an effort to regain control, to put the people back in charge of our democracy (Dean 1998).

James Moulton Thomas and I argued that, once suspicions form, normal organizational errors and inefficiencies feed beliefs in government cover-up (Harrison and Thomas 1997). We base this on case histories of UFOs and political assassinations. Bureaucracies do not do a good job of processing gluts of information under tight time deadlines. The FBI, under pressure to conduct a speedy investigation of the John F. Kennedy assassination, produced a lengthy report with many errors, omissions, and inefficiencies. Reports and evidence are misfiled or lost. Different spokespersons, each of whom has only a partial understanding of the situation, make conflicting pronouncements. Working under a crush of requests filed under the Freedom of Information Act, an overworked bureaucrat takes months to respond. Given the complexity of the U.S. government, I wonder if anyone within the government knows what the government knows about UFOs and, as we shall see, that includes at least one recent president! Of course, identifying SNA-FUs that can be misconstrued as evidence of duplicity does not eliminate the possibility of actual cover-up.

Certainly, many of the researchers who have pursued conspiracy theories are sincere and many self-proclaimed witnesses have truthfully reported events as they remember them. However, even sincere and honest people can be wrong, and when we move into murky areas such as crash retrievals there is increasing latitude for treachery and error. Much of the evidence of government cover-up comes from witnesses who refuse to reveal their identities or lack the means to verify their claims. It is extremely difficult to determine the authenticity and chain of custody of incriminating documents. Each informant who overstates his credentials, offers up a story that does not ring true, loses important evidence, or is denounced by other informants undermines the credibility of accusations against the government.

Michael Barkun writes that conspiracy theories are at once frightening and reassuring (2003: 4). A conspiracy theory is "frightening because it magnifies the power of evil, leading in some cases to an outright dualism in which light and darkness struggle for cosmic supremacy." It is reassuring because "it promises a world that is meaningful rather than arbitrary. Not only are events nonrandom, but also the clear indication of evil gives the conspiracist a definable enemy against which to struggle, endowing life with purpose." Is the truth *really* out there, and if so, when will it be revealed?

Eight

MATTERS OF LIFE AND DEATH

In the 1998 movie *Deep Impact*, world governments withhold the discovery that a huge asteroid is on a collision course with Earth. In true science fiction fashion, a snooping investigative reporter manages to force the issue. Once the President of the United States learns that the reporter knows about the impending catastrophe, he holds a news conference to warn the public. In his telecast from the White House, the President alerts the nation that if nuclear explosives fail to pulverize the asteroid or at least knock it off course, Earth may not survive the impact.

Government preparations, it turns out, must have been in progress for quite some time. The *Orion* rocket, a nuclear-propelled deep space dream machine that has been stuck on the drawing boards since the 1960s, is somehow completed to transport a work crew to the asteroid where they will drill holes and plant nuclear explosives. Meanwhile, caves located in Missouri have been prepared to hold one million people. This will include 200,000 people who were selected because they have the skills necessary to reestablish society, and 800,000 people who were chosen randomly on the basis of their Social Security numbers. Other countries, according to the President, have their own national redoubts, and people who are not selected for deep cover are told to look to local authorities for shelter. The audience understands that the local shelters offer scant hope for survival.

Surmounting many hurdles the astronauts aboard the *Orion* succeed in breaking the asteroid into two pieces and in a final suicide run they obliterate the largest of these. The remaining piece hits the Atlantic not far from Cape Hatteras. This triggers a tsunami that sends water as far inland as the Ohio Valley. Because of the heroic actions of these later-day "right stuff" astronauts, not everyone dies. The movie ends with enthusiastic crowds cheering the President at a rally on a badly battered Capitol Mall.

The trials of the self-sacrificing spacefarers in the *Orion* must have paled against the tribulations of the politicians and the bureaucrats who chose 200,000 people as the nucleus for postimpact society. Presumably, the authority for this selection came from the U.S. Congress, and the movie shows that its decisions were enforced by the military. As concerned citizens there are many questions that one should ask. What criteria did they use to select some scientists, historians, physicians, educators, theologians, and artists over others? Did they consider child-bearing qualifications and parenting skills? Were the selection criteria seen as fair by the people who were excluded as well as by the people who were chosen? How did the chosen ones survive two years of "button-up?" As we contemplate the enormity of such issues, we can see why the scriptwriters resorted to hand waving on the part of the President, and the audience's imagination.

Many of the new findings about our place in the universe are disconcerting. Since the 1970s, scientists have drawn attention to the frailty of Earth's ecosystem and the immense damage done to it by an exploding population. The same pictures of belching smokestacks that reassured people in the late 1930s that the great economic depression was lifting now look as dangerous as lit unfiltered cigarettes. Pandemics have decimated societies before and despite rapid advances in medicine could do so again, killing even more people. A whole parade of technological marvels that are intended to benefit humankind could backfire in ways that spells our doom (Rees 2003). Nuclear war is only one such risk. What will become of us? What can we do to mitigate disaster? Do our children and grandchildren have a chance? If, as suggested by the fate that befell New Orleans in 2005, we can't cope with hurricanes, how can we cope with cosmic catastrophes?

Apocalyptic Visions

Extreme events refer to large-scale disasters that cause many casualties and long-term disruptions. The worst imaginable case, an extinction level event, is one that threatens the continuation of the entire human race. We are still here to contemplate extinction level events but earlier forms of humans such as *Homo erectus* and Neanderthals did die off. Until relatively recently—well into the twentieth century—scientists viewed human evolution as occurring in a linear fashion with one set of ancestors evolving into another. In essence, through a gentle process where some genes proved more adaptive than others, early hunter-gatherers gave way to Mozart, Picasso, and Mother Theresa. Now some scientists are challenging this view (Tattersall and Schwartz 2001). They view the evolutionary tree as more like a bush, with common ancestors giving rise to different species of humans, and some of these coexisted at the same time. Quite possibly different "families of man" did not meld into one another nor did they just melt away. Rather, competitors may have perished in the Stone Age equivalent of nuclear war.

Apocalyptic visions are a part of many religions, but not all (Zen Buddhists do not get worked up about such things). The Bible is replete with famines, floods, and wars. It warns of the end of times, and raises such specters as the fiery pits of Hell. UFO religions are often predicated on millennial views: that the world as we know it is coming to an end (Wojcik 1997, 2003; J. R. Lewis 1995, 2003; Partridge 2004). Remember that apocalyptic visions permeate abductions. Details vary, but the common denominator is a world where the environment, wildlife, and civilization have been ruined, and the few people remaining must endure pain and misery (Mack 1999).

In Daniel Wojcik's usage, apocalypse refers to the "catastrophic destruction of world or current society, whether attributed to supernatural forces, natural forces, or human actions" (1997: 12). In the scientific worldview apocalypse is brought about by nature, while in the religious worldview it is brought about by God. In the religious view an apocalypse may occur no matter what action we take, a situation that encourages fatalism. Or, it may be that through ritual, prayer, and self-sacrifice we can forestall or even prevent the apocalypse. The apocalypse may presage the dawn of a great new era, if not for everyone, then at least for the faithful. A common pattern in UFO religions is that believers will survive the apocalypse and enjoy the fruits of a utopian new order. Wojcik describes apocalyptic visions within UFO circles as "a synthesis of Christianity, Theosophy, Spiritualism, Eastern religions, New Age notions, and ideas inspired by science fiction literature and popular films" (1997: 10).

In a his analysis of the Bible's Book of Revelation, Edwin F. Edinger describes an abundant apocalyptic literature that includes dreams, visions, and journeys where one is shown otherworldly secrets that culminate in the end of an age that does not choose to go quietly into the night (1999). He views the apocalypse as an archetype: an idea that resides in the collective unconscious of a culture. Archetypes are symbolic—the archetype of the apocalypse symbolizes major change—and archetypes make themselves manifest in several ways.

The archetype of the apocalypse, Edinger suggests, is evident in the breakdown of Western civilization; in heightened conflicts among religious groups; in books, movies, and television programs that focus on destruction; and in fictional or projected encounters between humans and aliens that do not work out well for us. Perhaps we can interpret the minor scars associated with alien implants as latter day equivalents of "the mark of the beast," and aliens harvest hybrid human babies just as God and the devil harvest souls.

Apocalyptic visions represent material from the unconscious entering awareness, and, in Edinger's opinion, demonstrate progress towards the emergence of the self, that part of the psyche that strives for unity, wholeness, and integration. This archetype represents shattering the world as it has been, followed by a reconstitution: movement towards a new sense of self and wholeness. Thus, Edinger's analysis is consistent with John Mack's view that visions of devastation can represent one step (among many) towards higher levels of psychological development (Chapter 6). Perhaps abductees' visions of the end of the world are sustained by a combination of doomsday science, religion, and the sense of a "quickening" or impending change that prevails in our culture right now.

One of the gloomiest scientific assessments of Earth's long-term prospects comes from astrobiologists Peter Ward and Donald Brownlee, who point out that we live on a planet and at a time that is unusually, perhaps uniquely hospitable to life (2002). They describe how Earth progressed from a hot, barren rock to a habitable location with an atmosphere, oceans, forests, lakes, and myriad forms of life, including complex forms characterized by consciousness and culture. This congeniality, they point out, will not prevail indefinitely. Over the coming millennia our descendants will first swelter, then freeze, then roast alive. Complex cycles based on the changing brightness of the Sun, plate tectonics, rock weathering, and alterations in the atmosphere and oceans will lead first to global warming, then to an ice age, and ultimately to high temperatures that first drive remaining life into the sea and then leave nothing but a hot, barren rock. As thousands and then millions of years pass, Earth will become increasingly less habitable, first losing its ability to support complex forms of life, and ultimately becoming incapable of hosting even single-celled bacteria. In effect, life's progress on Earth will be thrown into reverse gear and our planet will return to a hot, dry, lifeless cinder, before it is swallowed up in flame after our Sun becomes a red giant, perhaps six billion years from now.

Near Earth Objects

Despite the visible craters on the Moon, it has been only two hundred years or so that scientists have recognized that rocks could fall from the sky (J. S. Lewis 1996; Chapman 1998; Chapman et al. 2001). Farmers and field laborers were the first to report this, but their claims were discounted by the scientists of the day (J.S. Lewis 1996). The farmers had three strikes against them. They lacked education and did not have credibility. Their reports violated widely held Aristotelian notions of harmony and perfection in the universe. And, scientists had no ready explanations. Early laboratory experiments that involved dropping rocks failed to produce craters similar to those that we can see on the Moon, suggesting that the Moon's craters resulted from something else, such as volcanic activity. (These experiments failed because the laboratory rocks lacked the velocity to make craters.)

Craters on Earth are not necessarily easy to find. Since oceans cover approximately 72 percent of the Earth three out of every four craters is underwater. Over time, plate tectonics (the movement of large geological plates near the Earth's crust), soil erosion, and the growth of vegetation make the craters imperceptible. However, an impact can disrupt millions of years of gradual sedimentation and deposit certain rare metals such as iridium, thereby allowing scientists to find and date impact sites.

Asteroids and comets that come close to Earth are called Near Earth Objects or NEOs. It has only been twenty years or so—since researchers proposed that an NEO impact was largely responsible for the demise of the dinosaurs sixty-five million years ago—that science has better appreciated the threat to Earth of rocks from the sky. Almost everyone began to recognize a risk in 1994 when comet Shoemaker-Levy 9 crashed into Jupiter and created a splash whose volume equaled that of our entire planet.

Visualize a metal silhouette of a duck in a shooting gallery, attached to an endless belt and moving along at a set speed while a host of blindfolded people shoot in its general direction. Most of the shooters are armed with BB guns, a fair number have .22s, and a few have larger weapons. Because the shooters cannot see where they are aiming most of their bullets fly far wide of the mark. On occasion some projectiles whiz near the tin duck, and on even fewer occasions they hit. Since most of the projectiles are tiny, lightweight pellets, those that do hit do not do much damage. On rare occasions a ".22" hits and causes noticeable damage, and eventually a much larger and more destructive bullet will demolish a target.

Earth can be compared to the tin duck and asteroids and comets that fly by as the bullets. Only a tiny fraction of NEOs will ever enter our atmosphere. Of course at the cosmic level the scale is much larger than in the case of the shooting gallery, with some NEOs measured in terms of meters, kilometers, and billions of tons. The time scale is expanded, too, with, perhaps tens of thousands or millions of years passing between strikes that have global consequences.

By far most NEOs are cosmic BBs—small and weak. Our atmosphere protects us from objects up to about fifty meters in diameter as these are fully or almost fully incinerated when enter our atmosphere (D. Morrison 2001). We know of perhaps a million or so NEOs that are larger than the fifty-meter "entry-level" objects that can survive our atmosphere, and we estimate that there is perhaps a million more that we have yet to identify. Serious local damage can result from NEOs that are in the 300-meter range. This is the size of the object that exploded above Tunguska, Siberia in 1907, causing relatively little damage partly because it detonated well before it hit Earth and partly because it hit a remote, isolated area. The event would have been much more deadly, and better known, if it had occurred a few seconds later, over Imperial Russia's capital of St. Petersburg. Matters get very serious when we consider objects on the order of one kilometer or larger. We know of perhaps eleven hundred NEOs this size and suspect that that there are many others yet to be detected.

Since smaller NEOs are more common than larger ones the average expected time between impacts increases with NEO size. The average strength of those that reach the Earth on an annual basis is the same size as a rather wimpy atomic bomb, about five kilotons (that is, the equivalent of five thousand tons of dynamite). Earlier estimates suggested that a Tunguska-sized explosion would occur every few centuries, but more recent calculations suggest that we can expect these only once every thousand years. The truly devastating impacts that are associated with mass extinctions are separated on the average by millions of years. If, as some suspect, major impacts occur on a 26-million-year cycle, given that the last "really big one" occurred 65 million years ago, then maybe we are overdue.

Scientists who have calculated how Earth might be affected by the impact of NEOs of different sizes warn that the extent of damage is determined not only by size but by composition of the incoming object, its angle of entry, and precisely where it hits (Chapman 1998; Chapman et al. 2001). A three-hundred-meter (diameter) NEO impact would dig a crater five to ten kilometers across, ignite a fire at ground zero, and kick up enough dust to obscure sunlight but not enough to ruin crops. Locally, the ground would shake and the impact could create a tsunami.

A two-kilometer NEO, sometimes called a "civilization ender," would blast a crater approximately fifty kilometers across. Fires would ignite within hundreds of kilometers of ground zero, and tsunamis would cause flooding ten kilometers inland. Enough dust and debris would be hurled into the stratosphere to drop sunlight to the level of a very cloudy day, and worldwide agriculture would be threatened by summertime freezes. The ozone layer would be destroyed, and with it our protection from ultraviolet rays. An impact of this magnitude, on the order of fifteen megatons, should be expected once every 300,000 years.

A ten- to fifteen-kilometer NEO would qualify as an "extinctor" and it was an object of about this size that led to mass extinctions including that of the dinosaurs. This giant would smash a crater several hundred kilometers across. Earth would be plunged into a global firestorm, and tsunamis would inundate low-lying areas worldwide, establishing new shorelines perhaps a hundred miles inland. Enough dust would be thrown into the atmosphere to make it impossible to see, and whatever was left would descend into a global night. Resulting widespread local earthquakes and the addition of huge amounts of sulfuric acid to the oceans would not seem to matter a lot. Perhaps the biggest object that threatens Earth is a 35-kilometer comet called Encke, but if it actually strikes it will not do so until billions of years from now.

What is the likelihood of actually being killed by a NEO impact? One historical survey suggests small NEOs do very little personal harm—a child's hat was pushed off, a man was knocked out, a colt was killed—but in 1490 in Shansi, China, ten thousand people died in a rain of rocks (J. S. Lewis 1996). Taking future "big ones" into account, in the long run the chances of getting killed in an impact are about the same as the chances of dying in an airplane accident: in each case, about 1:20,000 (Chapman 1998). Compared to dying as a result of an NEO impact one is less likely to die as a result of a flood (1:30,000), tornado (1:60,000), venomous bite or sting (1:100,000), fireworks accident (1:1,000,000), or botulism (1:3,000,000). On the other hand, compared to dying in an impact, one is more likely to die as the result of a motor vehicle accident (1:100), homicide (1:300), fire (1:800), firearms accident (1:2,500), or electrocution (1:5,000). Keep in mind, though, that these statistics are based on very long stretches of time when nobody dies from an impact, punctuated by brief periods when there are enormous casualties (Chapman 1998; Chapman et al 2001).

Smaller impacts are much more likely than larger impacts so we can expect many regional disasters for each global disaster. Still, a relatively small impact at the wrong time and place could indirectly become a global catastrophe by triggering a nuclear war. This could be the outcome if an asteroid hit just inside the border of India or Pakistan, or perhaps North Korea. Such an impact could be very difficult to discriminate from a missile attack, especially in an age where the military can launch and then de-orbit large, dense artificial asteroids whose crushing effects on enemy territory would mimic those of an NEO impact.

Australian astronomer Ray Norris has identified events of a magnitude that would make even the most horrendous impact seem as exciting as a fender-bender in the parking lot (Norris 2000). These catastrophes could eliminate life on many planets. A supernova within fifty light years would reduce the amount of ozone in Earth's atmosphere by approximately 95 percent, increasing fourfold the amount of dangerous ultraviolet radiation that bombards Earth. After this continued for two years it would be followed by an eighty-year bombardment by the supernova's lethal cosmic rays. Other inhabited planets within fifty light years of the supernova also would be depopulated.

Gamma ray bursters are even more dreadful; the amount of energy released by a burster is on the order of five magnitudes the order of that released by a supernova (Norris 2000). Its effects would run from the center to the far reaches of a galaxy, exterminating life over many thousands of light years. On Earth, supernovas and gamma ray bursters should hit Earth's "reset" button every 200 million years but as far as Norris can tell this has not happened for about twenty times that long. Perhaps the calculations are unduly pessimistic, perhaps something that did not watch over the dinosaurs is watching over us, or perhaps we are lucky.

Planetary Defense

Astronomers are able to spot and track NEOs and estimate when, and to a lesser extent where, they will strike. The goal of the Spaceguard survey currently underway is to identify 90 percent of the Earth-threatening asteroids by the year 2008. Of course it will not be possible to identify every potential threat, such as those posed by "long period" comets that only infrequently head towards Earth. This means that in some cases we could have very little warning. If we want to minimize the number of potential "surprises" we need to pick up the pace: bring more telescopes and computers on line, and perhaps set up detecting and tracking equipment in orbit and on the Moon.

Usually we will learn of an impending strike decades, perhaps centuries, before the event. This is quite different from major earthquakes or volcanic eruptions (which are expected but whose date is unknown), diseases that may suddenly gain in virulence, or storms such as hurricanes and typhoons that can be predicted but only a few days before they strike. Generous advance notification makes is possible to engage in careful planning, and perhaps take steps that will allow our species to survive.

Scientists do have proposals for preventing NEO impacts (Schweikart et al. 2003). One possibility is to divert the NEO so that it passes harmlessly by. After the threat has been identified we can dispatch a rocket to explore it up close to help assess the risk and determine a course of action. Blowing it up is not always the best strategy because the net result may be that some or all of the pieces rain down on Earth, as happened in the movie *Deep Impact*. On the other hand, nuclear explosives launched from Earth or space could knock the object off course.

A small amount of force applied over a long period of time could change the NEO's trajectory. This might be accomplished by a rocket attached to the side, or a "mass driver" that relentlessly bombards the asteroid with small packets of debris. Push it with a laser. Pull it with a solar sail. Since asteroids contain untold amounts of precious metals such as platinum and iridium, send strip miners to peel away the valuables and reduce it to a harmless hulk. Fortunately, at least some of these methods involve technologies that we now have, or that will soon come on line. We already have some of the hardware that we need to deflect fairly large NEOs, but it could take years to actually mount a successful planetary defense mission.

Identifying a threat way in advance would allow planners to generate alternatives, consult, carefully weigh and assess new information, reach decisions, build consensus, and arrange for implementation. It would let governmental leaders set policy and establish coordination among various disaster and relief agencies, train rescue workers, and notify residents of at-risk areas. Assuming we are not blindsided by a comet, there would be ample opportunity to plan evacuation routes, build and stock shelters, and put rescue and relief services in place. Yet, in 2005, we discovered that despite widespread recognition that a powerful hurricane could devastate New Orleans, U.S. officials did little in the way of serious preparation and diverted planning funds to other projects.

Fatalities and injuries can be reduced to the extent that we can identify the impact zone and conduct an effective evacuation. The temptation to evacuate as large an area as possible will be balanced against a reluctance to disrupt the infrastructure. Additionally, not everyone responds to entreaties to evacuate; some, like the Harry Truman who met his demise in the Mount Saint Helens eruption, will refuse to leave; others will agree to be evacuated but then return to their homes. Risk perception (Is the threat real?), social influence processes (What are my friends doing?), and resources (Do I have transportation to a safe, welcoming destination?) are among the many influences that affect people's decisions to evacuate.

NEO impacts, like floods, volcanic eruptions, and tornadoes are the result of natural forces. Some people may attribute these natural disasters to a wrathful god, evil spirits, or the disgruntled ghosts of relatives. Supernatural interpretations become a problem when they direct attention and energy from rational searches for solutions. They may be particularly destructive if they invite attending to false prophets and substituting empty ritual for problem solving. Certainly, many people would think of the approaching asteroid or comet as a "message from the heavens" and of these some will be drawn into cults. Blaming the gods may foster to a sense of helplessness and reduce motivation to take effective action.

Under major threat it might be possible to establish survival communities, as was done in *Deep Impact*. Here we might find guidance from anthropologists, economists, sociologists, and others who have explored ways to establish sustainable human settlements in space (Finney and Jones 1984; Harrison 2001). In some respects, postimpact Earth may resemble an off-world destination: a dangerous place bombarded with harmful forms of radiation, toxic atmosphere, and little or no useful vegetation. There is a certain resemblance between survivors coping with a nuclear winter and the first human settlers on Mars coping with dust storms, and both groups would be concerned with increasing the habitability of their respective planets. But in two respects the postimpact Earthlings would have the advantage. First, they are likely to exist in far larger numbers than the humans on Mars. Second, they are likely to be much better off in terms of equipment and supplies, for example, having the opportunity to mine tons of copper from destroyed telephone lines. To support postimpact citizens on Earth we do not have to worry about the immense cost of lifting materials into orbit. At least under some conditions, within very few generations a relatively small number of people can grow into a community of viable size (Finney and Jones 1984).

In *Deep Impact*, society's nucleus was protected in limestone caves in Missouri. The U.S. government's mistake (although it got away with it) was putting all of its eggs in one basket, which increases the likelihood that a localized disaster following the asteroid strike could kill off the remaining population. Protecting people from an Earth-shaking event by sequestering them in limestone caves near one of the world's most dangerous earthquake faults, the New Madrid fault, seems a dubious strategy at best. Dispersal is a key to survival, so several medium-sized survival communities would be much better than one megashelter. Of course, the ultimate protection for humanity as a whole is dispersal beyond our home planet. Dispersal throughout the solar system would not necessarily protect us from all risks—nuclear war can be conducted in the skies, diseases that can be carried by ship can travel by spacecraft, and there is always the possibility of a supernova or other cosmic catastrophe. But, dispersed beyond Earth, we would be far better protected from extinction than we are right now.

Resurrection and Eternal Life

Death is nature's way of clearing debris and making way for fresh, new life. We die as a result of trauma, disease, and the cumulative processes of aging. We die from "the stoppage of circulation, the inadequate transport of oxygen to the tissue, the flickering out of brain function, the failure of organs, and the destruction of vital centers" (Nuland 1993: xviii). Although death certificates list specific causes, age and debilitation go hand in hand, and if we live long enough we just wear out. Autopsies show that by the time most people reach their eighties, whatever the proximate cause of death—choking on a piece of food, for example—their bodies are riddled with numerous time bombs that are close to detonation. These include highly occluded arteries that are ready to pinch off, entangled neurons in the brain, a tumor here, and a marginally functioning organ there. For most of us, death will not come easily; only one in five will be taken quickly and unawares. Invasive procedures, impersonal medical personnel, and pain are more common than dying peacefully, surrounded by friends.

All creatures have a powerful predisposition to stay alive as this encourages continuation of their species. But, unlike other animals, we are self-reflective and recognize that we will die and that our bodies will decay. What happens after we die? This is the kind of existential or "God" question that lies outside the realm of science. Or perhaps science can answer this question, but not in ways that we find satisfying. Remember that science is monistic: for all intents and purposes, brain and its processes create mind or at least without brain mind ceases to exist. This is illustrated in Sherwin Nuland's description of a man who had a painless but potentially fatal heart attack while playing tennis (1993). The tennis player saw the world gradually grow darker, as if someone were turning down a rheostat connected to the Sun. This process was slow, uniform, perceptible, and inexorable. This progressive darkening was the natural result of the loss of oxygen. The higher functions of the brain shut down so that the little oxygen remaining could support the vegetative functions that kept him alive. He was lucky: medically trained people were present nearby and provided emergency help, the ambulance arrived quickly, and he later regained consciousness in the hospital wondering about all the fuss.

If science is correct that the brain is a prerequisite for consciousness, our clearest glimpse of the hereafter is dreamless sleep. Death is a giant void—no memories, no thoughts, no emotions, no perceptions, and no sense of self. Somehow, the great void that extends to the indefinite past seems so different, so unimportant compared to that which reaches into the indefinite future. One of religion's trump cards is the promise of eternal life. Unlike science, religion subscribes to dualism—that is, that we have both a body and a mind (consciousness, spirit, soul). If these are separate, and one can exist independent of the other, then perhaps consciousness can survive death.

Life after death was a component of ancient Persian and Egyptian religions and the elaborate burial practices of the Egyptians were intended to ease the Pharaohs' journey to the afterworld. In the ancient world, the idea of reincarnation was popular, and it remains so in Hinduism, Buddhism, a few groups of Muslims (the Alevi of Turkey, the Druse of Lebanon), and some Native American religions today (Mills and Lynn 2000). Some of the most enthusiastic believers in reincarnation are native peoples in British Columbia. In Hinduism, when our *jiva* or souls outgrow our bodies, we move up the great hierarchy of life, eventually appearing, and then reappearing, as humans (Smith 1991). In effect, we go through endless cycles of life, death, and rebirth, until we achieve the status of humans.

Many Christians believe that because we are descendents of Adam, who transgressed in the Garden of Eden by eating the apple of knowledge, we are sinful by nature. God lives in Heaven, and eventually faithful Christians will join him there. God is wrathful and vengeful, but his vengeance has been deflected by Jesus' death on the cross, which atoned for the sins of the world. On Judgment Day the dead shall be resurrected, and everyone will undergo intense scrutiny. Those who are chosen will join God in fellowship in Heaven while others will be cast into the fiery pit of Hell.

For most Christians, access to the hereafter is conditional and selective. Despite God's infinite compassion, wisdom, and grace, Christians must earn their tickets upstairs. In some accounts the God of the Christians seems less impressed by behavior than by a strong faith predicated on accepting Jesus as Savior. On Judgment Day people with extensive histories of misdeeds, but who have undergone deathbed conversions, will enter Heaven along with people who have maintained unblemished records. The concept of judgment by a harsh, unyielding, and perfectionist God is so thoroughly frightening that many religions try to skirt this (Edinger 1999). Still, Judgment Day could occur at any time. This is symbolized in a painting of abandoned automobiles strewn around Los Angeles, left behind by their occupants who have ascended to heaven (Wojcik 1997; Edinger 1999).

Themes of salvation, resurrection and immortality appear in flying saucer religions. Members of Heaven's Gate believed that after taking poison and departing their human bodies they would move on to the next higher plane, spiritually if not physically aboard a UFO that was traveling in the wake of the Hale-Bopp comet (Chapter 7) For the followers of Rael (whom, you may recall, was contacted by the Elohim that arrived on Earth via flying saucer), cloning is the key to immortality (Palmer 2004). The religious significance of cloning is evident in the remarks of a Chicago physicist who was about to begin experimenting on human cloning. "We are going to becoming one with God. We are going to have almost as much knowledge and power as God. Cloning and the reprogramming of DNA is the first step" (Noble 1999: vii).

Be that as it may, it will be a while before medical science and technology closes this particular gap with religion. Many scientists, theologians and politicians are appalled by the idea of human cloning. What enthusiasts tend to forget is that cloning's success rate is low; particularly with mammals. It took 272 tries to produce Dolly, the first cloned sheep. Clones tend to have serious defects and to age rapidly. Cloning primates may be all but impossible (Noble 1999).

The Raellians have an equivalent of baptism, and it is called transmission (Palmer 2004). In this ritual, Rael, or one of his bishops, dips his or her hands in a bowl of water and then holds the initiate's head while both strive to communicate telepathically with the Elohim. This ritual recognizes the Elohim (who first visited Earth in the distant past) as humanity's creator, and also transmits the initiate's genetic code to them. It also gives the initiate a chance at resurrection. Whether or not eternal life is granted depends on the Elohim's assessment of the initiate's service to humanity. (As a practical matter, initiates make arrangements with undertakers to preserve a piece of skull that will be used for the actual cloning.) Resurrection is a three-step process: cloning, accelerated growth (on the Elohim's home planet, this is accomplished in a "babytron"), and then transferring personality, which has been stored on a computer, into the new body. When the new body shows signs of wearing out, the process is repeated.

After setting up a firm called Clonaid, the Raellians proclaimed success with Baby Eve, a clone of the dead daughter of influential grieving parents. But this victory was short-lived because they were unable to produce proof—the child had disappeared! Did she exist? Is she in hiding? As Palmer points out, "Miraculous babes appear and disappear like bubbles throughout the history of heresy. Prophets have placed high expectations upon infant avatars, divine boys, and new Eves to usher in a new age … Baby Eve appears to be yet another miraculous babe who mysteriously fails to materialize … At this juncture, it appears that Baby Eve may become one of the unsolved mysteries in the annals of ufological lore" (2004: 192, 194).

Like cloning, cryonic suspension offers the lure of a scientific path to resurrection, this time with no religious overtones. In the 1920s, a visionary physicist and mathematician by the name of John Desmond Bernal developed the idea of maintaining a disembodied brain in a vat where it would be bathed by cerebrospinal fluid and suffused with fresh blood (Parry 2004). Over the years, the chill of the deep freeze replaced the warmth of the vat. Food can be frozen and thawed, why not people? Research in the 1950s showed that rats and hamsters could be frozen stiff for a few minutes, and then revived by means of a quick thaw in what we now call a microwave oven. Unfortunately, many of the animals that had been treated this way were the worse for wear, some died, and none could be restored to life after they had been frozen for more than an hour.

Despite the spotty nature of this success and the differences between hamsters and people, the first posthumous volunteer underwent cryonic suspension in 1967 (Parry 2004). As soon as possible following death the decedents' blood vessels are filled with preservative, and his or her body temperature is lowered to -320° F. The person is kept frozen in liquid hydrogen until medical science is able to both reverse the initial cause of death and revive him or her. A modest but wise investment should pay for the storage and revival in, say, a century or two. Unfortunately, bodies stored at this very low temperature have a tendency to shatter, like glass. Furthermore, to reanimate frozen corpses medical science will have to discover how to undo the damage caused by the preserving fluid and control the bursting and separation of cells as they are unfrozen. It is possible to freeze and thaw isolated types cells and tissues (bones, skin, cartilage) without doing significant damage, because, unlike a brain or body, they are not comprised of different types of cells that freeze and thaw at different rates. Today the tissues that we can freeze and thaw are immortalized not by resurrection of the donor but through research that benefits many people (Parry 2004).

Longevity

Although we cannot rest assured about the survival of consciousness after death we can try to increase the length of time that we remain alive. We know this is possible because longevity has increased notably in the last century. The average life expectancy in developed countries rose from 47 years in 1900 to 80 years in 2000, while maximum age has remained constant at approximately 120. Claims that some people in remote areas of Europe and Asia live for 150 to 160 years are without foundation (Wick 2002).

Increased life expectancy is reflected in a growing number of centarians: people who achieve the age of 100. While the population is growing at about 1 percent per year, centarians are increasing at the rate of about 8 percent per year. In the United States, at the beginning of the twentieth century, about one person in 100,000 reached 100 while now it is about one person in 10,000. We can expect 800,000 members of the baby-boom generation to attain 100 years of age (Perls et al. 2002).

Genes exert a strong influence on longevity. Centarians tend to be clustered in relatively few families. Their parents have unusually long lives, as do their siblings. The centarians advantage is postponing or warding off the diseases and ailments that kill other people at a relatively early age. Then, at some point—perhaps 100, perhaps 105—their defenses no longer work and they die of the same medical conditions as everyone else. One possibility is that the same genetic mechanisms that postpone fatal illnesses allow people to reproduce later in life, thus giving them a reproductive edge over, say, people who cease having children at age 40 (Perls et al. 2002).

Better food, new surgical procedures, and a cornucopia of fantastic drugs increase life expectancy (Bova 1998). Medicine has already made tremendous advances against certain kinds of killers. Much of this reflects progress with childhood diseases, notably smallpox and polio. Wonder medicines including inoculations that ward off rabies, influenza, and pneumonia and antibiotics to cure infections mean that fewer people die of these. Other developments include open-heart surgery to replace brittle arteries, heart-lung and kidney transplants, dialysis, and radiation and chemotherapy to eradicate or slow the course of cancer.

Whereas we cannot prevent all forms of death—each year about 62,500 people in the United States are lost to traffic accidents and another 30,000 to suicide—maybe we can postpone deaths due to heart disease (which accounts for 43 percent of all deaths after age 65), cancer (16 percent), stroke (10 percent), pneumonia and flu (6 percent) and other natural killers (Broderick 1999). If cancer, heart attack, and all other diseases were completely eliminated, average life expectancy would increase by about 15 years over what it is today (Hayflick 1998).

Biotechnology, in Brian Sager's analysis, debuted in 1976 with the establishment of Genentech (Sager 2001). Over the first twenty-five years the number of companies focusing exclusively on biological products and processes rose to 5,500 and many thousands of products went under development. Four hundred therapeutic drugs are in the works; these are targeted at infectious disease, cardiovascular disease, and immunological and neurological disorders. Biotechnologists can reengineer molecular proteins, mimicking in one week what would take natural selection ten thousand years. Today, many medicines work for some people but not for others. (This is because people differ in terms of genetic makeup, resulting in unique sets of physiological pathways.) And, of course, we may be able to grow new cells, tissues, and organs "from scratch." One of the greatest barriers to progress, Sager believes, is the reluctance of investors to back products that have a long development time. Another is hesitancy on the part of a public that is somewhat wary of biotechnology, worrying, for example, that genetically engineered food could be detrimental to personal health.

If we are to increase life span greatly we must conquer the external and internal processes that lead to aging and cellular death. Just like organs, muscles, and joints, genes are subject to continuous wear and tear. Part of this reflects instability in the biological molecules themselves and part of this reflects environmental assaults (Bova 1998; Hayflick 2003). Earth's thick atmosphere protects us partially, but not entirely, from ionizing radiation that causes damage by stripping electrons from atoms within the cell. This occurs daily, especially in intense sunlight at high elevations, and can be very dangerous for space travelers who venture beyond the Van Allen belts in the Earth's magnetosphere. Radiation could be a major showstopper in our efforts to disperse beyond Earth.

Each night the DNA goes to work repairing the damage of the day: proofreading to identify cells with defective genetic material and if not patching them up then replacing them with new ones. While these keep us in relatively good shape to reproductive age, the proofreading and repair systems themselves wear out. Over time they make more and more mistakes and find it increasingly difficult to maintain the pace required to cope with cascading errors. Given enough repetitions, the cells lose fidelity. This is analogous to a picture that has been photocopied thousands of times, each time becoming a little less accurate, with the results that the final copy is blurred, perhaps beyond recognition.

Even in the absence of aging, normal cells will die. DNA strands include telomeres that are, in essence, tinier strands reminiscent of shoelaces that prevent individual strands of DNA from looping and sticking to one another (Bova 1998; Hayflick 2003). Over time, these become shorter and shorter with the result that they can no longer do their work. In effect, the cell's nucleus includes a counter (not a timer) that limits the number of times that cell can reproduce. Certain kinds of cancerous cells can reproduce themselves forever. Although "eternally young," their unrestrained growth allows them to engulf and destroy vital centers.

The good news is that scientists are starting to understand some of the processes that lead to cellular aging and death. The bad news is that it may not be possible for us to extend cellular life indefinitely. One of the world's greatest authorities on cellular aging, Leonard Hayflick, places this achievement on the order of turning lead into gold (2003). Many suspected mechanisms lead to aging and death and extending life expectancy significantly will depend on a concerted, multipronged effort. We are conspicuously lacking in specifics, and the procedures that encourage cellular longevity may also trigger wild, cancerous growth.

Eternity in a Computer

A cyborg is a living organism that has been augmented by technology. In a sense, many of us alive today are cyborgs: contact lenses allow us to see clearly, tiny electronic aids improve our hearing, and tooth implants enable old-timers and prize fighters to enjoy barbecued ribs and corn on the cob. We have already made great progress developing structural parts to replace bones and joints (for example, artificial hips), mechanical parts to replace muscles (for example, power-activated arms), and even electronic parts that substitute for neural functioning (pacemakers). We have made limited progress with devices intended to help the blind "see" and we speculate about chip implants to improve memory (Sager 2001).

Wouldn't it be advantageous to live inside, say, a tireless, indestructible, and perpetually thin titanium robot? Or, how about basking forever within reverberating electronic circuits where every whim is satisfied by rich and responsive virtual reality (Paul and Cox 1996; Broderick 1999, 2001)? The advantages of cyber-life might include 360-degree vision; endless strength, stamina, and agility; speed-of-light communication with anyone anywhere; freedom from fatigue, disease, and illness; no need for diet or exercise regimens, and no body image problems. Learning would be instantaneous and effortless and memory would be flawless. Huge libraries could be uploaded into memory and everyone could be a superb scientist, mathematician, engineer, philosopher, humanist, theologian, artist, writer, and bridge champion.

In theory, we would have very little to worry about psychologically. Cyber-environments could be engineered to provide stimulation without undue stress but you yourself could be adjusted to revel in great stress. If your microchip had a close brush with a magnet then perhaps a small patch would cure your damaged psyche. Suicides could be undone by uploading a back-up copy of the temporarily deceased's mind. Damien Broderick predicts "high level artificial intelligence that surpasses human intelligence, augmented human abilities made possible by the implantation of computer chips, transfers of human minds to computers" will allow us to "live, work and play inside rich ... machine-generated virtual realities" and afford us "possible contact with galactic civilizations" that already have made the transition to postbiological intelligence (2001: 22-23).

Since the 1950s computers have improved in every way imaginable: operating speed, random access memory, storage memory, and software. Meanwhile, the cost (especially in terms of inflation-adjusted dollars) is plummeting. Now our best supercomputers perform several trillion operations per second. If we can make them two hundred times as effective, we can, in theory, approximate the human brain. In his discussion of universal robots (that is, robots that can do all sorts of things, not just repetitiously weld fenders onto cars), Hans Moravec points out that at ten-year intervals thousand-dollar computers will achieve the capabilities of lizards, mice, and monkeys (1999). Somewhere around 2040 they will attain the computational powers of humans, in essence replicating 300 million years of human evolution in half a century. Right now, giant computers are so expensive that they must be dedicated to major scientific problems; later they will become cheap enough to replace people.

Frank Tipler reasons, "A human being is a purely physical object, a biochemical machine" that is "completely and exhaustively described by the known laws of physics" (1995: 1). Our sense of ourselves results from a computer program being run in a computing machine called the brain. In his highly mathematical treatment, Tipler argues that massive computers may make it possible to resurrect everyone who has ever lived and keep them alive if not beyond the collapse of the universe than at least for a "virtual" eternity. His point of departure is that a computer emulation of a person is the same as the person. If we run enough computer emulations, then we will resurrect everyone who has ever lived. The computers will be left running indefinitely. If in fact the universe eventually collapses, there will be an "omega point" that involves a slowing of time so that subjectively life never ends.

There are many different models for the brain but most discussions of life in a computer involve updated versions of old-fashioned "switchboard" model. The computer scientists' version is that the brain is a machine like a computer and both process information. Computers can emulate brains because each can be understood in terms of binary operations or "flops" per unit time. If a computer can attain the processing rate of the brain it will be conscious and (if properly programmed) capable of human thought. Once computers gain sufficient capacity and speed, some speculate, we can upload personalities into them.

Unlike computer scientists, psychologists have a differentiated and nuanced view of intelligence. Before uploading becomes possible, qualitatively different forms of intelligence must be translated to digital operations. This includes holistic, artistic, and intuitive thinking as well as ordered serial information processing. There are other imperfections in brain-computer analogies, including the role of biochemical substances known as endocrines in emotions, and the possibility that consciousness depends upon quantum processes. But assuming that the computer is a perfect analogue to the brain (or that holistic functioning, endocrinology, and quantum-level activity can be duplicated within computers), how do we transfer personality from the brain to the computer? The details are fuzzy but the notion is scanning the brain, molecule by molecule, and feeding the results into a computer.

Maybe someday we can program artificial intelligence that will display emotions and engage in social behaviors that are highly suggestive of personality. Still it will be more than a little difficult to convince everyone that these entities are aware, conscious, and self-reflective. This could be particularly true if consciousness rests on subatomic, quantum processes and requires faithfully representing subatomic particles and their relationships to one another. This is not an abstract, tangential matter if you are thinking of making the transition personally. Even though the new uploaded version mimics your personality perfectly, would it be conscious? Would it be you, your twin, or something unprecedented? Would knowing that this alter ego would continue after your body died remove the sting of mortality? What if the transfer process depended on your biological death? As Damien Broderick asks, "Would you be prepared to terminate your own stream of awareness just so that some other person (with the same memories, admittedly) could awaken to an adventure in virtual reality, to endless machine life?" (2001: 208).

Widespread cyber transfer would depend on several conditions (Paul and Cox 1996). The technology must be inexpensive and widely available. Demand would be such that billions of units must be made available, almost overnight. It must be ecologically sustainable. The transfer process must be easy, painless, and reassuring. Finally, life must be better after transfer than before it. We can augment individual minds, hook different minds together, form supercolonies, and hook them to the Internet.

Predictions of virtual immortality are based on the steady doubling of computer power. There is a strong conviction that trends in progress today will continue tomorrow, that there will be no annoying limitations, no intervening events that will slow us down. Such thinking once assured us that the skies would be filled with personal helicopters, that we would build a trans-Atlantic tunnel, and that atomic power would blast canals through mountain ranges and power handwarmers to keep people comfortable at brisk November football games (MacKenzie 1996). These were natural, logical extrapolations of the science of the day. Of course, in retrospect, people could not have personal helicopters, because that would clutter the skies. Of course there was no need for a trans-Atlantic tunnel, once huge fleets of jets carried people from New York to Paris. Of course radiation made the use of atomic explosives for construction work totally unacceptable. Oftentimes linear extrapolations fail because they do not recognize that the predicted result hinges on interplay of many different factors: scientific, political, economic, and psychological.

The Postbiological Universe

Steven J. Dick raises the interesting possibility that since they are older than ours, most extraterrestrial civilizations have already made the transition to artificial forms of intelligence, that we exist in a postbiological universe where the psychology of biological beings no longer rules (2002). A postbiological universe is not one totally devoid of biological intelligence (after all, we are here) nor is it necessarily free of lower life. Rather, the majority of life has evolved beyond flesh-and-blood intelligence. Biological and postbiological life will live in harmony. Pressures of the marketplace will eliminate companies that produce surly, incompetent, contentious, or treacherous robots (Moravec 1999). Rather than regard robots as competitors or alien forms of intelligence, we should consider them our children and take great pride when they outperform us.

Dick points out that we do not really have good models of cultural evolution, but proposes the "Intelligence Principle" for organizing long-term cultural development. Specifically, the maintenance, improvement, and perpetuation of intelligence is the central driving force of cultural evolution, and to the extent that intelligence can be improved it will be improved (Dick 2002). In the future, our most rapid gains may be in the area of artificial intelligence. There are many unknowns and there may be ethical and legal brakes that will postpone the transition, but, given enough time, Earth, too, could become postbiological.

Nine

PREPOSTEROUS OR PRUDENT?

Evan Seamone, attorney and officer in the U.S. Army, has identified legal bases for preventing and mitigating major disasters (2003). Self-preservation is an imperative that mandates the involvement of international, national, and regional authorities. Self-preservation supersedes other treaties and laws. Killing in self-defense is justifiable, and when the alternative is death from starvation, cannibalism tends to be overlooked. Governments at all levels are responsible for keeping their people alive and must cooperate with one another to prevent or minimize disasters that cut across governmental boundaries. They also have the duty to "expect the unexpected," as illustrated in the history of U.S. civil defense that sought, well within the depths of the American heartland, protection against enemy air raids during World War II. The situation becomes complicated in the case of an impending asteroid impact or invasion from outer space, because the extremely low probability of such an event offsets the devastating results if the event were to occur. Planning, in Seamone's view, is considered "preposterous" when there are too many unknowns, but "prudent" given sufficient information to develop a workable plan. Is planning for cosmic events preposterous or prudent?

It is very difficult to interest people in serious planning for an asteroid impact, contact with extraterrestrials, and other cosmic events (Harrison 2003). People who lack foresight (the ability to think beyond the immediate here and now) and practical people who are highly involved in day-to-day existence are not likely to give much thought to remote possibilities. Thanks to the giggle factor most politicians and scientists will push such problems aside. The giggle factor refers to the raised eyebrows, stony silence, ridicule, and laughter that are attached to ideas and projects that fall outside of the normal range of discourse. The very ideas of asteroid impacts and extraterrestrial intelligence have "science fiction" rings to them. It is all too easy to associate these events with millennial cults and end-of-the-world prophecies and dismiss them as the province of cranks and flakes.

Many people shy away from disaster planning because they downplay the dangers inherent in a situation, or assume that everything will "work out" (as it often does). Yet, despite supreme confidence that she was unsinkable, the *Titanic* went to the bottom of the Atlantic after clipping an iceberg in the North Atlantic in 1912. Sometimes signs of danger are ignored even as deadly events become transparent. During the 1900 Galveston hurricane, men ignored their wives' entreaties to stay home and either help them shore-up the house or evacuate and trudged off to work, in some cases up to their thighs in water. For one group in Galveston, the moment of truth came when a restaurant's roof collapsed, killing five patrons, and for another group a corpse that floated into the railroad station waiting room was the first "intimation" of disaster (Larson 1999).

Planning for a cosmic event is either episodic (everyone works hard for a few days and then forgets about it) or proceeds at a glacial pace. Holding discussions once a year and trying to work through the United Nations are excellent ways to contain runaway progress. Admittedly, in some cases there are so many unknowns that it is difficult to plan prudently.

Some of the challenges of dealing with unprecedented events are revealed in efforts to protect U.S. citizens from nuclear war. The sociologist Lee Clarke has reviewed these plans and has found them lacking (Clarke 1999). Over the years, defense planners proposed building shelters that would protect people from the blast and fallout. Around 1950, for example, the government built sinister, windowless, blockhouse-like office buildings that were intended to survive atomic bombing but abandoned the tactic when hopelessly potent H-bombs came on line. In the 1960s, wealthy and nervous suburbanites built home fallout shelters. Owners wondered if they could really shoot their less wealthy or insightful neighbors who came seeking sanctuary. Ultimately, many of these underground chambers saw service as rumpus rooms and storage facilities. Numerous civil defense strategies were considered, but nobody, it seemed, was interested enough to pay for an extensive system of effective public shelters.

Then, officialdom lit upon the idea that evacuation would solve the problem (Clarke 1999). Just as authorities could evacuate beach communities on the shores of Long Island, New York in the face of an impending hurricane, they could move people from Manhattan to Albany just before the warheads hit. A dual theory of disaster planning took hold: protecting people from hurricanes, earthquakes, or other natural disasters is not that different from saving them from nuclear conflagration. If we can do the former, we can accomplish the latter.

Choosing a hurricane as a prototype for a nuclear attack creates an "affinity" between the two events (Clarke 1999). We assume that our experience with hurricanes, which is considerable (but not considerable enough, as shown when Hurricane Katrina hit New Orleans in 2005), offers a firm basis for protecting ourselves from nuclear war, a type of catastrophe that we have yet to experience. The illusory similarity makes it possible to develop reassuring plans of action. Endorsed by experts and released by the government, the plan proves that government is "doing something" to protect people from catastrophe.

The superficial similarities between the two events—hurricanes and nuclear attacks—at once creates the illusion that the plan is based on experience and diverts attention from the tremendous differences between the two threats. Hurricanes cannot strike within thirty minutes of their detection, cannot be retargeted to annihilate populations that have moved elsewhere, or lead to two-year nuclear winters.

Fantasy documents refer to plans that we develop in the absence of a firm knowledge base. Although they may succeed, such documents rest on flimsy conceptual schemes and insufficient data and for these reasons often fail when put to the test. Fantasy documents are "imaginative fictions about what people hope will happen" (Clarke 1999: 16). They are "whimsical speculations, flights of fancy in which scenarios are imagined with little regard to the usual constraints of 'reality'" (41). The fantasy part is that "most things will work right the first time, that most of the critical contingencies are known and have been prepared for" (30). Reactor meltdowns, nuclear wars, and giant oil spills are areas where we lack sufficient experience to plan effectively. Certainly, preparing for an asteroid impact or an encounter with creatures whose psychology and culture is not known to us are other areas where planning must proceed under conditions of high uncertainty.

Still, as Edward Cornish, editor of *The Futurist*, points out, foresight and planning will help us manage the future (Cornish 2004). We can profit from the lessons of explorers that undertook great expeditions of the past: anticipate future needs, use poor information if necessary, and expect the unexpected. Try to get a balance between imagination and reality, and think in the long term as well as the short term. Futurists have many tools for achieving all of this: quite a few of these are based on analyzing trends. In some cases trend analysis would be helpful: for example, understanding trends in SETI search technology might lead us to conclude that by a particular date we will have a fairly definitive answer to the question: "Are there other civilizations out there that use microwave radio technology?" Yet trend analysis is not applicable to all of the issues before us: the discovery of extraterrestrial intelligence or detection of an errant comet headed in our direction would be, for all intents and practical purposes, "one-off" or singular events. But even in these cases we can conduct thought experiments. We can draw on past experience—for example, historical precedents such as Europeans arriving in the Americas or the spread of ideas from one culture to another. Also, mathematical modeling may help us decide if, shortly after discovering one extraterrestrial culture, we are likely to discover many others. Perhaps scenario building is the most useful tool for us. This involves imagining a future event in some detail (for example, an asteroid hitting Helsinki), then working through the various implications. Cornish points out that even imperfect planning moves us beyond fatalism or helplessness and helps us prepare for effective action.

Planning for Contact

Serious planning for the discovery of extraterrestrial life followed close on the heels of the scientific papers that established the feasibility of interstellar communication via radio. The first radiotelescope search, Project Ozma, had already begun in time to influence the Brookings Report on how peaceful space exploration might affect human affairs. Commissioned by NASA and prepared by a large team of experts and consultants led by psychologist Donald Michael, the report was presented to the eighty-second Congress (Committee on Science and Astronautics 1961). This report offered a wide range of ideas—such as communications satellites—that were futuristic at the time but that have long since become everyday working technology. Encountering extraterrestrial intelligence was included, but this was only a tiny part of the report—a few paragraphs, really—suggesting that preparing the public for contact was not the primary purpose of this document. The Michael committee saw radio communication as the most likely way that contact could occur (although it added that we might find extraterrestrial artifacts on the Moon or other planets) and stressed that contact could be confirmed at any time. They felt that the consequences were largely unpredictable and could vary profoundly across cultures and groups. Confronted by a superior society, some societies have disintegrated, but others have survived, although in changed form. The report urged ongoing studies to prepare us, intellectually and emotionally, for the great discovery.

Philip Morrison, Frank Drake, Carl Sagan, and other early SETI scientists recognized that their work could have profound consequences for humanity, so they enlisted the help of anthropologists, lawyers, political scientists, psychologists, and sociologists (Morrison et al. 1977). In the late 1970s, Mary M. Connors, working at NASA Ames Research Center, outlined many of the issues that absorb planners today (Harrison 1997). She drew a distinction between immediate effects of contact, measured in days, weeks, and months, and long-term effects measured in years, decades, and centuries. Early effects were likely to include rumors, clogged telephone circuits, heightened emotionality, and demands for vigorous government actions. Long-term effects would begin after the initial excitement waned and as the discovery infiltrated not only science and technology but also religion and the arts: in short, almost every aspect of human life and endeavor.

In the late 1990s Ivan Almar and Jill Tarter constructed the Rio Scale for estimating the likely impact of an announcement of the discovery of extraterrestrial life (forthcoming). Named after a conference in Brazil, the Rio Scale was modeled after the earlier Torino Scale that had been designed to assess the risk associated with potential asteroid strikes (Binzel 1997). The latter proposed multiplying the likely force of the impact (based on the asteroid's size) by the probability that the object would hit Earth. Thus, the larger the object, and the more certain that it will hit Earth, the greater the threat.

The Rio Scale is based on estimates of the credibility and potential consequences of the discovery of extraterrestrial life. Credibility is synonymous with believability: thus an announcement by a respected scientist who presented good evidence would be more credible than an announcement by a middle school science teacher who lost his confirming videotape. Impact depends on the type of discovery (for example, an omnidirectional beacon as compared to a specific message aimed at Earth), the way in which the discovery is made (a radiotelescope search or reinterpretation of ancient documents), and the location of the intelligence (a neighboring star or a distant galaxy). The Rio Scale is intended to set an appropriate level of alertness on the part of scientists and help reporters understand the event's significance. It emphasizes microwave and optical SETI but also acknowledges SETA, or the search for extraterrestrial artifacts, and the possible discovery of alien intelligence within our solar system.

SETI Planning Efforts

Planning undertaken by astronomers revolves around the standard microwave detection scenario. The working assumption is that by means of a radiotelescope we will discover a carrier wave or "dial tone" from a civilization that is hundreds, perhaps thousands of light years away. Because our two cultures will be so radically different it could take us years to decode this message, if this is possible at all. Since radio waves travel at the speed of light it is doubtful that we could enter into a true dialogue with a civilization that far away.

John Billingham developed a decision tree to guide our responses to microwave transmissions (Billingham 2002). He distinguishes, for example, between eavesdropping on a signal between two distant civilizations and receiving a transmission intended for Earth. If we eavesdrop we may want to withhold responding, since there is no evidence that they have discovered us. If we are specifically targeted there is no advantage to "playing possum" since they already know that we are here. Similarly, the decision tree leads to different reactions to a simple signal as compared to one that is rich in content. (More information-rich or informative signals require more detailed and nuanced responses.) And, of course, our reactions would be very different to friendly versus threatening messages. Billingham explicitly applies decision theory to microwave SETI but notes that it could be extended to other search procedures. Planning for active SETI—powerful broadcasts to the stars—is in its infancy. Opinion is divided on whether active SETI is an inordinate risk or logical next step, and, in any event, there is no easy way to determine who speaks for Earth.

By far the most sustained planning under the orthodox SETI scenario is conducted under the auspices of the Permanent SETI Committee of the International Academy of Astronautics. This Committee meets annually in conjunction with the International Astronautical Federation Congress. Typically, each Congress includes a half-day session on the anthropological, economic, legal, political, psychological, and sociological aspects of SETI. Over the years, discussions have ranged over many issues including public attitudes and support for SETI, conduct of the search, news dissemination and rumor control, deciphering message content, and framing a model reply. There is no single report that summarizes all of the work of the SETI Committee, but periodically, papers presented at International Astronautical Federation meetings are published in special editions of the journal *Acta Astronautica*. The flavor of much of this research is captured in my 1997 work, *After Contact:*

The Human Response to Extraterrestrial Life, and John Billingham's *Societal Implications of the Detection of an Extraterrestrial Civilization* (Harrison 1997; Billingham et al. 1999).

One of the SETI Committee's greatest contributions so far is the development of postdetection protocols that it hopes will be followed if the discovery occurs (Lyall 2000). These protocols require careful verification of the discovery so as not to raise a false alarm (SETI searchers are rightfully fanatic about this) and announcing the discovery to the world as a whole so as not to give any one country an advantage. Because they know that the discovery will affect everyone, the committee tries to engage the United Nations in the planning process. This could help move the protocols from voluntary agreement to law. The committee has strategies for working with the media to minimize false alarms and misinformation and discourage the kind of reporting that could lead to panic.

Since search method determines search outcome, it makes sense for astronomers to plan within the limits of radio and optical SETI. Their equipment positions them to find a dial tone at a distance. It is not helpful for detecting a huge world ship lurking at the outer perimeter of our solar system, a message from ancient astronauts inscribed in a dark corridor within a pyramid, or the Space Brothers' Web site.

Planning for a dial tone at a distance shows that the scientists who are conducting the search are accountable, that they recognize the possible consequences of their work, and that they seek to minimize risk. The scenario is itself is comforting. "They" will not know that we have found them and, if they somehow find out, it should be all but impossible (we suppose) for them to get here. Finally, linking planning to a scientific search strategy signals to both scientists and the public that SETI researchers are engaged in a legitimate scientific activity, that they are not fringe scientists or crackpots.

Donald Tarter suspects that SETI searchers will be in for a rude awakening by ham-handed governmental authorities if and when an extraterrestrial signal is acquired (2000). As long as SETI remains little more than an exercise the government can afford to treat the activity with benign neglect. As soon as detection occurs, he believes, no national leader would risk leaving the matter entirely within the hands of the scientific community. To gain control over the situation, government officials will seek debriefing and security agents will monitor signals at the observatory or with their own equipment. Government analysts will work night and day. Whereas Donald Tarter does not use the phrase "government cover-up," he does expect that the government will attempt "information management" and security agencies will do much of the enforcement. He expects that scientists will be forced to sign secrecy oaths, government spokespersons will replace science educators, and officials will monitor the media. Any hint of danger in the signal itself, or any unrest among the populace, will increase the strength of government regulation.

One of the most detailed discussions of secrecy is that offered by Allen Tough (1990). He begins by reviewing many justifications for secrecy. Astronomers will maintain secrecy because they are afraid that if their findings are incorrect they will be subjected to ridicule and embarrassment. The government will remain silent so that people won't panic; so that extraterrestrial culture will not have an adverse impact on our philosophy, theology, or economy; so that by entering into an alliance with extraterrestrials we can gain a competitive military or economic edge on other countries; and so that we will not be duped by a seemingly friendly form of intelligence that arrives in a "Trojan Horse" and then turns against us.

Tough then explains the flaws in each of these justifications. He urges astronomers to share all of their observations, no matter how weird or unbelievable, since we really don't know how we will discover extraterrestrials. Expectations that people will panic are rarely met and today people are very aware of the possibility of extraterrestrials. Although competition and secrecy may be advantageous in the short run, openness and international cooperation may better maximize long-term benefits. Tough's advocacy of openness is admirable but Donald Tarter's forecast may be closer to the mark. Governments tend to rely on precedent and prefer consultants who are highly trustworthy (no loose cannons), two practices that will encourage government intervention and information control.

Efforts useful for planning have increased in recent years. In 1999, NASA sponsored a workshop on the cultural aspects of astrobiology; although there was no funding to publish the report, it is accessible on the NASA astrobiology Web site and a brief description appeared in a magazine (Harrison et al. 2002). In 2000, the Foundation for the Future, a Bellevue, Washington think tank issued an edited volume on what SETI might lead to one thousand years from now (Tough 2000). Douglas A. Vakoch, a psychologist associated with the SETI Institute, has developed and led a number of symposia and panels (including at American Anthropological Association meeting) whose results will eventually appear as published conference proceedings. His leadership is bringing a wider range of social scientists into the planning effort.

The Contact Planning Group

If planning in the tradition of the SETI Committee is methodical and conservative, then planning in the tradition of the Contact Planning Group (CPG) that assembled twice in the late 1990s was fast and furious. Financed by a Silicon Valley entrepreneur, this group met to develop a broad spectrum of planning scenarios and to outline multiple strategies for managing contact with nonhuman forms of intelligence, including that of the extraterrestrial variety. There were two ground rules. First, all ideas brought forth in the discussion could be used by any participant in any way he or she saw fit. Second, although participants were free to disclose their own participation in the CPG, members signed legally binding agreements that they would not reveal the identities of the other participants. This second rule was intended to prevent participation from damaging anyone's career, and to assure that the results of the meeting would stand by themselves, neither strengthened nor weakened by the reputations of the participants. The following account is based on private notes augmented with other material.

Critical Uncertainties

The CPG discussed three critical uncertainties that would affect human reactions to nonhuman intelligence. These are the speed with which the contact scenario unfolded, the familiarity of the nonhuman intelligence, and perceptions of the net effects of the event.

Like any other event, contact could occur in a fast way or a leisurely way. The discovery could take the form of a sudden insight that immediately follows a demarcated event, or it could consist of a dawning awareness, based on the slow accrual of evidence that "we are not alone." Sudden insight will be more disruptive than a dawning awareness. If we gradually become aware of alien intelligence and have time to adjust to the event, we should be less disrupted than if, like one of the central characters in the movie *Independence Day*, we wake up to one morning to face an alien invasion. As noted by Michael Barkun, some conspiracy theorists suggest that the government, working through the media, is preparing us for contact (2003). Whereas this strikes me as very unlikely, advance contemplation should help desensitize people, thus reducing the intensity of their reaction if contact should occur.

Our current technology may place us on a slow trajectory. If we find traces of past life on Mars, if we find evidence of simple forms of life on extrasolar planets, then we should be better conditioned for the discovery of extraterrestrial intelligence. Indeed, the fact that the search proceeds at the limits of our technology and hence yields ambiguous evidence may help us ease into the new era. As more evidence is accumulated, as different interpretations are tried and discarded, scientists could converge inexorably on the conclusion that we are not alone. Slowly, one person after another realizes that we share the universe with other intelligent life, easing our transition into the postcontact world. (Think of the benefits of slowly entering a cold swimming pool as compared to jumping in from a diving board!) The major disadvantage of the slow trajectory is that it provides greater opportunity for secrecy, manipulation, and cover-up.

Familiarity refers to people's sense that "they" are like "us." We should find it easier to deal with forms of intelligence that seem familiar to us—for example, flesh-and blood (or flesh-and-blood substitute) humanoids that communicate with us via radio, as compared to weird or ephemeral beings that communicate telepathically. If "the other" is really strange we may become fearful and lose hope of communicating and finding common grounds.

Net effects refer to our perceptions of whether, in the final analysis, the overall consequences for humanity will be favorable or unfavorable. Will we be granted access to advanced science and technology? Will we be accorded membership in some sort of interstellar federation or galactic club? Will we be contained on our planet, somehow abused, or even destroyed? Will they play tricks or make fun of us? Whether most of us perceive extraterrestrials as benevolent or malevolent—as angels or demons—could have an overriding effect on our reactions.

Both astrobiology and SETI are peaceful scientific activities that practitioners consider safe. Instead of being considered one of the better prototypes for understanding the response to extraterrestrial life, the public's panicky response to Orson Welles's *Invasion from Mars* broadcast (based on a novella entitled *War of the Worlds*) is the worst example because given the standard detection scenario contact will not begin with an invasion. With the exception of Michael Michaud, who had a distinguished career with the Department of State, few members of the SETI Committee remind us that we should prepare for the worst (Michaud 1972, 1977).

Perhaps there is something fundamental in the human psyche that responds negatively to the prospect of extraterrestrial life (D. Tarter 2000). When he heard about the Arecibo transmission, the British Astronomer Royal at the time fretted that we might attract the attention of a violent or berserk civilization. A leading scientist and educator, Robert Sinsheimer, described SETI as one of the three most dangerous types of research. He felt that SETI, nuclear weapons development, and recombinant DNA technology should be banned at once (Billingham 2002). Timothy Ferris feared not that aliens would be different from us, but that they would turn out to be bigger and more brutal bullies armed with bigger clubs (Ferris 1992). Roberto Pinotti expects that the two most prominent effects of contact will be a "crisis of authority," which includes science, religion, and sociopolitical structures, and that Earth's super powers would quickly be reduced to the status of "Andorra, Monaco, and the Republic of San Marino" (1990: 163). He adds "today's establishment worldwide would have everything to lose from any form of contact with ETI, since it would be the first victim in a frontal collision between different civilizations" (164). Astronomer and skeptic Donald Menzel commented that the public is afraid of "saucers"—and we need only a match to set off a nationwide panic that could far exceed that touched off by Orson Welles' s *Invasion from Mars* radio broadcast in 1938 (Pinotti 1990). Menzel certainly did what he could to convince the public that UFOs do not exist.

Ironically, a threat from outer space might increase rather than decrease international stability. People that do not necessarily see eye-to-eye sometimes reconcile to eliminate threats. This occurred during World War II when the United States, the United Kingdom, and many other nations joined with the Soviet Union to defeat Germany, Italy, and Japan. President Ronald Reagan understood this unifying effect, and publicly commented that an attack from outer space could cause the United States and the Soviet Union to work cooperatively. Addressing high school students and faculty in Fallston, Maryland on 4 December 1985 he said, "…When you stop to think that we're all God's children, wherever we live in the world, I couldn't help but say to [Russian President Gorbachev] just think about how easy his task and mine might be in these meetings that we held if suddenly there was a threat to this world from some other species from another planet outside in the universe. We'd forget all the little differences that we have between our countries and we would find out once and for all that we really are all human beings here on this Earth together" (quoted in Pinotti 1990: 164-165). In a public response, Gorbachev agreed, but stated that he did not think that an invasion was imminent (Pinotti 1990).

The CPG reinforced the view that we must be prepared for the worst: ready to counter both direct and indirect threats. Direct threats are those that come from the extraterrestrial life itself. These would include, for example, any type of hostile activity including frightening communications and military or other action that is contrary to human welfare. Simple examples would be their establishing a military base within our solar system or occupying some parts of Earth. Other threats could come in the form of disrupting the international political system, perhaps through diplomatic support or technical aid for hostile nations or terrorist groups. Indirect threats could take the form of releasing well-intentioned information that undermines human institutions and values.

Sectors

Rather than looking at the direct effects of contact on humanity as a whole, the CPG explored how different contact scenarios would affect different sectors—Government, Science, Business, Media, and Religion—and how the responses of these different sectors would shape public reaction. There was a sense that although certain sectors might form alliances and cooperate, they would also pursue selfish interests.

If the newly discovered intelligence were benevolent, Government would attempt to extract useful knowledge, and if it were malevolent, Government's first goal would be to protect its citizens. The greater the perceived threat, the more likely Government will centralize and take sharp, decisive action, and the more likely Donald Tarter's predictions of government oversight will come true (2000). Among key Government organizations that will shape Americans' responses are political institutions such as the U.S. Congress, administrative bodies such as the U.S. Department of State, Homeland Defense, the FBI and the military. An ill-prepared or poorly functioning government could easily transform a promising event into a disaster.

Government's first concern will be protecting its own authority, which could be quite difficult if there is no clear and obvious way to do this. Extrapolating from the work of psychologist Irving Janis, Government's response under conditions of ambiguity and uncertainty would depend on the speed of the unfolding of events (Janis and Mann 1985). If contact unfolds in a slow and leisurely way we can expect denial, rationalization, buck-passing, and other activities that effectively avoid addressing the issue. If, on the other hand, an unprepared Government were confronted with a rapidly evolving scenario, we could expect panicky, ineffective decision making. Government is unlikely to respond effectively to the extent that it refuses to accept evidence that violates preconceptions, that it is dominated by self-serving people and agencies, that it is slowed by cumbersome bureaucratic procedures, and that it has low credibility in the eyes of the people (Harrison 2003).

Widespread beliefs in government conspiracies and cover-ups will prove troublesome if Government tries to reassure people that it has everything under control. As noted in Chapter 7, perceptions of government dishonesty and duplicity have reached crisis proportions and could contribute to any of a number of catastrophes, including overreaction to the confirmation of alien intelligence. The CPG suggested that perceptions of government manipulation and cover-up would be particularly strong in the case of a malevolent intelligence and a leisurely time line.

Science, according to the CPG, would want to learn as much as possible about nonhuman intelligence, irrespective of whether or not it took a benevolent or malevolent form. Each of the other sectors would rely heavily on science for assessing the situation and for developing ways to communicate. Participants thought that scientists might come closest to matching a superior form of intelligence and for this reason, if none other, would make the best communicators and good-will ambassadors.

Less pleasingly, Science might overstate the threat in order to receive the massive infusion of resources that Science enjoys when called upon to resolve a crisis. The CPG expected that if the intelligence were perceived as malevolent, we should anticipate a strong alliance involving Government, Science, and the Military. This would be especially true in a rapidly unfolding situation.

Business, according to the CPG, would try to learn as much as it could in order to protect economic interests. On the one hand, Business would prosper if incoming extraterrestrial technology makes it possible to offer new products and services. On the other hand, Business would suffer if we receive word of new technologies that make current industries obsolete. In order to forestall a stock market crash, Business may be tempted to suppress information, especially about contact with a malevolent form of intelligence. Moreover, Business may try to maintain a level playing field by doing what it could to keep a superior civilization out of the marketplace. Even under a rapidly deteriorating situation involving a strange and malevolent form of intelligence some companies will offer products intended to mitigate disaster. Under almost any conditions there will be voracious markets for movies, books, novelties, and toys.

Media is important in its own right, and as an interface between the different sectors and the public. Media can disseminate accurate and complete information, or it can be used to manipulate public opinion.

As an ally of Government, Science, and Business, Media can ease public apprehensions. The higher the status of the specific newspaper or TV news program, the more likely it is to reflect the views of the establishment. (For this reason we can count on the *The New York Times* and the *Washington Post* to reinforce the restrained views of mainstream science, while tabloids will wax prosaic about the paranormal and seamier aspects.) Still, Media may be torn between accurate, responsible reporting and getting the story out quickly and in ways that attract wealthy sponsors and huge audiences.

Religion, according to the CPG, would be interested in any form of contact that could substantiate or disprove important religious beliefs. We can expect religious leaders to look very carefully for signs that are consistent or inconsistent with specific teachings and prophecies. There may be strong pressures to deify or demonize "the other," and it would be incumbent on responsible religious leaders to resist this. In the case of a malevolent form of intelligence, religious leaders may be called upon to strengthen society's backbone and generate hope. Agnostics and atheists should not overlook the power of religion to provide people with solace and strengthen public resolve under conditions of threat.

Of the different sectors, apart from Science, it is Religion and Media that have received substantial attention outside of the CPG. The report submitted to Congress floated the idea that members of fundamentalist religious groups would respond badly to contact (Committee on Science and Astronautics 1961). The report's author, Donald Michael, pointed out that antiscience sects were gaining members throughout the world. He did not have a flattering impression of the intellectual levels of either the shepherds or the flocks, and stated that they would find the news "electrifying." He realized that some religious groups already believe in life on other worlds, so we should expect different religious groups to respond in different ways.

Later surveys suggest that many Christians have relaxed attitudes toward the discovery of extraterrestrial life. Michael Ashkenazi conducted interviews with twenty-one theologians, seventeen of whom believe that extraterrestrial intelligence exists, and found Buddhism and Hinduism among the religions that already accept the idea of extraterrestrial life or will not be particularly troubled by confirmation of its existence (1992). He was more concerned by Christianity, Judaism, and Islam, which believe that man is created in God's image. Ashkenazi expects that Catholicism and other hierarchically organized Christian religions will interpret the event and make policy and then church members will fall in line. Protestant sects are varied and autonomous, and are likely to react in different ways, with fundamentalist and dogmatic sects reacting vehemently.

Victoria Alexander mailed questionnaires to a national sample of clergy including 563 Protestant ministers, 396 Roman Catholic priests, and 41 rabbis (1998). Of the 1,000 surveys, 230 were returned. Although described as a UFO survey, the questions were couched in terms of an "advanced extraterrestrial civilization." Although not all respondents were thrilled by the prospect of extraterrestrial life, most of the U. S. clergy who returned their questionnaires did not feel that their faith or that of their congregation would be compromised. Just 3 percent of the Protestant ministers, 1 percent of the Catholic priests and 11 percent of the rabbis (that is, one rabbi) strongly agreed that "Official confirmation of the discovery of an advanced, technologically superior extraterrestrial civilization would have severe negative effects on the country's moral, social, and religious foundations." In comparison to these miniscule percentages, 48 percent of the respondents disagreed and 29 percent strongly disagreed with the same statement. Would their congregations perceive contact as a threat? Not really—15 percent thought yes, 18 percent were unsure, and 67 percent thought no. Would the discovery cause their congregations to question their fundamental beliefs regarding the origin of life? Eight out of ten ministers, priests and rabbis thought not. And on it went: 70 percent of the respondents thought that contact would not endanger organized religions and 77 percent indicated that they would not be shaken by genetic similarities between humans and extraterrestrials. For every respondent who thought that extraterrestrial claims of responsibility for life on Earth would cause a religious crisis, two respondents thought that it would not.

On the whole theologians and clergy express openness and even positive attitudes towards the discovery of extraterrestrial life. Of course, imagining an event and actually experiencing it can be quite different. How many young men have craved to participate in battle, only to reassess their position once engaged in a bayonet charge or pinned down by machine gun fire?

Some of the respondents to Alexander's survey did think that the discovery would cause a crisis. And, as is always a problem with survey research, we do not know the views of the high proportion of people who failed to complete the questionnaire. One of these potential informants declined because he did not want to participate in a "trick of the devil." For people who support SETI, the problem is not "religion" but some religious groups. A leader of a relatively small and unimportant sect could gain power and do great damage by effectively combining fundamentalism, fire-and-brimstone preaching, and television to build fear, hatred, and despair.

Response Strategies

The CPG covered more than one large pad of poster paper with scribbles and diagrams detailing how various combinations of speed, familiarity, and net affect were likely to impact different sectors before it turned to strategies for managing contact and its aftermath. It reviewed four strategies: cooperation, adaptation, containment, and fight. The value of each strategy depended upon how contact occurred, and each strategy required different policies, personnel, and resources. Each strategy included shaping public perceptions of the situation, maintaining social cohesion and international stability, and assembling and positioning the resources necessary to respond effectively to the hypothetical event.

Cooperation was the preferred strategy if contact were voluntary on our part, if "they" appeared to be friendly, and if people expected a positive overall net effect. Government and science would work together to strengthen channels of communication with the intelligence. Through Media, Government would give the public as much accurate information as possible. Government would build "informational alliances" with other governments and insure that everyone shared in the benefits. Religion would preach the value of cooperation with extraterrestrials, expand its belief system to incorporate the new reality, and, along with Government, emphasize the public's moral responsibility and the need to treat extraterrestrials respectfully. Major world religions would be on guard against the emergence of potentially dangerous cults. Media would stress the value of infusing new ideas within society, and the "story of the millennium" would be one of new times and new hope.

Adaptation is promising if there is time to react, the form of intelligence is at least somewhat familiar, and if there is a hint of coercion on their part. Government would show strong leadership, mobilize all intelligence assets, and attempt to reassure the public. Science would strive to "make the strange familiar," that is, interpret the intelligence in terms of known quantities and use procrustean techniques if necessary to make the situation seem as similar as possible to past situations that were well understood. Religion would discover how to reduce public fear and mistrust, strengthen the public's sense of humanity, and resist attempts to deify or demonize the intelligence. Mainstream religion would stand guard against a proliferation of cults. Media would develop a "resilient" communications strategy but the overall message would still be "new times and new hope." People might have to prepare for wide-scale change and perhaps even sacrifice.

Containment is the most promising strategy if the alien intelligence is strange, hard to understand, and possibly hostile and if the situation unfolds slowly over time. Government would centralize, assert strong leadership, and limit the public's access to knowledge. Science would try to get as much information as possible about the other's strengths and vulnerabilities and gain insight into their technology. Religion would try to reduce public fear and mistrust and strengthen people's sense of humanity. Fight is the only option in the face of an unambiguous alien attack: suffice it to say that if they are as advanced technologically as many people expect, we would enter the fight as underdogs, unlikely to emerge victorious.

Perhaps the course of interstellar affairs will not be entirely smooth even if we meet friendly, communicative, benevolent others (Harrison and Dick 2000). During the first phase, we will be highly enamored of extraterrestrial intelligence. This will reflect, in part, our tendency to admire older, wiser, richer, and more powerful individuals, and in part the high expectations regarding the benefits that we hope for from our new partnership. At some point, however, extraterrestrials are likely to fall short of our expectations. Maybe they will not have the information that we seek; perhaps we will fall short of their expectations and they will withhold their largesse. Or, perhaps after they create a positive first impression they will reveal a flaw in their character or society. This will lead to a second phase, marked by suspicion, cynicism, and negative emotions (all proportional to the heights of earlier expectations). Yet, unless we break off communication, this, too, will pass. We will ease into the third phase as we develop a fuller and more differentiated view of what they are like. At that point extraterrestrials will no longer be seen as devils or gods, but as complex creatures and entities with unique and subtle patterns of strengths and weaknesses.

First contact, if it occurs at all, will occur in our future. Any difficulties that we experience will be partly due to extraterrestrials and partly of our own making. We can shift from being part of the problem to becoming part of the solution by means of serious planning. We have the capacity to develop strategies and tactics that can maximize benefits and prevent, minimize, contain, or reverse damages. We can make more intelligent or less intelligent choices (Harrison 2003). For this reason, it is important that we proceed with planning efforts. How do we accelerate the search? How do we recognize signs of intelligence when we encounter it? What kinds of research can we undertake right now to understand extraterrestrial intelligence if and when we encounter it later on? How do we ensure that the discovery is for the benefit of all humankind? If we like what we find, how do we compose a model reply? How do we establish positive, mutually beneficial relationships with societies that are radically different from our own? And, how can the scientists who conduct the search establish a dialogue with the public, so people will be well prepared if and when contact occurs? A dialogue is not to be confused with telling people how it is or what they should do. It requires listening carefully to what the people have to say.

Effective planning requires an open mind. This means broadening our horizons beyond the standard scientific detection scenario and thinking through a wide range of possibilities, including some of the less plausible or palatable alternatives. We need experimentation and rehearsal, to become proficient at thinking broadly and flexibly, analyzing unexpected or unusual situations, generating "out of the box" solutions, and doing the necessary groundwork for an effective response.

We cannot anticipate every situation but we can develop a tool kit so that we can respond flexibly when the time arises. This tool kit would include a reservoir of experts, mobilization procedures, strategies for simplifying the situation (for example, by minimizing interference from the public) and ways to buy time (early warning procedures, rumor control).

Overall, planning should take into account multiple search strategies, recognize that either "we" or "they" could take the initiative, and acknowledge that contact and its aftermath will depend upon the nature of extraterrestrial civilization, the way that contact unfolds, and the civilizations and individuals involved. These efforts must admit the possibility that we cannot be certain of what we may find (or what may find us) and that "contact" could involve spacecraft or evolve in totally unexpected ways. By including possibilities that strike us as implausible, we may be able to forestall the "Titanic Effect." This occurs when an event is considered so unlikely that it is given no further thought. Because the idea that the *Titanic* might sink was so unthinkable, she sailed without adequate safety precautions. Indeed, lifeboats were removed to give passengers a larger promenade area and better ocean views. Other events considered as impossible were the meltdowns at Three Mile Island and at Chernobyl, the chemical plant venting poisonous gas in Bhopal India, and the explosion of the space shuttle *Challenger* (Clarke 1999). We have the foresight to prepare for a lengthy roster of environmental and man-made events, and encountering extraterrestrial intelligence should be added to this list.

Much planning draws on historical events involving the meeting of two radically different cultures, such as the arrival of Spaniards in the New World, the British and Dutch in Africa, the British in Australia, and the Americans in Japan (Dick 1996; Harrison 1997). Since extraterrestrials are not expected to arrive in person, special attention is paid to the flow of ideas across cultures; for example, the arrival of the Arabic numerical system in Europe (Dick 1996). In these comparisons it is assumed that the extraterrestrial society is vastly advanced in terms of science and technology; hence, "they" are cast in the role of the wealthy and powerful Europeans. Humans are cast in the technologically inferior roles.

Drawing on the human experience so far, the expectation is that the technologically superior culture will overwhelm the technologically inferior culture. Do these precedents represent a reliable body of knowledge, or are they mere "affinities" that only superficially resemble actual contact? Does our knowledge base at this point support functional plans or only symbolic documents? Historical precedents give us our only experiential basis right now, but we must be aware that extrapolations yield only rough approximations of what might happen following real contact, so we have to take these approximations with a grain of salt.

—*Ten*—

STAR WARS

Colin Bennett proposes that 12:30 P.M. on Thursday, 20 November 1952 was one of the defining moments of the twentieth century (2001). That was when George Adamski, arguably the first self-proclaimed contactee, met Orthon, who had come to Earth aboard a flying saucer from Venus. Bennett proposes this because aliens have been a prominent part of our culture ever since. They are among us, if not exactly like the Space Brothers who drove Adamski in a black 1954 Pontiac sedan, then in our imaginations, stories, and dreams. For over fifty years political parties, scientific theories, fads, and fashions have come and gone, but flying saucers remain. Whatever arrived here in 1952 came to Earth to stay and has been a source of fear, inspiration, and derision ever since.

Cosmic evolution, modern astronomy, space exploration, and new threats to Earth are among the forces that encourage us to reassess our place in the universe. These scientific discoveries captivate our imagination and hint of new solutions to old questions about who we are, where we came from, and what will become of us. They have infiltrated religion and folklore and have lead people to new truths that are validated by their perceptions, memories, and cultural if not empirical facts. Our heightened fascination with realms beyond Earth shows no signs of tapering off, and will rise to new peaks if extraterrestrial life is discovered.

Today it is tempting to view science as the final arbiter of truth, the gold standard against which all ideas are gauged, the best model for all forms of inquiry (Bauer 2001). Science, as it applies to contemporary discussions of our place in the universe, includes all sorts of ideas that would have amused or befuddled scientists of earlier generations. Concepts such as superposition, complementarity, uncertainty, nonlocality, and entanglement, notes Dean Radin, create a "new reality that fades before us like a Cheshire cat" (2006: 220). These ideas run contrary to the assumptions of classical physics and common sense, and have significantly softened scientists' sense of the absolute. Whether or not we are in the midst of a paradigm shift that will prompt science to embrace the paranormal or are undergoing a flurry of New Age ideas, the "new physics" makes it easy to expect that science can provide definitive answers to life's most baffling questions. Right now, many people are willing to run ahead of the data and, if credentialed scientists do not agree with their ideas, conclude that their critics are narrow-minded, misguided, or do not understand the potential of the latest theories. In fact, science cannot address all questions right now and there may be some issues that forever remain outside of science's grasp. But many scientists are convinced that eventually science will be able to answer all questions that are worth asking—that is, questions that we can explore through empirical means.

Religion has been with us for all time, although its specific manifestations have varied over the years. Religion persists because it offers cosmological ideas and ethical prescriptions that constitute useful blueprints for effective living and because when successful it promotes both mental health and social harmony. Fundamentalists who are bound by a literal interpretation of the Bible and who deny scientific findings are offset by theologians, religious leaders, and congregations that maintain religious values while accepting cultural relativism, burgeoning science, and runaway technology. For them, religion is fluid and dynamic and takes nature into account. Surveys find relaxed attitudes among theologians, ministers, rabbis, and priests. In recent years the Catholic Church has stepped up efforts to embrace both religion and science, and the Pope's own observatory participates in the search for extraterrestrial life. New theologies such as cosmotheology are sensitive to science, ecumenical in approach, and emphasize not the uniqueness of Christ, but the universality of God's work (Hoffman 2004b). There is a strong sense of history, a view to the future, and a ministry of hope.

It is certainly possible to study UFOs scientifically, but most discussions are dominated by anecdotes that bear an unmistakable resemblance to folklore and myth. Extraterrestrial entities puportedly watch us, study us, and intervene in our history. They offer us moral guidance and, under some conditions, salvation. Such myths have parallels in different cultures and at different times (Bierlein 1993). There are several possibilities here—for example, they may be similar because stories migrate from one culture to another, or they may appear independently at different times and places because they cater to widespread and enduring human needs. Under the second of these explanations UFOs and abductions are space-age versions of earlier myths, such as dazzling performances by angels and nocturnal visits by old hags who half-suffocated Victorian gentlemen. Of course, consigning UFOs to myth infuriates UFOlogists who are convinced that flying saucers are nuts-and-bolts spacecraft arriving from distant solar systems and entirely worthy of scientific attention. The widespread skeptical view that UFOs are imaginary would cause no end of mischief in the unlikely event that the extraterrestrial hypotheses were to prove true.

At first glance, modern science appears to be dabbling in myth. One reason, of course, is that much folklore masquerades as history and science. Another is that visions of hyperspace, parallel universes, nonlocality, quantum entanglement, and the like resonate with beliefs in "alternative realities" or "other planes of existence" that pervade religion and folklore. It is difficult, right now, to tell exactly where these ideas might lead. However, scientists and skeptics do not confuse anecdote with history and science; nor—with some notable exceptions—do they dwell upon a possible connection of quantum physics and the paranormal. For many contemporary scientists higher dimensions are useful hypothetical constructs, and not necessarily the stage for macro-events, such as battle between gods, realms of the dead, conduits for mental telepathy, or interstellar shortcuts. Scientists study transcendent experiences, too, but as the product of biology, culture, and human psychology, not as union with spiritual entities. Scientists study the end of the world, but as the result of natural physical causes and human error, not as retribution from a wrathful God. Scientists who are interested in immortality (or at least unprecedented longevity) believe that this might be brought about through biotechnology, not through prayer. And, from the scientific view, any superhuman forms of intelligence that exist beyond Earth are hypothetical, and, if they really do exist, are the products of evolution, not of supernatural forces. Any similarities between science and myth are superficial and should not mask crucial differences in assumptions, theories, and research.

Researchers who use scientific methods to search for life beyond Earth (including those who search for extraterrestrial probes in our solar system) strive valiantly to distance themselves from religion and myth. They work hard to make sure that their ideas are not confused with the uncritical wishful thinking that they see as prominent within UFOlogy and fret continuously about confusing SETI and UFOlogy in the public mind. At the heart of this campaign is a relentless emphasis on the scientific stature of SETI: the scientific method, replication and verification, peer review, and strict protocols to prevent premature claims. I know of no other area where scientists work so hard to explain away their own findings and steer away from false claims.

Many astronomers and other scientists have had "bad experiences with aggressive [UFOlogists] accusing us of all kinds of nasty things and not taking their ideas seriously" and for this reason avoid talking to them (Grinspoon 2003: 351). SETI scientists are closely identified with the skeptics' cause, and some serve on Paul Kurtz's Committee for the Scientific Investigation of Claims of the Paranormal and write articles for the *Skeptical Inquirer*. Minimizing the "UFO taint" has been a constant uphill battle. Countless documentaries on "life in the universe" have included both SETI and UFOlogy without adequately distinguishing between the two. Careful research and wild claims are intermingled. The inherently conservative nature of science places SETI at a disadvantage against unruly competitors who all too often stress sensationalistic but unproven ideas.

The Global Brain

Are cosmic and biological evolution the result of blind and impersonal forces, or do they reflect a larger plan and purpose? Can we explain religious and mystical experiences in terms of neurology or is there more to it? Must we rely on telescopes and other scientific instruments or will extrasensory perception allow us to communicate with distant entities? Should we pray to God for everlasting life, or are we better off investing our time and energy in biotechnology and computer science? Such are the controversies that rage as we come of age in the universe.

To approach this in a humorous vein, we might compare the contributions of science, religion, and folklore to simultaneous acts in a three-ring circus. In these traveling shows of yesteryear, three acts appeared simultaneously in three separate rings. One ring, for example, might feature a man in formal attire walking on his index fingers, the second a trained bear, and the third, a troupe of clowns. Naturally, the spectators' attention is drawn to the nearest ring, but it takes very little effort to glimpse acts in elsewhere in the tent.

Similarly, we might view science, religion, and folklore as occupying three separate rings, each presenting its own conception of the universe and our place within it. In this cosmic circus, self-selection would place spectators close to their favored ring, yet all but the most focused spectators will occasionally catch acts in neighboring rings. As in the case of the tent circus there is suspense, superhuman performances, illusion, and comic relief. Sometimes spectators cringe and avert their eyes. Acts change frequently, and there are sideshows galore. Barkers make or imply promises that are rarely kept for the patrons who pay the entrance fee.

In a less playful mood, we might view science, religion, and myth as competing efforts, and consider ourselves in the midst of a war over what form of superior intelligence (if any) reigns in the universe. This particular brand of Star Wars is fought entirely by humans and is largely self-perpetuating while extraterrestrials, God, and UFO passengers are obscured in the shadows. It is a multifaceted war waged on many fronts. Although heated and impassioned, this battle is not fought with spaceships and death rays, but with theory and conjecture, scientific data and personal experience, flawless logic and overpowering emotion, scrupulous research and outrageous deception, and with words and images. At stake is our view of reality. Do we live in a fully reducible but perhaps sterile universe of particles and waves, a spiritual cosmos ruled by God the transcendent, or a mythical kingdom ruled by ancient astronauts and iconic grays? At this point in history, each of the three contenders has enough power to keep the controversy going, but none of them has enough strength to score a knockout blow.

Or, we might view our transition from citizens of Earth to citizens of the universe as dependent on the collective thinking that Howard Bloom describes as the Global Brain (2001). This is a metaphor for the emerging collectively intelligent network of billions of minds (not just human minds but minds from all species), knowledge bases, and computers. Many species pool sensory data, share information, and make group decisions. Roughly 3.5 billion years ago, when life was appearing on Earth, the Global Brain was already taking shape. Bloom finds evidence of cooperative synergistic thinking in the fossilized remains of trilobites and dinosaurs, and throughout history ranging from ancient Mesopotamia to today's world. People gathered in small nodes that became larger with the advent of cities. These nodes were linked together as a result of explorers, invaders, and traders. Now we live on a heavily populated planet that is all but saturated with high-band, high-volume communications systems. Analyzing today's Global Brain, Bloom explores the effects of intermingling of minds in local communities, nation states, and continents, as well as worldwide.

One of the attractions of Bloom's analysis is his clever characterization of the various social roles that are required for advancing knowledge. In his system, "diversity generators" propose new ideas. They spawn variety and spark new hypotheses in the communal mind. "Faustians" cross borders (such as between science and religion), introducing new ideas to audiences that have never before heard of them. "Flockers" are conformists who prefer the comfort of established knowledge. These are the good students of this world, who never ask questions but score well on multiple-choice tests. "Resource shifters" direct money and personnel to support ideas that are seen as promising in light of prevailing worldviews.

Resources are distributed unequally, with mainstream science receiving the lion's share. Very little money goes for paranormal research but estimates of support are grossly overrated (Radin 1997). In his discussion of UFOs and academia, Stuart Appelle points out that UFOlogy's marginal status severely limits its opportunities to develop quality research (Appelle 2000). Public funding is not available. Mainstream science has quality control mechanisms to police membership within the field and imposes peer review on published articles. UFOlogy lacks ways to exclude incompetent researchers and is highly vulnerable to hoaxes and tricks. Universities stand ready to prepare the next generation of astrobiologists, but there is no recognized path to professional UFOlogy. Mainstream science journals are archived in libraries around the world and made available at special rates to members of professional associations. Few university libraries choose to subscribe to UFO journals, and UFO archives are likely to be shuffled from place to place before they end up in the incinerator. Scientific UFOlogy models itself after mainstream science, but since society defines it as a marginal, low-status activity, it is hard pressed to match science's practices.

Pitted against diversity generators, conformity enforcers press people and ideas into common molds, oftentimes in rather brutal ways. The freedom to challenge establishment thinking, to explore new ideas, depends very much on time and place. Here, Bloom takes his cue from ancient Greece. During good times, an "Athenian" strategy prevails and outsiders bearing new ideas are welcome. Different groups are allowed to form, churn out new ideas, and enter into tournaments. During bad times, a Spartan strategy wins. New ideas are unwelcome; one philosophy (or political system or scientific model) fits all. The smallest sin— deviation from group thinking—invites punishment.

Opposing factions, Bloom continues, enter into "intergroup tournaments" to see which group can come up with the best ideas. Tournaments force teams to think critically and refine their ideas. How strong would today's science or religion be if each was not engaged in a tournament with the other? Today tournaments take place at scholarly meetings and within the pages of academic journals. Many other tournaments take place on television, and in this arena science does not have an advantage. Since the primary goal of television is to entertain, programs tend to be dominated by highly imaginative individuals who make sensationalistic claims while one token skeptic is on hand to provide "balance."

When advertising executive Alex Osborn introduced brainstorming as a group decision-making tool, he wanted problem-solving groups to get as many varied ideas on the table as possible. He thought that the more ideas that were brought forth, the greater the number of good ideas that could be culled from the pool (1957). Osborn encouraged people to offer ideas without self-censorship and to build upon each other's thinking whenever possible. Even silly ideas are welcome, because they encourage out-of-the box thinking and may lead to useful suggestions. Because of its inhibiting effect on creativity, criticism should be withheld; later on, ideas can be evaluated in terms of their sensibility and practicality (Osborne 1957; Cornish 2004). Even in our highly permissive society, quality should still count. Most people prefer not to look foolish or incompetent and for this reason should be concerned about the quality of their ideas. Whereas we may have given up on pre-twentieth century conceptions of progress, we have not abandoned hope for thorough and convincing answers to questions. Finally, without high-quality ideas we cannot plan wisely and make sound decisions. Bad ideas lose wars, put companies out of business, land people in jail, destroy fortunes, and wreck reputations.

Imagination

Imagination is indispensable for science, religion, business, government, literature, the creative and performing arts, and every other sphere of inquiry or activity. Fantasy plays an essential role in discovery and invention. Imagination may lead to a radical new insight, but more commonly rests on looking at an old idea in a new way or connecting formerly unrelated ideas. An excellent example of the far-reaching effects of looking at something in a new way is Edwin Hubble's realization in the early 1920s that he was not viewing a cluster of stars within our Milky Way but looking at one of countless distant galaxies (Shermer 2006). Borrowing—that is, taking an idea from one field and applying it to another—is important in the creative process. It is the novel combination of elements that yields the breakthrough.

Where do people get the ideas that fuel their thinking on cosmic issues? The brief answer is *everywhere*: refereed books and articles in scholarly journals, popular accounts on television and in the press, the Holy Bible, pulp fiction, T-shirt slogans, comic books, and the neighbor next door. Today, notes Michael Barkun, many people's belief systems are improvised; that is, assembled from bits and pieces from a wide variety of disparate sources (2003). His particular interest is conspiracy theories, but we might note that in addition to improvised politics, there are improvised or "do it yourself" religions and for that matter, cosmologies. Improvised belief systems are exactly what they sound like: a little bit of this, a little bit of that. For most people these consist of ideas that are accessible, which means that they are common themes in the mass media or readily found on the Internet. People then tinker with these ideas, trying various permutations and combinations until they discover a package that "feels" right. The end result of this wildly eclectic process is an individualistic or idiosyncratic worldview that does not fit into an easily understood category, and, like DNA, is not duplicated in many other people. The overall assemblage may be chaotic and riddled with inconsistencies, gaps, and other flaws, but, for the individual, it works.

Ideas migrate from one place to another, oftentimes distorted somewhat in transit. As already noted, UFOlogy has three tracks: the scientific (empirical studies of UFOs), the spiritual (transformative effects of abductions) and the political. Barkun also describes how conspiracy thinking, formerly centering on Freemasons, Jesuits, the Illuminati, and other political groups, has now influenced political thinking about UFOs (2003). Originating in right-wing politics, this type of thinking entered the UFO community where it fanned beliefs that governments are withholding the truth. Rapidly proliferating theories cast wider and wider nets, encompassing larger and larger numbers of conspirators, including aliens that are thinly disguised versions of traditional human scapegoats.

Like many other social scientists, Barkun finds it convenient to separate "mainstream" views, which are promulgated by the cultural elite and widely accepted within a society, from "deviant" views, maintained by hippies, clairvoyants, theosophists, and other formerly small and circumscribed groups of people. The beliefs that help define such groups— transcendence through LSD, telepathic communication, ascended masters, reincarnation—constitute stigmatized knowledge, defined as such because it is ignored or rejected by the mainstream (Dean 1998; Barkun 2003). Until recently, these ideas had currency only within their respective groups; only infrequently did outsiders, who usually responded with disbelief or derision, notice them. Now the barriers between these groups are dissolving and the stigmatized knowledge is spreading from one group to another. The formerly segregated deviant subgroups now have common cause and support one another.

Stigmatized knowledge is entering mainstream society and may be infiltrating science, although not on a large scale. This is suggested by the supermind theories that are presented as scientific, written by people with good credentials, and sometimes published by a respectable university press. As you may recall, these theories suggest that, as individuals, we are enmeshed in a larger web of consciousness, and because of this entanglement we can tap into hidden realities. Past-life regressions, reincarnation, telepathic communication, near-death experiences, communication with the dead, and other anomalistic, paranormal, or occult phenomena are explained by these theories. Stigmatized knowledge—which most scientists reject—is the bedrock of these theories, the justification for their existence.

Of course, new developments could remove the stigma, allowing the formerly stigmatized knowledge to pass into the mainstream. We all have our pet ideas, but we cannot predict with great certainty exactly what science will find. Perhaps we should be mindful of Hans Moravec's caution that "Credulity, psychological quirks, social role playing, subliminal cueing, probability misjudgments, experimental errors and charlantry alone may explain worldwide belief in the supernatural—but not yet conclusively. The study of life and mind is in such early days that paranormal effects could be partying under science's nose" (Moravec 1999: 88).

Failures of Imagination

Imagination may fail us, and the most obvious example is the rigid person with a narrow set of interests who ignores or instantly rejects new ideas. The archetype here is the smug, know-it-all scientist whose thinking is crippled by encrusted knowledge and who always follows a predictable path. In his discussion of reports of meteors landing in rural areas, John S. Lewis complains that even modern-day experts can be "snotty ignoramuses who have never been out at night" (1996: 163):

> Over and over we find the eyewitness reports followed a few days later by a letter to the editor in which some Dr. Defensor Veritas points out that the fire the farmer put out could not possibly have been started by the meteorite he picked up in the same place because it is 'well known that meteorites

are cold when they fall, and that frost often grows on their surfaces.' As for reports of injuries or fatalities reported in other languages or (even worse) in other centuries, clearly the observers must have been little more than superstitious, credulous, impressionable children. It is easier to scoff at the credentials of witnesses than to accommodate the observation within the expert's theory. (J. S. Lewis 1996: 163)

In his discussion of strategies for envisioning the future, Edward Cornish provides many illustrations of experts whose predictions have been far off the mark (Cornish 2004). These include nuclear physicists who thought it would be impossible to tap atomic energy, people who thought automobiles would never replace horses and buggies, and a whole host of luminaries that deemed heavier-than-air travel impossible (even as the Wright brothers were taking flight). Generally, forecasters are better extrapolating trends than imagining major breaks with past technology. For example, at the end of the nineteenth century, prognosticators correctly predicted improvements in trains and ships, but missed the significance of automobiles. Almost nobody foresaw the massive changes that computers would bring. Still, when Cornish reviewed published predictions made in the late 1960s about life now, he concluded that about two-thirds of the predictions were correct (Cornish 2004). Like religious prophets, futurists tend to get in trouble when they become highly specific about dates and numbers.

Certainly, we are well advised to keep an open mind, especially in areas where there are so many unanswered questions. As David Bohm pointed out, "Thinking within a fixed circle of ideas tends to restrict the questions to a limited field. And if one's questions stay in a limited field, so do one's answers" (quoted in Wyller 1996: 214). But imagination can also fail us in a different way, and that is when we become so enamored of an exotic idea that we overlook evidence to the contrary. This happens when we cling to a pet illusion and overlook discordant facts. As evidence mounts that the idea is faulty, we resort to multiple fallback positions, each of which is less defensible than the proceeding. We rely on ever more arcane and convoluted theories and clutch ever more tenuous "facts" just to keep the belief alive. This is evident in continued beliefs in alien abductions, despite growing evidence that these are fully explained by cultural and psychological factors.

An inability to break a counterproductive mindset is revealed in reactions to the Vatican's disclosure of the Third Secret of Fatima (Matter 2001). The apparition of the Blessed Virgin that appeared at Fatima, Portugal in 1917 entrusted young Lucia with prophecies that were relayed to the public through the bishops. The first parts of Mary's message dealt with two horrific wars and the conversion of Russia followed by peace. The third part or "secret" as written by Lucia was sealed in an envelope and was to be revealed to the public on Lucia's death or in 1960, whichever came first. In 1960, Pope John XXIII reviewed the message, and then sent the document back to the archives. Entrusted from pope to pope, the Third Secret of Fatima became one of the great conspiracy theories of the twentieth century. The source of much rumor and speculation, it became increasingly contentious over time. Finally in early 2000, Pope John Paul II authorized the secret's release. People were warned that the document should be interpreted as metaphorical rather than literal, and that in any event the major prediction had already become a part of the Catholic Church's past.

The day that the prelates released the secret document on the Internet, the Vatican's Web site crashed. Lucia had been shown a vision of the Holy Father in an apocalyptic setting. There, afflicted with pain and sorrow, he was gunned down by assassins. In fact, an assassination attempt had been made on John Paul II in 1981 and he had recovered, but there remained many discontinuities between prophecy and fact. Releasing the Third Secret of Fatima did little to calm speculation and soon people complained that the version released by the Vatican was nothing more than a smoke screen to hide the real secret, one far more portentous and horrific. Thus, conspiracy theorizing about the Third Secret of Fatima continued unabated (Matter 2001).

Quality Control

One of the biggest issues in quality control is who does the evaluation and what standards they use. Scientists and skeptics eschew religious worldviews and complain that people accept misleading and flimsy evidence about UFOs and other paranormal phenomena. They bemoan the public's lack of scientific literacy, oftentimes instigated and supported by an irresponsible media or at least one that is far more concerned with entertainment than with enlightenment. University-based theologians try to distance themselves from Bible-thumping fundamentalists who accept creation science, and express annoyance at scientists who focus on religion in its popular and superstitious forms. Scientists tend to see people who are given to religion and folklore as gullible and driven by wish, while people given to religion see scientists as preoccupied with only a narrow sliver of reality.

Science insists on empirical methods to validate its theories. Religion looks for coherence, consistency, explanatory power, resonance with internalized standards of truth, and consonance with other knowledge that is available at the time. Within folklore, many claims are validated in ways that mimic procedures of science, but awkwardly applied and invoking lower criteria or standards. In folklore, longevity and repetition help define truth (Barkun 2003). Stories that have been around a long time, that are told and retold, that are easily accessed on the Internet, and that are reinforced by the media come to be regarded as fact.

We live at a point in time where we are much more adept at generating ideas than evaluating them. In a sense, rapidly accumulating knowledge has primed the pump of imagination but we do not yet have enough findings to hold imagination in check. As the self-correcting processes of science continue, many of the ideas that hopefuls have put on the table will have to be withdrawn. Future historians may look back at an increase, followed by a decrease in interpretations of our place in the cosmos.

As we move from youth to maturity we go through periods where options first increase then decrease. Dating and mating is one example. As we enter the marriage marketplace, we encounter more and more prospects, but as we become more and more serious about a specific potential partner, other prospects drop out. Career development is another example. At first, children view work as what their parents do, but as they gain experience outside the home they discover more alternatives. It is no longer assumed that one will follow in a parent's footsteps. One could become a teacher, physician, or military officer. But before too long reality constraints kick in. If the person lacks the grades for medical school or cannot pass the physical to become a military officer, only teaching remains. Of course, this accordion effect (expansion followed by contraction) is not inviolable. People get divorced and reenter the marriage marketplace, and changing economic conditions have forced many middle-aged persons to generate new career options.

Howard McCurdy describes how, in the 1950s, Wernher von Braun, Hermann Oberth, and other visionaries initiated a campaign to interest the public in space exploration (1997). They wrote popular books, published articles in widely distributed magazines, and participated in engaging television programs. Through inspiring words and lavish illustrations they generated interest in space exploration. They raised such prospects as huge fleets of spaceships taking people to the Moon and Mars where they would establish large, comfortable, futuristic, and aesthetically pleasing bases. This publicity encouraged people to develop many visions of our future in space. The reality, of course, was that space exploration was expensive, dangerous, and never came close to meeting the high expectations. Hypothetically, we had many exciting futures in space, but in reality, few if any of these visions have materialized.

Perhaps we can compare the current state of affairs in our understanding of the universe with that which prevailed in archaeology at the end of the nineteenth century (Colavito 2005). At that time, preliminary findings encouraged the imagination to roam, leading to much speculation about lost civilizations and reinforcing myths and themes that later held sway in science fiction and popular culture. Thus, people were attracted to far-fetched theories that we now politely refer to as "alternative history." Although our knowledge of astronomy and biology is burgeoning, the emerging picture of our place in the cosmos remains ambiguous and incomplete. Are the nanostructures identified in Martian meteorites fossils or uninteresting physical structures? If the initiation of life and evolution in the direction of intelligence are common, why have we yet to confirm the existence of even one extraterrestrial civilization? Does modern physics offer us ideas that can be transformed into faster-than-light travel, or new, encompassing theories of consciousness that could account for ESP and other occult effects? Does the seeming order of the universe indicate a superhuman form of intelligence, if not an anthropomorphic God?

A hundred or a hundred and fifty years ago archaeologists were assembling pieces of a jigsaw puzzle that would help reveal ancient history, and today astronomers and many other scientists are finding pieces of a puzzle whose completion will clarify our place in the universe. Just as, at an earlier time, prominent gaps encouraged imaginations to roam, the missing pieces of today's great puzzle encourage speculation and improvisation. As scientists find more pieces of the puzzle, the gaps will fill in, if never quite complete, a picture of our place in the cosmos. In the past scientific information has supplanted myth and we may expect this to happen again. Shared definitions of reality will always remain a matter of degree, but with more evidence it becomes increasingly difficult to support alternative history, pseudoscience, and myth. Scientific discoveries will reduce or at least undercut the number of idiosyncratic, transient, half-real phantom universes that flit in and out of people's minds. Scientists are the most promising traffic cops to eliminate the traffic jam and restore the flow of high-quality ideas.

Memetics

Both biological organisms and ideas are capable of reproduction. Evolutionary biologist Richard Dawkins pursued this idea in his book, *The Selfish Gene,* and since its appearance many writers have followed his lead (Dawkins 1976). Our point of departure is Susan Blackmore's *The Meme Machine,* a work that explains why some ideas thrive and others fail, why some good ideas never catch on and why bad ideas can persist despite being riddled with errors or having no basis in fact (Blackmore 1999). Over the years memes have been defined as ideas and objects, elements of thought, and units of culture, and I think of them as items of information. For Blackmore, memes are units of imitation—values, customs, rituals, fads, beliefs, and stories—that are passed from one person to another. If an idea originates and remains locked in your head it doesn't count, but if you learned it from someone else or pass it on it qualifies as a meme. We are bombarded by memes all of the time, and every idea in this book is a meme.

Memes vary in terms of fidelity, fecundity, and longevity. Fidelity refers to the accuracy with which it is reproduced. A high-fidelity meme has no errors or distortions. It closely approximates the original. Thus, a story that remains intact as it is passed from person to person is high fidelity; a story that loses details, is embellished, or is changed to meet people's expectations is low fidelity. Fecundity refers to the meme's ability to generate other memes. One tale of an eerie experience, for example, seems to give rise to yet another. Longevity, of course, refers to durability over time. Memes that appear in the Bible or peer-reviewed journals last longer than those promulgated in the back pages of this week's *People* magazine.

Like genes, memes are subject to variation, selection, and retention. Think, for example, about how stories change as they pass from person to person, each person hearing the story somewhat differently, each putting his or her spin on subsequent versions. Some variations of the story will catch on while less appealing versions will drop out. Memes that fit well within a particular worldview and resonate with people's expectations and values may survive for a very long time.

Early discussions linked memes to reproductive fitness, but Blackmore views them as independent replicators, that is, capable of being copied in their own right. In genetics, DNA is machinery for replication. In memetics, books, newspapers, letters, radio and television broadcasts, faxes, and of course the Internet spread ideas. Memes spread even when they work against genetic survival. Consider that memes favoring same-sex marriages gained acceptance in 2004, even though homosexuality does not yield biological offspring. From the gene's view all that matters is that it be passed down from one generation to another, and from the meme's point of view, all that matters is that it find as many hosts as possible. Revising our views of our place in the universe can be viewed in terms of the generation of memes and their movement from place to place. Which memes are likely to be accepted and thrive? Which memes must struggle to gain acceptance or rapidly disappear from view in a sea of more popular ideas?

In the long run, truthful memes—that is, fact-based memes that accurately reflect reality—have the best chance of survival. After all, these should work better than memes that are based on misperceptions of reality or are simply made up. But in discussions of our place in the universe, ideas run way ahead of the facts and when data do exist there may be sharp disagreements over their interpretation. When it is hard to distinguish quality objectively, which memes are likely to catch on?

We are inclined to propagate memes that make us feel good, meaning that memes suggesting that a universe that is brimming over with purpose, meaning, and promise are more likely to survive than those suggesting that the universe is pointless. We tend to accept and propagate the memes of people that we like. This is because we are more likely to seek out and attend to the views of warm-hearted and generous people rather than people who are selfish and cold. The memes of the warm, fuzzy prophet who expresses open concern about the future of humankind will be dispersed more widely than the memes of someone who comes across as cold, insensitive, and selfish. "Fast talkers" and "good talkers" may outperform inarticulate people who are smarter and have better command of the facts. The widespread dispersal of Carl Sagan's memes rested in part on genuine affection for him by his television audiences coupled with his ability to express scientific memes in ways that people could grasp and repeat. Carl Sagan in science, Huston Smith in religion, and Jacques Vallee in UFOlogy qualify as "meme fountains," generating idea after idea. Quality considerations aside, the sheer volume assures that many of these ideas will take hold.

People who control meme reproductive mechanisms are well positioned to get their ideas spread. Publishers, the owners of television networks and production companies, actors and actresses, newscasters and commentators, popular writers and journalists pass their memes to millions of people at a time. In the short run, at least, Larry King's shoot-from-the-hip ideas reach far more people than better but less widely circulated ideas presented in a lecture hall. However, King's memes are rapidly replaced with new ideas while those that enter into the scholarly literature may have more sticking power.

Blackmore points out that we tend to imitate altruistic people who have our best interests at heart; unfortunately, some people give a convincing appearance of altruism while pursuing selfish ends. Cult members who do not realize that their leader is out to exploit them may propagate that leader's dangerous ideas. Memes that are not capable of disproof can survive for a very long time. A meme on the verge of dying out can mutate and regain strength in its new form. This occurs, for example, when the world does not end at a prophesized date and the prophet rationalizes the failure and sets a new date. A true meme ("This is amazing technology!") can provide cover for a false meme ("It came from outer space!"). One formula for widespread memes, is "Take a highly emotional, naturally occurring human experience with no satisfactory explanation, provide a myth that appears to explain it, and include a powerful unseen force that cannot easily be tested" (Blackmore 1999: 182). Social conformity enters in also; we tend to be rewarded for selecting the same memes as everyone else. Very much a partisan, Blackmore believes that memetics helps explain why science offers a better kind of truth.

As we come of age in the universe, many of the ideas that heat today's discussions will prove worthless and will be abandoned. Like disintegrating musket balls lodged in ancient oak trees, they will have served—or failed to have served—their purpose at an earlier point in time. In the mean time, keeping an open mind may give us a fresh take on human existence and prepare us for discoveries that are yet to come.

⋆⋆⋆⋆⋆

EPILOGUE

In September 2005, Bill Clinton commented on life in the universe, UFOs, Area 51, and Roswell (Wozniak 2005). The former U.S. President, allowing that his views might be considered "flaky," was convinced, on the basis of scientific findings, that within the lifetimes of many people who are alive today, scientists will discover some form of extraterrestrial life. Clinton also confessed that, as president, he tried to find out more about UFOs. He concluded that the crash landing at Roswell was an illusion. However, many people in his administration were convinced of alien artifacts at Area 51 in Nevada. He sent someone to Area 51 "to figure it out" but his emissary reported that it was simply a secret defense installation where they did boring work. If there were UFO secrets, Clinton said, they were "concealed from me too," adding that he would not be the first American president "that underlings had lied to, or that career diplomats had simply waited out." There "may be some career person sitting around somewhere, hiding these dark secrets from elected presidents ... if so, they successfully eluded me ... and I am embarrassed to tell you that I did try to find out." Clinton hoped that we would continue to explore the boundaries of human existence, both on Earth and beyond the skies.

REFERENCES

Achenbach, Joel. 1999. *Captured by Aliens: The Search for Life and Truth in a Very Large Universe.* New York: Simon and Schuster.

Alcock, James F. 2001. "Science vs. Pseudoscience, Nonscience and Nonsense." In *Skeptical Odysseys: Personal Inquiries by the World's Leading Paranormal Inquirers,* ed. Paul Kurtz, 37-46. Amherst, NY: Prometheus Books.

Alexander, Victoria. 1998. "The Alexander UFO Religious Crisis Survey." http://wwweb.com/kelleher/articles alexander/survey_religion.html. Accessed 14 April 2006.

Almar, Ivan, and Jill Tarter. Forthcoming. "The Discovery of ETI as a High-Consequence Low Probability Event." *Acta Astronautica.*

Alper, Gerald. 2005. *The Paranoia of Everyday Life: Escaping the Enemy Within.* Amherst, NY: Prometheus.

American Society of Missiology. Mission statement. http://www.asmweb.org/default.htm. Accessed 17 April 2003.

Appelle, Stuart. 2000. "Ufology and Academia: The UFO Phenomenon as a Scholarly Discipline." In *UFOs and Abductions: Challenging the Borders of Knowledge,* ed. David M. Jacobs, 7–30. Lawrence: University Press of Kansas.

Appelle, Stuart, Steven Jay Lynn, and Leonard Newman. 2000. "Alien Abduction Experiences." In *Varieties of Anomalous Experiences: Examining the Scientific Evidence,* eds. Etzel Cardena, Steven Jay Lynn, and Stanley Krippner, 283–314. Washington, DC: American Psychological Association.

Armstrong, Karen. 1993. *A History of God: The 4,000-Year Quest of Judaism, Christianity, and Islam.* New York: Ballantine Books.

———. 2005. *A Short History of Myth.* Edinburgh: Cannongate.

Aronoff, Jodi, Stephen Jay Lynn, and Peter Malinoski. 2000. "Are Cultic Environments Psychologically Harmful?" *Clinical Psychology Review* 20, no. 1: 91–111.

Ashkenazi, Michael. 1992. "Not the Sons of Adam: Religious Responses to ETI." *Space Policy,* 8, no. 4, 341-349.

Bainbridge, William Sims. 2004. "Religion and Science." *Futures* 36, no. 9: 1009–1023.

Baker, Robert A. 1987–1988. "The Aliens Among Us: Hypnotic Regression Revisited." *Skeptical Inquirer* 12, no. 2 (Winter): 147–162.

———. 1997. "Studying the Psychology of the UFO Experience." In *The UFO Invasion: The Roswell Incident, Alien Abduction, and Government Coverup*, eds. Kendrick Frazier, Barry Karr, and Joe Nickel, 230–234. Amherst, NY: Prometheus.

Balch, Robert W. 1995. "Waiting for the Ships: Disillusionment and the Revitalization of Faith in Bo and Peep's UFO Cult." In *The Gods Have Landed: New Religions from Other Worlds*, ed. James R. Lewis, 137–166. Albany: State University of New York Press.

Barbour, Ian G. 2000. *When Science Meets Religion*. San Francisco: Harper San Francisco.

———. 2002. *Nature, Human Nature, and God*. Minneapolis, MN: Fortress Press.

Barkun, Michael. 2003. *A Culture of Conspiracy: Apocalyptic Visions in Contemporary America*. Berkeley, CA: University of California Press.

Bauer, Henry H. 2001. *Fatal Attractions: The Trouble with Science*. New York: Paraview.

Behe, Michael J. 1996. *Darwin's Black Box: The Biochemical Challenge to Evolution*. New York: Touchstone.

Benford, Gregory. 1999. *Deep Time: How Humanity Communicates across the Millennia*. New York: Perennial.

Bennett, Colin. 2001. *Looking for Orthon*. New York: Paraview.

Berlitz, Charles, and William Moore. 1980. *The Roswell Incident*. New York: Grosset and Dunlap.

Bierlein, J. G. 1994. *Parallel Myths*. New York: Ballantine Wellspring.

Billingham, John. 2002. "Pesek Lecture: SETI and Society; Decision Trees." *Acta Astronautica* 51, no. 10: 667–672.

Billingham, John, Roger Heyns, David Milne, Stephen Doyle, Michael Klein, John Heilbron, Michael Ashkenazi, Michael Michaud, Julie Lutz, and Seth Shostak. 1999. *Societal Implications of the Detection of an Extraterrestrial Civilization*. Mountain View, CA: SETI Institute Press.

Binzel, Richard P. 1997. "A Near Earth Object Hazard Index." *Annals of the New York Academy of Science* 822: 545-551.

Blackmore, Susan. 1999. *The Meme Machine*. Oxford: Oxford University Press.

———. 2001. "Why I Have Given Up." In *Skeptical Odysseys: Personal Accounts by the World's Leading Paranormal Inquirers*, ed. Paul Kurtz, 85–94. Amherst, NY: Prometheus Books.

Bloom, Howard. 2001. *The Global Brain: Evolution of the Mass Mind from the Big Bang to the Twenty-first Century*. New York: John Wiley & Sons.

Boden, M. Tyler, and Howard Berenbaum. 2004. "The Potentially Adaptive Features of Peculiar Belief." *Personality and Individual Differences* 37, no. 4: 707–719.

Bonting, Sjörd L. 2003. "Theological Implications of Possible Extraterrestrial Life." *Zygon* 38, no. 3: 587–602.

Borgo, Alejandro J. 2005. "What Should We Do With Skepticism?" *Skeptical Inquirer* 29, no. 4: 51–53.

Bova, Ben. 1998. *Immortality: How Science is Extending Your Life Span—and Changing the World.* New York: Avon Books.

Bower, Bruce. 2003. "Words Get in the Way: Talk is Cheap, but it Can Tax Your Memory." *Science News,* 19 April: 250.

Boyle, Alan. 2005. "Would You Pay to Send Messages into Space?" *Cosmic Log,* 18 March. http://www.msnbc.com/id/7180932. Accessed 30 January 2006.

Bracewell, Ronald. 1975. *The Galactic Club: Intelligent Life in Outer Space.* San Francisco: San Francisco Books.

Broderick, Damien. 1999. *The Last Mortal Generation.* Adelaide: New Holland Books.

———. 2001. *The Spike: How Our Lives Are Being Transformed by Rapidly Advancing Technologies.* New York: Tom Doherty Associates.

Bynum, Joyce. 1993. "Kidnapped by an Alien: Tales of UFO Abductions." *ETC: A Review of General Semantics* 50, no. 1: 86.

Cardena, Etzel, Steven Jay Lynn, and Stanley Krippner, eds. 2000. *Varieties of Anomalous Experiences: Examining the Scientific Evidence.* Washington, DC: American Psychological Association.

Chaisson, Eric J. 2001. *Cosmic Evolution: The Rise of Complexity in Nature.* Cambridge, MA: Harvard University Press.

Chapman, Clark R. 1998. Statement on the Threat of Impact by Near Earth Asteroids: Comments before the Subcommittee of the Committee on Science of the U.S. House of Representatives. May 21.

Chapman, Clark R., Daniel D. Durda, and Robert E. Gold. 2001. "The Comet Impact Hazard: A Systems Approach." South West Research Institute White Paper. http://www.boulder.swri.edu/cark/neowp.html. Accessed 14 April 2001.

Cheney, Margaret. 2001. *Tesla: Man Out of Time.* New York: Touchstone Books.

Christian, David. 2004. *Maps of Time: An Introduction to Big History.* Berkeley: University of California Press.

Ćirković, Milan M. 2004. "The Temporal Aspect of the Drake Equation and SETI." *Astrobiology* 4, no. 2, 225–231.

Clancy, Susan A. 2005. *Abducted: How People Come to Believe They Were Kidnapped by Aliens.* Cambridge, MA: Harvard University Press.

Clancy, Susan A., Richard J. McNally, Daniel L. Schachter, Mark F. Lenzenweger, and Roger K. Pittman. 2002. "Memory Distortion in People Reporting Abduction by Aliens." *Journal of Abnormal Psychology* 111, no. 3, 455–461.

Clark, Jerome. 2003. *Strange Skies: Pilot Encounters with UFOs.* New York: Citadel.

Clarke, Lee. 1999. *Mission Improbable: Using Fantasy Documents to Tame Disaster.* Chicago: University of Chicago Press.

Colavito, Jason. 2005. *The Cult of Alien Gods: H. P. Lovecraft and Extraterrestrial Pop Culture.* Amherst, NY: Prometheus.

Collins, Harry W., and Trevor Pinch. 1992. *The Golem: What You Should Know About Science*. Cambridge: Cambridge University Press.

Committee on Science and Astronautics. 1961. *Proposed Studies on the Implications of Peaceful Space Activities for Human Affairs*. U.S. House of Representatives, Eighty-Seventh Congress, First Session, 24 March 1961.

Cornet, Bruce, and Scot L. Stride. 2003. "Solar System SETI Using Radio Telescopes." *Contact in Context*. Saddle River, NJ: SETI League.

Cornish, Edward. 2004. *Futuring: The Exploration of the Future*. Bethesda, MD: World Future Society.

Corso, Philip, and William J. Birnes. 1997. *The Day After Roswell*. New York: Pocket Books.

Craig, Roy. 1995. *UFOs: An Insider's View of the Official Quest for Evidence*. North Denton: University of North Texas Press.

Crombag, H. F. M., W. A. Wafenaar, and P. J. Von Kopler. 1996. "Crashing Memories and the Problem of Source Monitoring." *Applied Cognitive Psychology* 10, no 2: 95-104.

Cusack, Thomas R., and Richard A. Stoll. 1994. "Collective Security and State Survival in the Interstate System." *International Studies Quarterly* 38, no. 1: 33–59.

Darling, David. 2001. *Life Everywhere: The Maverick Science of Astrobiology*. New York: Basic Books.

Davies, Paul. 1984. *God and the New Physics*. New York: Simon and Schuster.

Davis, Eric W. 2004. *Teleportation Physics Study. Special Report. AFRL-PR-ED-TR-2003-0034*. Air Force Research Laboratory, Air Force Material Command, Edwards Air Force Base, CA.

Dawkins, Richard. 1976. *The Selfish Gene*. Oxford: Oxford University Press.

Dean, Jodi. 1998. *Aliens in America: Conspiracy Cultures from Outerspace to Cyberspace*. Ithaca, NY: Cornell University Press.

Deardorff, J., B. Haisch, B. Maccabee, and H. E. Puthoff, 2005. "Inflation-Theory Implications for Extraterrestrial Visitation." *Journal of the British Interplanetary Society* 58: 43–50.

Dein, Simon, and Roland Littlewood. 2005. "Apocalyptic Suicide: From a Pathological to an Eschatological Interpretation." *International Journal of Social Psychiatry* 51, no. 3: 198–210.

Denzler, Brenda. 2001. *The Lure of the Edge: Scientific Passions, Religious Beliefs, and the Pursuit of UFOs*. Berkeley: University of California Press.

DePalma, M. T., M. McCall, and G. English. 1996. "Increasing Perceptions of Disease Vulnerability through Imagery." *Journal of the American College of Health* 44, no. 5: 226–234.

DeVore, Irven. 2001. "Extraterrestrial Intelligence? Not Likely." *Annals of the New York Academy of Sciences* 950, no. 1: 276–278.

Diamond, Jared. 2005. *Collapse: How Societies Choose to Fail or Succeed.* New York: Viking.

Dick, Steven J. 1996. *The Biological Universe: The Twentieth Century Extraterrestrial Life Debate and the Limits of Science.* Cambridge: Cambridge University Press.

———. 2000a. "Cosmic Humanity," In *When SETI Succeeds: The Impact of High Information Contact,* ed. Allen Tough, 93–101. Bellevue, WA: Foundation for the Future.

———. 2000b. "Cosmotheology: Theological Implications of the New Universe." In *Many Worlds: The New Universe, Extraterrestrial Life and the Theological Implications,* ed. Steven J. Dick, 191–211. Radnor, PA: The John Templeton Foundation Press.

———. 2002. "SETI and the Postbiological Universe." Paper presented at the annual meeting of the SETI League, Little River, NJ.

Don, Norman S., and Gilda Moura. 1997. "Topographic Mapping of UFO Experiences." *Journal for the Study of Scientific Exploration* 11, no. 4: 435–453.

Donald, Merlin. 2001. *A Mind So Rare: The Evolution of Human Consciousness.* New York: Norton.

Donderi, Don. 2000. "Science, Law and War: Alternative Frameworks for the UFO Evidence." In *UFOs and Abductions: Challenging the Borders of Knowledge* ed. David M. Jacobs, 56–81. Lawrence: University Press of Kansas.

Downing, Barry. 1997. *The Bible and Flying Saucers.* 2nd ed. New York: Marlowe and Company.

Drake, Frank, and Dava Sobel. 1992. *Is Anyone Out There? The Scientific Search for Extraterrestrial Intelligence.* New York: Delacorte Press.

Druffel, Ann, and D. Scott Rogo, 1980. *The Tujunga Canyon Contacts.* Englewood Cliffs, NJ: Prentice–Hall.

Edinger, Edward F. 1999. *Archetype of the Apocalypse: Divine Vengeance, Terrorism, and the End of the World.* Chicago: Open Court.

Fernandes, Joaquim, and Fina D'Armada. 2005. *Heavenly Lights: The Apparitions of Fatima and the UFO Phenomenon.* Victoria, BC: EcceNova Editions.

Ferris, Timothy. 1992. *The Mind's Sky: Human Intelligence in a Cosmic Context.* New York: Bantam Books.

Finney, Ben, and Eric M. Jones. 1984. *Interstellar Migration and the Human Experience.* Berkeley: University of California Press.

Fitzgerald, Randall. 1998. *Cosmic Test Tube: Extraterrestrial Contact, Theories and Evidence.* Los Angeles: Moonlake Media.

Fowler, Raymond. 1979. *The Andreasson Affair.* Englewood Cliffs, NJ: Prentice Hall.

Freitas, Robert A., Jr. 1983. "The Case for Interstellar Probes." *Journal of the British Interplanetary Society* 36, November: 490–495.

Freitas, Robert A., Jr., and Francisco Valdes. 1985. "The Search for Extraterrestrial Artifacts (SETA)." *Acta Astronautica* 12, no. 12: 1027–1034.

Friedlander, Michael W. 1995. *At the Fringes of Science.* Boulder, CO: Westview Press.

Fuller, John. 1966. *The Interrupted Journey*. New York: Dell.

Gabriel, Theodore. 2003. "The United Nuwabian Nation of Moors." In *UFO Religions*, ed. Christopher Partridge, 149–161. London: Routledge.

Garry, Maryanne, Charles G. Manning, Elizabeth F. Loftus, and Steven J. Sherman. 2001. "Imagination Inflation: Imagining a Childhood Event Inflates Confidence that It Occurred." *Psychonomic Bulletin and Review* 3, no. 2: 208–214.

George, Marie I. 2005. *Christianity and Extraterrestrials? A Catholic Perspective*. New York: iUniverse.

Gerrig, Richard J., and Bradford H. Pillow. 1998. "A Developmental Perspective on the Construction of Disbelief." In *Believed-In Imaginings: The Narrative Construction of Reality*, ed. Joseph de Rivera and Theodore R. Sarbin, 101–120. Washington, DC: American Psychological Association.

Goffman, Erving. 1986. *Frame Analysis*. Boston: Northeastern University Press.

Goldberg, Carl. 2000. "The General's Abduction by Aliens: Four Levels of Meaning in Alien Abduction Reports." *Journal of Contemporary Psychotherapy* 30, no. 3: 307–320.

Goode, Erich. 2000. *Paranormal Beliefs*. Prospect Heights, IL: Waveland Press.

Greene, Brian. 2004. *The Fabric of the Cosmos: Space, Time, and the Texture of Reality*. New York: Vintage.

Grinspoon, David. 2003. *Lonely Planets: The Natural Philosophy of Alien Life*. New York: Ecco/HarperCollins.

Guthke, Karl S. 1960. *The Last Frontier: Imagining Other Worlds from the Copernican Revolution to Modern Science Fiction*. Ithaca, NY: Cornell University Press.

Haines, Richard F. 1979. *Observing UFOs: An Investigation Handbook*. Chicago: Nelson Hall.

———. 1999. *CE-5: Close Encounters of the Fifth Kind*. Naperville, IL: Sourcebooks.

Haines, Richard F., and Jacques F. Vallee. 1990. "Photo Analysis of an Aerial Disk Over Costa Rica." *Journal of Scientific Exploration* 4, no. 1: 71–74.

Halpern, Paul. 2004. *The Great Beyond: Higher Dimensions, Parallel Universes, and the Extraordinary Search for a Theory of Everything*. New York: Wiley.

Hamer, Dean. 2004. *The God Gene: How Faith is Hardwired in Our Genes*. New York: Doubleday.

Hansen, George P. 2001. *The Trickster and the Paranormal*. Philadelphia: Xlibris.

Harpur, Partrick. 2003. *Daimonic Reality: A Field Guide to the Otherworld*. Ravensdale, WA: Pine Winds Press.

Harrison, Albert A. 1997. *After Contact: The Human Response to Extraterrestrial Life*. New York: Plenum.

———. 2000. "The Relative Stability of Belligerent and Peaceful Societies: Implications for SETI." *Acta Astronautica* 46, no. 10–12: 707–712.

———. 2001. *Spacefaring: The Human Dimension.* Berkeley: University of California Press.

———. 2003. "Confirmation of ETI: Initial Organizational Response." *Acta Astronautica* 53, no. 3: 229–236.

———. 2005. "Beyond God's Planet: Values in a Populated Universe." In *Values and Evaluating,* ed. Rudi Keller and Winder McConnell, 61–83. Tubingen und Basil: A Francke Verlag.

Harrison, Albert A., Kathleen Connell, and Gregory K. Schmidt. 2002. "Rethinking Our Place in the Universe: Exploring the Societal Implications of NASA's Astrobiology Program." *Space Times,* January–February: 4–9.

Harrison, Albert A, and Steven J. Dick. 2000. "Contact: Long-Term Implications for Humanity." In *When SETI Succeeds: The Impact of High Information Contact,* ed. Allen Tough, 7–31. Bellevue, WA: Foundation for the Future.

Harrison, Albert A., and James Moulton Thomas. 1997. "The Kennedy Assassination, Unidentified Flying Objects, and Other Conspiracies: Psychological and Organizational Factors in the Perception of Cover-Up." *Systems Research and Behavioral Science* 14, no. 2: 113–128.

Hawkins, Michael. 1997. *Hunting Down the Universe: The Missing Mass, Primordial Black Holes, and Other Dark Matters.* Reading, MA: Helix Books.

Hayflick, Leonard, 1998. "How and Why We Age." *Experimental Gerontology* 33: no. 7-8: 639–653.

———. 2003. "Living Forever and Dying in the Attempt." *Experimental Gerontology* 38: 1231–1241.

Henry, Lucy A., and Gisli H. Gundjonsson. 2003. "Eyewitness Memory, Suggestibility, and Repeated Recall Sessions in Children with Mild and Intellectual Disabilities." *Law and Human Behavior* 27, no. 5: 481–505.

Hoffman, Thomas. 2004a. "A Brief Handbook of Protestant Exomissiology." Master's thesis, The University of Houston: Clear Lake.

———. 2004b. "Exomissiology: The Launching of Exotheology." *Dialog: A Journal of Theology* 43, no. 4: 324–337.

Hood, Ralph W., Jr., Bernard Spilka, Bruce Hunsberger, and Richard Gorsuch. 1996. *The Psychology of Religion: An Empirical Approach.* New York: The Guilford Press.

Hopkins, Budd. 1983. *Missing Time.* New York: Berkeley Books.

———. 1987. *Intruders.* New York: Ballantine.

———. 2000. "Hypnosis and the Investigation of UFO Abduction Accounts." In *UFOs and Abductions: Challenging the Borders of Knowledge,* ed. David M. Jacobs, 192–214. Lawrence: University Press of Kansas.

Hopkins, Budd, David L. Jacobs, and Ron Westrum. 1992. *Unusual Personal Experiences: An Analysis of the Data from Three National Surveys Conducted by the Roper Organization.* Las Vegas, NV: Bigelow Holding Companies.

Horgan, John. 1997. *The End of Science: Facing the Limits of Knowledge in the Twilight of the Scientific Age.* New York: Broadway Books.

———. 2003. *Rational Mysticism: Dispatches from the Border between Science and Spirituality.* Boston: Houghton Mifflin.

Howard, Andrew, Paul Horowitz, David Wilkinson, Charles M. Caldwell, Edward J. Groth, Norm Javosik, David W. Latham et. al., 2004. "Search for Nanosecond Optical Pulses from Nearby Solar Type Stars." *The Astrophysical Journal*, 8, no. 1: 1270-1284.

Hoyle, Fred, and Chandra Wickramasinghe. 1993. *Our Place in the Cosmos.* London: Dent.

Hoyt, Diana. 2000. *UFOCRITIQUE: UFOs, Social Intelligence, and the Condon Report.* Master's thesis, Virginia Polytechnic Institute and State University.

Huyghe, Patrick. 2001. *Swamp Gas Times: My Two Decades on the UFO Beat.* New York: Paraview Press.

Jacobs, David M. 1992. *Secret Life: First Hand Documented Accounts of UFO Abductions.* New York: Simon & Schuster.

———. 1998. *The Threat: The Secret Agenda; What Aliens Really Want.* New York: Simon & Schuster.

———, ed. 2000a. *UFOs and Abductions: Challenging the Borders of Knowledge.* Lawrence: University Press of Kansas.

———. 2000b. "Introduction." In *UFOs and Abductions: Challenging the Borders of Knowledge*, ed. David M. Jacobs, 1-6. Lawrence: University Press of Kansas.

———. 2000c. "The UFO Abduction Controversy in the United States." In *UFOs and Abductions: Challenging to Borders of Knowledge*, ed. David M. Jacobs, 192–214. Lawrence: University Press of Kansas.

Janis, Irving L., and Leon Mann. 1985. *Decision Making: Psychological Analysis of Conflict, Choice and Commitment.* Homewood, IL: The Free Press.

Jarvis, William E. 2003. *Time Capsules: A Cultural History.* Jefferson, NC: McFarland and Company.

Jungerman, John A. 2000. *World in Process: Creativity and Interconnection in the New Physics.* Albany: State University of New York Press.

Kaminar, Wendy. 1999. *Sleeping with Extra-Terrestrials: The Rise of Irrationalism and Perils of Piety.* New York: Pantheon.

Kelleher, Colm, and George Knapp. 2005. *Hunt for Skinwalker: Science Confronts the Unexplained at a Remote Ranch in Utah.* New York: Paraview.

Klerkx, Greg. 2004. *Lost in Space: The Fall of NASA and the Dream of a New Space Age.* New York: Pantheon.

Koltko-Rivera, Mark E. 2004. "The Psychology of Worldviews." *Review of General Psychology* 8, no. 1: 3–58.

Krupp, E. C. 1995. "Negotiating the Highwire of Heaven: The Milky Way and the Itinerary of the Soul." *Vistas in Astronomy* 39, no. 4: 405–430.

Kuhn, Thomas S. 1970. *The Structure of Scientific Revolutions.* 2nd ed. Chicago: University of Chicago Press.

Kurtz, Paul. 1988. *Forbidden Fruit: The Ethics of Humanism.* Amherst, NY: Prometheus.

———. 1991. *The Transcendental Temptation: A Critique of Religion and the Paranormal,* Amherst, NY: Prometheus.

———. 1992. *The New Skepticism: Inquiry and Reliable Knowledge.* Amherst, NY: Prometheus.

Larson, Eric. 1999. *Isaac's Storm: A Man, A Time, and the Deadliest Hurricane in History.* New York: Vantage Books.

Launius, Roger D. 1998. *Frontiers of Space Exploration.* Westport, CT: Greenwood Press.

———. 2005. "Perceptions of Apollo: Myth, Nostalgia, Memory, or All of the Above?" *Space Policy* 21: 129–139.

Lewis, James R. 1995. *The Gods Have Landed: New Religions from Other Worlds.* Albany: State University of New York.

———. 2003. "Legitimating Suicide: Heaven's Gate and New Age Ideology." In *UFO Religions,* ed. Christopher Partridge, 103–128. London: Routledge.

Lewis, John S. 1996. *Rain of Iron and Ice: The Very Real Threat of Comet and Asteroid Bombardment.* Reading, MA: Addison Wesley.

Liebman, Julie I., Marcia J. McKinley-Pace, Anne Marie Leonard, Laura A. Sheesley, Casey L. Gallant, Mary E. Renkey, and Elyse Brauch Lehman. 2002. "Cognitive and Psychosocial Correlates of Adults' Eyewitness Accuracy and Suggestibility." *Personality and Individual Differences* 33, no. 1: 149–166.

Lindley, David. 2001. *Boltzman's Atom: The Great Debate that Launched a Revolution in Physics.* New York: The Free Press.

Lorenzen, Coral, and Jim Lorenzen. 1977. *Abducted: Confrontations with Beings from Outer Space.* New York: Berkeley Books.

Lovelock, James E. 1986. *Gaia: A New Look at Life on Earth.* New York: Oxford University Press.

Lyall, Francis. 2000. "Communications with Extraterrestrial Intelligence: A New Dimension of Space Law." *Acta Astronautica* 46, no. 10-12: 751–757.

MacFarlane, Thomas J., ed. 2001. *Einstein and Buddha: The Parallel Sayings* New York: Ulysses Press.

Mack, John E. 1994. *Abduction: Human Encounters with Aliens.* New York: Scribners.

———. 1999. *Passport to the Cosmos: Human Transformation and Alien Encounters.* New York: Crown.

———. 2000. "How the Alien Abduction Phenomenon Challenges the Boundaries of Our Reality." In *UFOs and Abductions: Challenging to Borders of Knowledge,* ed. David M. Jacobs, 241–262. Lawrence: University Press of Kansas.

MacKenzie, Donald. 1996. *Knowing Machines: Essays on Technical Change.* Cambridge, MA: The MIT Press.

Malin, Michael C., and Kenneth S. Edgett. 2000. "Evidence for Recent Ground Seepage and Surface Runoff on Mars." *Science* 288, no. 5475: 2230–2335.

Masse, W. B. 1995. "The Celestial Basis of Civilization." *Vistas in Astronomy* 39, no. 2: 461–477.

Mastrappa, R. M. E., H. Glanzberg, J. N. Head, H. J. Melosh, and W. L. Nicholson. 2001. "Survival of Bacteria Exposed to Extreme Acceleration: Implications for Panspermia." *Earth and Planetary Science Letters* 189, no. 1-2: 1–8.

Matheson, Terry. 1998. *Alien Abductions: Creating a Modern Phenomena.* Amherst, NY: Prometheus.

Matter, E. Ann. 2001. "Apparitions of the Virgin Mary in the Late Twentieth Century: Apocalyptic, Representation, Politics." *Religion* 31: 125–153.

McConnell, Brian. 2001. *Beyond Contact: A Guide to SETI and Communicating with Alien Organizations.* Sebastapol, CA: O'Reilly and Associates.

McCurdy, Howard E. 1997. *Space and the American Imagination.* Washington, DC: Smithsonian Institution Press.

McNally, Richard J., Natasha B. Lasko, Susan A. Clancy, Michael L. Macklin, Roger K. Pittman, and Scott P. Orr. 2004. "Psychophysiological Responding during Script-Driven Imagery in People Reporting Abduction by Space Aliens." *Psychological Science* 15, no. 7: 493–497.

Michalak, Stanley. 2004. "Post-democratic Cosmopolitans: The Second Wave of Liberal Internationalism." *Orbis*, Fall: 593–607.

Michaud, Michael A. G. 1972. "Interstellar Negotiation." *Foreign Service Journal,* December 10–14: 29–30.

———. 1977. "Negotiating with Other Worlds." *The Futurist* 7: 71.

———. 1995. "Towards a Grand Strategy for the Species." *Earth Oriented Applied Space Technology* 2: 213–219.

———. 2003. "Ten Decisions that Could Shake the World." *Space Policy* 19, no. 2: 131–136.

———. 2005. "Active SETI Is Not Scientific Research." SETI League Guest Editorial. http://www.setileague.org/editor/activeseti.htm. Accessed 30 January 2006.

Millis, Marc G. 2004. "Prospects for Breakthrough Propulsion Physics." NASA Technical Memorandum 2004-213082, NASA Glenn Research Center.

Mills, Antonia, and Steven Jay Lynn. 2000. "Past Life Experiences." In *Varieties of Anomalous Experience*, ed. Etzel Cardena, Steven Jay Lynn and Stanley Krippner, 283–314. Washington, DC: American Psychological Association.

Mitchell, Edgar D, and Dwight Williams 1996. *The Way of the Explorer.* New York: Putnam.

Modelski, George, and Gardner Perry III. 2002. "Democratization in Long Perspective Revisited." *Technological Forecasting and Social Change* 69, no. 4: 359–376.

Moldwin, Mark. 2004. "Why SETI is Science and UFOlogy is Not." *Skeptical Inquirer* 28, no. 6: 40–43.

Moravec, Hans. 1999. *Robot: Mere Machine to Transcendent Mind.* Oxford: Oxford University Press.

Morrison, David. 2001. "Asteroid and Comet Impact Hazards: Ten Frequently Asked Questions about NEO Impacts." http://impact.arc.nasa.gov/introduction/faq-neo.html. Accessed 23 July 2001.

———. 2005. "Only a Theory? Framing the Evolution/Creation Issue." *Skeptical Inquirer* 29, no. 6: 35–41.

Morrison, Philip, John Billingham, and John Wolfe, eds. 1977. *The Search for Extraterrestrial Intelligence.* NASA SP 419. Washington, DC: National Aeronautics and Space Administration.

Morse, Melvin, and Paul Perry. 2000. *Where God Lives: The Science of the Paranormal and How Our Brains Are Linked to the Universe.* San Francisco: HarperCollins/Cliff Street Books.

Moseley, James W., and Karl T. Pflock. 2002. *Shockingly Close to the Truth: Confessions of a Grave-Robbing Ufologist.* Amherst, NY: Prometheus Books.

NASA, 2006. "Stardust: Answering Cosmic Questions." http://www.nasa.gov/missionpages/stardust/main/index.html. Accessed 30 January 2006.

Newberg, Andrew, Eugene D'Aquili, and Vince Rause. 2001. *Why God Won't Go Away: Brain Science and the Biology of Belief.* New York: Ballantine Books.

Noble, David F. 1999. *The Religion of Technology: The Divinity of Man and the Spirit of Invention.* New York: Penguin.

Nocks, Lisa. 1998. "The Golem: Between the Technological and the Divine." *Journal of Social and Evolutionary Systems* 21, no. 3: 281–303.

Norenzayan, Ara, and Richard E. Nisbett. 2000. "Culture and Causal Cognition." *Current Directions in Psychological Science* 9, no. 4: 132–135.

Norris, Ray P. 2000. "How Old is ET?" In *When SETI Succeeds: The Impact of High Information Contact*, ed. Allen Tough, 103–106. Bellevue, WA: Foundation for the Future.

Nuland, Sherwin B. 1993. *How We Die: Reflections on Life's Final Chapter.* New York: Vintage Books.

O'Connor, Kieron P., and Frederick Aardema. 2005. "The Imagination: Cognitive, Pre-cognitive, and Meta-cognitive Aspects." *Consciousness and Cognition* 14, no. 2: 233–256.

O'Murchu, Diarmuid. 2004. *Quantum Theology: Spiritual Implications of the New Physics.* New York: Crossroad Publishing Company.

Osborne, Alex. 1957. *Applied Imagination.* New York: Scribners.

O'Sullivan, Maureen. 2003. "The Fundamental Attribution Error in Detecting Deception: The Boy-Who-Cried-Wolf Effect." *Personality and Social Psychology Bulletin* 29, no. 10: 1316–1327.

Palmer, Susan J. 2004. *Alien's Adored: Rael's UFO Religion.* New Brunswick, NJ: Rutgers University Press.

Parnell, June. 1998. "Measured Personality Characteristics of Persons who Claim UFO Experiences." *Psychotherapy in Private Practice* 6, no. 3: 159–165.

Parry, Bronwyn. 2004. "Technologies of Immortality: The Brain on Ice." *Studies in the History and Philosophy of Biological and Biomedical Sciences* 35, no. 2: 393–413.

Partridge, Christopher. 2004. "Alien Demonology: The Christian Roots of the Malevolent Extraterrestrial in UFO Religions and Abduction Spiritualities." *Religion* 34, no. 3: 163–189.

Patry, Alain C., and Luc G. Pelletier. 2001. "Extraterrestrial Beliefs and Experiences: An Application of the Theory of Reasoned Action." *The Journal of Social Psychology* 141, no. 2: 199.

Paul, Gregory S., and Earl D. Cox. 1996. *Beyond Humanity: Cyberevolution and Future Minds*. Hingham, MA: Charles River Associates.

Peebles, Curtis. 1994. *Watch the Skies!* Washington, DC: Smithsonian Institution Press.

Perls, Thomas, Robin Levenson, Meredith Regan, and Annibale Puca. 2002. "What Does It Take to Live to 100?" *Mechanisms of Aging and Development* 123, 2-3: 231–242.

Persinger, Michael. 2000. "The UFO Experience: A Normal Correlate of Brain Functioning." In *Varieties of Anomalous Experiences: Examining the Scientific Evidence*, eds. Etzel Cardena, Steven Jay Lynn and Stanley Krippner, 262–302. Washington, DC: American Psychological Association.

Peters, Ted. 1977. *God's Chariots? Flying Saucers in Politics, Science and Religion*. Atlanta, GA: John Knox Press.

———. 1998. *Science & Theology: The New Consonance*. Boulder, CO: Westview Press.

Pflock, Karl. 2001. *Roswell: Inconvenient Facts and the Will to Believe*. Amherst, NY: Prometheus Books.

Pinotti, Roberto. 1990. "ETI, SETI, and Today's Public." *Space Policy* 6, no. 2: 161–167.

Pipes, Daniel. 1997. *Conspiracy Theories: How the Paranoid Style Flourishes and Where it Comes From*. New York: The Free Press.

Polkinghorne, John. 1998. *Belief in God in an Age of Science*. New Haven, CT: Yale University Press.

Radin, Dean. 1997. *The Conscious Universe: The Scientific Truth of Psychic Phenomena*. San Francisco: Harper Edge.

———. 2006. *Entangled Minds: Extrasensory Experiences in a Quantum Reality*. New York: Paraview.

Ramachadan, V. S., and Sandra Blakeslee. 1998. *Phantoms in the Brain: Probing the Mysteries of the Human Mind*. New York: William Morrow and Company.

Randle, Kevin D., Russ Estes, and William P. McCone. 1999. *The Abduction Enigma: The Truth Behind the Mass Alien Abductions of the Late Twentieth Century*. New York: Forge Books.

Raup, David M. 1991. *Extinction: Bad Genes or Bad Luck?* New York: W. W. Norton, 1991.

Ray, James Lee. 1998. "Does Democracy Cause Peace?" *Annual Review of Political Science* 1: 27–46.

Raybeck, Douglas. 2000. *Looking Down the Road: A Systems Approach to Futures Studies.* Prospect Heights, IL: Waveland Press.

Redfern, Nick, and Andy Roberts. 2003. *Strange Secrets: Real Government Files on the Unknown.* New York; Paraview.

Rees, Martin. 2003. *Our Final Hours.* New York: Basic Books.

Reeves, Byron, and Clifford Nass. 1996. *The Media Equation: How People Treat Computers, Television and New Media Like Real People.* Cambridge: Cambridge University Press.

Relyea, Harold C. 2003. "Government Secrecy: Policy Depths and Dimensions." *Government Information Quarterly* 20, no. 4: 395–418.

Ring, Kenneth H. 1992. *The Omega Project: Near Death Experiences, UFO Encounters, and Mind at Large.* New York: William Morrow and Company.

Riordan, M., and L. Hoddeson. 1997. *Crystal Fire.* New York: W. W. Norton and Company.

Ross, Hugh. 1989. *The Fingerprint of God.* Orange, CA: Promise Publishing Company.

Rue, Loyal. 2005. *Religion is Not about God: How Spiritual Traditions Nurture our Biological Nature and What to Expect When They Fail.* New Brunswick, NJ: Rutgers University Press.

Ruppelt, Edward J. 1956. *The Report on Unidentified Flying Saucers.* New York: Doubleday.

Russell, Peter. 2005. *From Science to God: A Physicist's Journey into the Mystery of Consciousness.* New York: New World Library.

Ryback, Timothy W. 1999. *The Last Survivor: Legacies of Dachau.* New York: Vintage.

Saffary, Roya, Renu Nandakumar, Dennis Spencer, Frank T. Robb, Joseph M. Davila, Martin Swartz, Leon Ofman, Roger H. Thomas, and Jocelyn DiRuggerio. 2002. "Microbial Survival of Space Vacuum and Extreme Ultraviolet Radiation: Strain Isolation and Analysis during a Rocketflight." *FEMS Microbiology Letters* 215, no. 1: 163–168.

Sagan, Carl. 1978. *Murmurs of Earth.* New York: Random House.

Sagan, Carl, and Ann Druyan. 1997. *The Demon-Haunted World: Science as a Candle in the Dark.* New York: Ballantine Books.

Sager, Brian. 2001. "Scenarios on the Future of Biotechnology." *Technological Forecasting and Social Change* 68, no. 2: 109–129.

Saliba, John A. 1995a. "Religious Dimensions of UFO Phenomena." In *The Gods Have Landed: New Religions from Other Worlds,* ed. James R. Lewis, 15–64. Albany: State University of New York Press.

———. 1995b. "UFO Abductee Phenomena from a Sociopsychological Perspective: A Review." In *The Gods Have Landed: New Religions from Other Worlds,* ed. James R. Lewis, 207–250. Albany: State University of New York Press.

————. 2003. "The Psychology of UFO Phenomena." In *UFO Religions*, ed. Christopher Partridge 346–369. London: Routledge.

Sarbin, Theodore R. 1998a. "Believed-In Imaginings: A Narrative Approach." In *Believed-In Imaginings: The Narrative Construction of Reality*, ed. Joseph de Rivera and Theodore R. Sarbin, 15–31. Washington, DC: American Psychological Association.

————. 1998b. "Poetic Construction of Reality." In *Believed-In Imaginings: The Narrative Construction of Reality*, ed. Joseph de Rivera and Theodore R. Sarbin, 297–307. Washington, DC: American Psychological Association.

Schachter, Daniel L. 2001. *The Seven Sins of Memory: How the Mind Forgets and Remembers*. Boston: Houghton Mifflin.

Scharper, Stephen B. 1994. "The Gaia Hypothesis: Implications for a Christian Political Theology of the Environment." *Cross Currents* 44: 207–222.

Scheibe, Karl E. 1998. "Replicas, Imitations and the Question of Authenticity." In *Believed-In Imaginings: The Narrative Construction of Reality*, ed. Joseph de Rivera and Theodore R. Sarbin, 47–70. Washington DC: American Psychological Association.

Schuessler, John F. 1998. *The Cash-Landrum UFO Incident*. La Porte, TX: Geo Graphics.

Schwartz, Berthold E. 1988. *UFO Dynamics: Psychiatric and Psychic Aspects of the UFO Syndrome*. Moore Haven, FL: Rainbow Books.

Schweikart, Russell L., Edward T. Lu, Piet Hut, and Clark R. Chapman, 2003. "The Asteroid Tugboat." *Scientific American*, 289, no. 5: 54-61.

SciFi.com. 2002. "The Roper Poll: UFO's and Extraterrestrial Life." http://www.scifi.com/ufo/roper. Accessed 20 May 2006.

Scully, Frank. 1950. *Behind the Flying Saucers*. New York: Henry Holt.

Seamone, Evan R. 2003. "The Duty to 'Expect the Unexpected': Mitigating Extreme Natural Threats to the Global Commons Such as Asteroid and Comet Impacts with the Earth." *Columbia Journal of Transnational Law* 41: 735–794.

Sherman, S. J., R. B. Cialdini, D. Schwartzman, and K. D. Reynolds. 1985. "Imagining Can Heighten or Lower the Perceived Likelihood of Contracting a Disease: The Mediating Effect of Ease of Imagery." *Personality and Social Psychology Bulletin* 11: 118–127.

Shermer, Michael. 1997. *Why People Believe Weird Things*. New York: W. H. Freeman and Company.

————. 1999. *How We Believe: The Search for God in an Age of Science*. New York: W. W. Freeman and Company.

————. 2004. *The Science of Good and Evil*. New York: Times Books.

————. 2006. *Science Friction: Where the Known Meets the Unknown*. New York: Times Books.

Shlain, Leonard. 1998. *The Alphabet Versus the Goddess: The Conflict Between Word and Image*. New York: Penguin Compass.

Shostak, Seth 2001. "The Outlook for Cosmic Company." *Annals of the New York Academy of Science* 950: 289-295.

Shostak, Seth 2004. "When Will we Detect the Extraterrestrials? *Acta Astronautica*, 55, no. 3-9: 753-758.

Slayton, Donald K., and Michael Cassutt. 1994. *Deke!* New York: Forge Books.

Smith, Huston. 1991. *The World's Religions*. San Francisco: Harper San Francisco.

———. 2001. *Why Religion Matters: The Fate of the Human Spirit in an Age of Disbelief*. San Francisco: Harper San Francisco.

Sparks, William B., and Holland C. Ford. 2001. "Imaging Spectroscopy for Extrasolar Planet Detection." *The Astrophysical Journal* 578: 543–564.

Spence, Donald P. 1998. "The Mythic Properties of Popular Explanations." In *Believed-In Imaginings: The Narrative Construction of Reality*, ed. Joseph de Rivera and Theodore R. Sarbin, 217–228. Washington, DC: American Psychological Association.

Staley, James T. 2003. "Astrobiology, The Transcendent Science." *Current Opinion in Biotechnology* 14, no. 3: 347–354.

Steiger, Brad, and Hayden Hewes. 1997. *Inside Heaven's Gate*. New York: Signet Books.

Stride, Scot L. 2001. "Instrument Technologies for the Detection of Extraterrestrial Interstellar Robotic Probes." *Proceedings of the SPIE: International Society for Optical Engineering* 4273: 178–189.

Strieber, Whitley. 1987. *Communion: A True Story*. New York: Avon.

———. 1988. *Transformations*. New York: Avon.

Sturrock, Peter A. 1999. *The UFO Enigma: A New Review of the Physical Evidence*. New York: Warner Books.

Suedfeld, Peter. 2001. "The Sensed Presence." Keynote address presented at the 2001 meeting of the Society for Clinical and Experimental Hypnosis, San Antonio, Texas.

Swords, Michael D. 2000. "UFOs, the Military, and the Early Cold War Era." In *UFOs and Abductions: Challenging the Borders of Science*, ed. David M. Jacobs, 82-121. Lawrence: University Press of Kansas.

Tarter, Donald E. 2000. "Security Considerations in Signal Detection." *Acta Astronautica* 46, 725–728.

Tarter, Jill. 2001. "The Search for Extraterrestrial Intelligence." *Annual Review of Astronomy and Astrophysics* 39: 511–548.

———. 2003. "Earth's Radio Wave Halo." *Astrobiology Magazine*, August 29: 1.

Tattersall, Ian, and Jeffery Schwartz. 2001. *Extinct Humans*. Boulder, CO: Westview Press.

Tipler, Frank J. 1995. *The Physics of Immortality: Modern Cosmology, God, and the Resurrection of the Dead.* New York: Anchor.

Tough, Allen. 1990. "A Critical Examination of the Factors that Might Encourage Secrecy." *Acta Astronautica* 21, no. 2: 97–102.

———, ed. 2000. *When SETI Succeeds: Implications of High Information Contact.* Bellevue, WA: Foundation for the Future.

———. 2005. "Invitation to ETI." http://www.ieti.org/. Accessed 8 April 2006.

Ulmschneider, Peter. 2003. *Intelligent Life in the Universe: From Common Origins to the Future of Humanity.* New York: Springer Verlag.

Vallee, Jacques F. 1993. *Passport to Magonia: On UFOs, Folklore, and Parallel Worlds.* Chicago: Contemporary Books.

———. 1999. "Physical Analyses in Ten Cases of Unexplained Aerial Objects with Material Samples." In *The UFO Enigma: A New Review of the Physical Evidence,* ed. Peter A. Sturrock, 234–256. New York: Warner Books.

Vergano, Dan. 2004. "Air Force Report Calls For $7.5M to Study Psychic Teleportation." *USA Today.* http://www.usatoday.com/tech/news/2004-11-05-teleportation_x.htm. Accessed 5 November 2004.

Victor, Jeffrey S. 1998. "Social Construction of Satanic Ritual Abuse and the Creation of False Memories." In *Believed-In Imaginings: The Narrative Construction of Reality,* ed. Joseph de Rivera and Theodore R. Sarbin, 191–216. Washington, DC: American Psychological Association.

von Däniken, Erich. 1973. *Chariots of the Gods?* New York: Bantam.

von Ludwiger, Illobrand. 1998. *Best UFO Cases: Europe.* Las Vegas, NV: National Institute for Discovery Science.

Wade, Jenny. 1996. *Changes of Mind: A Holonomic Theory of the Evolution of Consciousness.* Albany: State University of New York Press.

Walton, Travis. 1978. *The Walton Experience.* New York: Berkeley Books.

Ward, Peter, and David Brownlee. 2000. *Rare Earth: Why Life is Uncommon in the Universe.* New York: Copernicus.

———. 2002. *The Life and Death of Planet Earth: How the New Science of Astrobiology Charts the Ultimate Fate of Our World.* New York: Times Books.

Warren, Donald I. 1970. "Status Inconsistency Theory and Flying Saucers." *Science* 170: 599–603.

Webb, Jeffrey B. 2004. *The Complete Idiot's Guide to Christianity.* New York: Alpha Books.

Wells, Gary L., and Elizabeth A. Olson. 2003. "Eyewitness Testimony." *Annual Review of Psychology* 54: 277–295.

Wheen, Francis. 2004. *Idiot Proof: Deluded Celebrities, International Power Brokers, and the Erosion of Common Sense.* New York: Public Affairs.

White, Frank. 1987. *The Overview Effect: Space Exploration and Human Evolution.* Boston: Houghton-Mifflin.

Wick, Georg. 2002. "Anti-aging Medicine: Does it Exist? A Critical Discussion of Anti-Aging Health Products." *Experimental Gerontology* 37, no. 8-9: 1137–1140.

Wickramasinghe, Chandra. 2004. "The Universe: A Cryogenic Habitat for Microbial Life." *Cryobiology* 48, no. 2: 113–125.

Wierzbicki, James. 2002. "Weird Vibrations: How the Theremin Gave Musical Voice to Hollywood's Extraterrestrial 'Others'; Electronic Music from 1950s Science Fiction Films." *Journal of Popular Film and Television* 30: 125–135.

Williams, Richard S. 2000. "A Modern Earth Narrative: What Will Be the Fate of the Biosphere?" *Technology in Society* 22, no. 3: 303–339.

Wilson, David Sloane. 2002. *Darwin's Cathedral: Evolution, Religion, and the Nature of Society.* Chicago: University of Chicago Press.

Wojcik, Daniel. 1997. *The End of the World as We Know It: Faith, Fatalism and Apocalypse in America.* Amherst, New York: New York State Universities Press.

———. 2003. "Apocalyptic and Millenarian Aspects of American UFOism." In *UFO Religions*, ed. Christopher Partridge, 274-300. London: Routledge.

Wong, Pak-Chung, Kwong-Kuk Wong, and Harlan Foote. 2003. "Organic Data Memory Using the DNA Approach." *Proceedings of the ACM* 46: 95–97.

Wozniak, Lara. 2005. "Clinton's Worldview: Part Two." http://www.finacenasia.com/articles/4E718926–9027–7E17–4B7EF9778FE76A1C.cfm. Accessed 14 September 2005.

Wulff, David M. 2000. "Mystical Experiences." In *Varieties of Anomalous Experiences: Examining the Scientific Evidence*, ed. Etzel Cardena, Steven Jay Lynn, and Stanley Krippner, 397–440. Washington, DC: American Psychological Association.

Wyller, Arne A. 1996. *The Planetary Mind.* Aspen, CO: MacMurray & Beck.

Young, John. 1998. "Rescuing the 'Other' in Liberal and Conservative Dialogue: A Phenomenological Approach." Master's thesis, Union Theological Seminary. http://www.tikaro.com/thesis. Accessed 7 April 2003.

Zaitsev, Alexander L. 2002. "Design and Implementation of the First Theremin Concert for Aliens." Sixth International Space Arts Workshop, Paris, 17 March.

Zaitsev, Alexander, Charles M. Chafer, and Richard Braastad. 2005. "Making a Case for METI." SETI League Guest Editorial, March. http://www.setileague.org/editor/meti/htm. Accessed 30 January 2006.

Ziegler, Charles A. 1997. "Analysis of the Roswell Myth: A Traditional Folk Motif in Modern Garb." In *UFO Crash at Roswell: The Genesis of a Modern Myth*, eds. Benson Saler, Charles A. Ziegler, and Charles B. Moore, 30-73. Washington, DC: Smithsonian Institution Press.

Ziman, John. 1978. *Reliable Knowledge: An Exploration of the Grounds of Belief in Science.* Cambridge: Cambridge University Press.

Zimmer, Troy A. 1984. "Social Psychological Correlates of Possible UFO Sightings." *Journal of Social Psychology* 123, no. 2: 201–207.

————. 1985. "Belief in UFOs as Alternative Reality: Cultural Rejection or Disturbed Psyche?" *Deviant Behavior* 6: 405–419.

INDEX

Index

Moore, William, 138
Morality, 82, 91, 97, 98, 100-101, 118
Moravec, Hans, 160, 193
Mormons, 95
Moroni, 95
Morrison, Philip, 169
Morse, Melvin, 109
Mount Ranier, 62
Mount Saint Helens, 52
Mount Wilson Observatory, 9
MSNBC, 52
Murmurs of Earth, 53
mysticism, 88, 101, 105-109, Thomas
    Edison and, 5; hallucinations and
    106
myth, 5-6, 11, 18, 29, 30, 77, 82, 84,
    86, 89, 126, 186, 187, 197; central,
    82, 84; science and, 6, 27, 30
nanotechnology, 73
NARCAP, 60
NASA, 11, 15, 28, 42, 46, 71, 72, 90,
    91, 92,134, 168, 192, 172
Nass, Clifford, 18
National Academy of Sciences, 135
National Institute for Discovery Science,
    80, 130
National Public Radio, 35
Neanderthals, 144
near death experiences, 109, 110
Necronomicon, 29
NEOs (Near Earth Objects), 12, 56,
    143-144,147-150, 166, 167, 169;
    likelihood of dying from, 149; pro-
    tection from, 151-153
Nettles, Bonnie Lu, 129
neurotheology, 106-109
New Age, 27, 84, 111
New Madrid Fault, 153
New Orleans, 144, 151, 167
New physics, 32, 109, 186, (see ironic
    science)
New Religious Movements, 83 (also see
    cults)
New York Times, 41, 178
news, entertainment and, 36
Newton, Isaac, 34, 125
Niven, Larry, 31
Nixon, Richard, 131

Noah's Ark, 93
Nobel Prize, 21
Noble, David F., 5, 91
Nocks, Lisa, 18
Noetic Institute, 92
Noosphere, 109
Norris, Ray, 97, 150
nuclear war, 150, 175, 167
Nuland, Sherwin, 154
O'Murchu, Diarmuid, 102
Oak Ridge Observatory, 50
Oberth, Hermann, 196
Observatories, Evpatoria, 51; Hat Creek,
    48; Keck, 9; Mount Wilson, 9; Oak
    Ridge, 50
Observer-dependent explanations, 65-70,
    74-79
Oh God, 80
Omega point, 161
opinion leaders, 24
Orion, 143-144
Orson Welles, 174, 175
Orthon, 185
Osborne, Alex, 191
OSETI (Optical SETI), 49-50
Othello Effect, 78
OURS Foundation, 30
overview effects, 92
OWL (Overwhelmingly Large Tele-
    scope), 47, 71
Ozma, Project, 168
Palmer, Ray, 123
Palmer, Susan 96, 127, 156
Panspermia, 54-56
Pantheism, 111
Paradigm shifts, 33-34, 125, 186
Paranoid thinking, 140-141
Paranormal, 26-27, 37, 38, 187
Parapsychology, 39
Parker, Calvin, 112
Parnell, June, 77
Partridge, Christopher, 99-100
Passport to Magonia, 126
Passport to the Cosmos, 113, 117
Peculiar beliefs, 119
Pele, 4
People Magazine, 198
perception, 15, 16, 75, 79